Heidegger

Heidegger
Thinking of Being

Lee Braver

polity

First published in 2014 by Polity Press

Reprinted 2014, 2015

Polity Press
65 Bridge Street
Cambridge CB2 1UR, UK

Polity Press
350 Main Street
Malden, MA 02148, USA

ISBN-13: 978-0-7456-6491-0 (hardback)
ISBN-13: 978-0-7456-6492-7 (paperback)

A catalogue record for this book is available from the British Library.

Typeset in 10.5 on 12 pt Palatino
by Toppan Best-set Premedia Limited
Printed and bound in the United States by Courier Digital Solutions

The publisher has used its best endeavours to ensure that the URLs for external websites referred to in this book are correct and active at the time of going to press. However, the publisher has no responsibility for the websites and can make no guarantee that a site will remain live or that the content is or will remain appropriate.

Every effort has been made to trace all copyright holders, but if any have been inadvertently overlooked the publisher will be pleased to include any necessary credits in any subsequent reprint or edition.

For further information on Polity, visit our website: www.politybooks.com

What the hell – this one's for me. I wrote the damn thing after all.

Contents

Contents

Acknowledgments

I want to thank my children, Sophia, Julia, and Ben, and my wife, Yvonne, for their patience and support.

Abbreviations

BQ	*Basic Questions of Philosophy: Selected "Problems" of "Logic"*
BT	*Being and Time*
BW	*Basic Writings*
CP	*Contributions to Philosophy*
DT	*Discourse on Thinking*
EF	*The Essence of Human Freedom: An Introduction to Philosophy*
EGT	*Early Greek Thinking: The Dawn of Western Philosophy*
EHP	*Elucidations of Hölderlin's Poetry*
ET	*The Essence of Truth*
FS	*Four Seminars*
HCT	*History of the Concept of Time*
HH	*Hölderlin's Hymn "The Ister"*
HR	*The Heidegger Reader*, ed. Figal
ID	*Identity and Difference*
IM	*An Introduction to Metaphysics*
KPM	*Kant and the Problem of Metaphysics*, 5th edn, enlarged
M	*Mindfulness*
MFL	*The Metaphysical Foundations of Logic*
N	*Nietzsche*, vol. denoted by Roman numeral
OBT	*Off the Beaten Track*
OWL	*On the Way to Language*
PLT	*Poetry, Language, Thought*
PM	*Pathmarks*
PR	*The Principle of Reason*
PT	*The Piety of Thinking*
PWD	*Philosophical Writings of Descartes*, 3 vols.

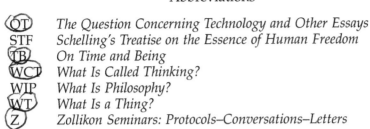

QT   *The Question Concerning Technology and Other Essays*
STF   *Schelling's Treatise on the Essence of Human Freedom*
TB   *On Time and Being*
WCT *What Is Called Thinking?*
WIP *What Is Philosophy?*
WT   *What Is a Thing?*
Z   *Zollikon Seminars: Protocols–Conversations–Letters*

Note: Smaller, numbered divisions within some texts are referred to using the following symbol: ¶

Introduction: An Initial Orientation

Martin Heidegger (1889–1976) is, by many estimations, the most important philosopher of the twentieth century, at least in what is known as the continental tradition. His work forms the connecting point of most of the major schools of the time. His early work brings together the dominant influences of the late nineteenth and early twentieth centuries – neo-Kantianism, existentialism, hermeneutics, and phenomenology – whereas his later thought is the dominant influence on much of what followed – post-modernism, post-structuralism, and deconstruction, as well as later forms of hermeneutics and phenomenology. Little in twentieth-century continental philosophy can be fully understood without a solid grasp of Heidegger's ideas.

This is what I try to provide the reader with in this book. There are certainly limits to how much I can cover of Heidegger's work, both in depth and breadth; his collected works amount to more than one hundred volumes, after all. But I will try to discuss many of his main ideas, the central themes he returns to again and again. No single book could hope to convey the nuances and complexities of his thought. This book is certainly not meant to be a substitute for reading Heidegger but an aid to doing so, a companion to give you an initial orientation to your own reading of his difficult works.

For they are disorienting indeed. Heidegger spends a great deal of time studying the history of philosophy, and I think it's fair to characterize this as a love–hate relationship. On the one hand, he is a relentless critic of the tradition, tirelessly berating past philosophers (with the exception of the pre-Socratics) for neglecting the question of being, his one unwavering focus. Philosophers have generally taken a particular understanding of what it means to be – usually something like a substance which is self-sufficient and self-enclosed – and applied it to everything that is. Heidegger's task, as he announces in his first book, *Being and Time*, is to reawaken this question that has been forgotten and ignored.

Yet, on the other hand, he constantly expresses enormous admiration for the great philosophers, seeing some of the best clues as to how to answer and even how to ask this question in the history of philosophy. These are the people who came closest to asking it, and even their negligence is informative. What they overlooked is not random but forms specifically shaped gaps in their thought and if we pay attention to both what they say and what they don't say, we can look through these holes to see the outlines of what they passed over and around.

The point is that Heidegger sees the vast majority of past philosophy as operating on the basis of certain deeply flawed assumptions. If we are to avoid their mistakes, we must not take over their taken-for-granted presuppositions. But, because of the ubiquity and depth of these presuppositions, a work that thinks without them will look exceedingly strange to eyes that have learned to see by their light. Like Plato's philosopher who, upon escaping the cave, must let his eyes adjust a while to the sunlight, so reading Heidegger requires a fundamental adjustment of our expectations and ways of reading and thinking.

Part of this readjustment is linguistic. He believes that our vocabulary and grammar tend to focus only on certain phenomena and contain hidden presuppositions about how they behave, just the presuppositions that he is taking pains to avoid. So if the way he expresses his ideas is not to betray the very ideas he's trying to express, Heidegger needs to come up with new terms (or use old terms very differently) and new ways of speaking and writing. This is probably the most notorious and off-putting feature of Heidegger's writings. You almost have to learn a new language – Heideggerese – just to read his works. And a vocabulary cheat-sheet won't solve the problem because the *grammar* of Heideggerese, the way he puts the words and sentences together, is also unusual. Most philosophy is hard to read but Heidegger's linguistic practice clashes with the ways we are used to reading, making his writing terrifically frustrating.

Another part of the readjustment is conceptual. Heidegger's thought moves in strange ways. For one thing, he is rather suspicious of logical argumentation. This does not mean that he eschews argumentation entirely – there are plenty of arguments to be found in his work, and many of them are quite good – but he does think that there are limitations to this way of thinking. Reason is an important tool in understanding the world, but it is only one tool, and many situations call for others. For example, moods and feelings can reveal much about the world, much that reason is simply blind to. In general, rational thought disengages from activity and involvement to weigh ideas disinterestedly. While this does reveal important facts, it covers over others, features that are only present or visible when we are engaged and involved. Thus, he isn't rejecting reason; I'm not sure what such a move would even look like. Instead, he's rejecting the exclusive reliance on it. Truth is more varied than this.

This approach is largely due to phenomenology, the school of thought founded by his teacher, Edmund Husserl. As we will see in Chapter 1, this form of philosophy favors careful description of experience exactly as it shows itself over argumentation. Rather than relying on reason to tell us how the world must or ought to be, we attend to our experience to tell us how the world actually is. Following this approach consistently means that if things show up irrationally or arationally, then that is how things are. It also means that whatever discloses the world to us is a legitimate means of access to truth and reality, so emotions, works of art, and historical texts, for example, all stand shoulder-to-shoulder with reason as ways of discovering truths. This gives Heidegger's work the appearance of an irresponsible cultivation of irrationality to some, but it also imbues it with a breadth and humanity that has few rivals in the canon.

That may sound strange given his almost monomaniacal pursuit of a single topic throughout his entire long career: the question of being. Heidegger never tires of thumping on this question as the one essential issue for all of philosophy, indeed, for human life, but this claim makes more sense when we get an idea of what he means. Being, for Heidegger, means to become manifest or to appear to us. He fully subscribes to phenomenology's rejection of all that transcends experience, such as Plato's Forms or Kant's noumena. These do not appear in experience so we cannot study them or incorporate them into a theory. Whatever God knows is His business; if it does not impact my life then it is not a phenomenon for me and so I have no business making claims about it. Phenomena – that which appears – is equivalent to that which is.

an insight Heidegger credits the ancient Greeks with discovering (BT 51/28) and Husserl with recovering, although he came to consider Husserl unequal to the insight.

Heidegger's work studies all the different kinds of beings there are by examining all the various ways things can appear to us, and these prove to be extraordinarily various and rich. His thought accommodates every different kind of entity, respecting the profound differences among them without trying to reduce them to a few broad principles or only one. Thus, although the topic of being might sound extremely narrow, it actually covers everything, and in such a way as to highlight rather than wash out the vibrant bountiful diversity of reality. In particular, it captures the world's diversity far more successfully than philosophers who tend to see everything in terms of a single idea, like participation in the Forms, or substance, or mathematically measurable features, another deep flaw of the tradition. Phenomenology is the great enemy of reductionism in all its forms.

Martin Heidegger was born to a sexton in Messkirch, Germany in 1889. He initially studied theology at the University of Freiburg but later switched to philosophy, eventually becoming heir apparent to Husserl, one of the most prominent figures of the day. Heidegger assumed Husserl's Chair at Freiburg upon Husserl's retirement on the strength of his first book, *Being and Time* (1927). The story goes that he had to rush the unfinished book into print in order to secure the Chair since, while he had achieved an impressive reputation at the University of Marburg on the basis of his teaching, he needed a major publication for the promotion. The book was an instant success, catapulting Heidegger to world prominence, and it retains its position as one of the greatest books of the twentieth century.[2]

Heidegger joined the Nazi party in 1933 with considerable enthusiasm. He was elected Rector of the University of Freiburg where he implemented Nazi educational policies, though there is some uncertainty about how thoroughly. While he resigned the Rectorship in early 1934, he remained a member of the Nazi party, albeit with apparently little enthusiasm. The precise reasons for his resignation and his disillusionment with the party are also a matter of debate, as we will see in Chapter 8.

Around the end of the 1920s and the beginning of the 1930s his work underwent what some have called a *Kehre* or turn, although the nature, extent, and even the existence of such a change is hotly debated among Heidegger scholars. His writing style certainly changed, becoming, if anything, more difficult. He came to favor essays and lecture courses to massive tomes, although apparent attempts at full-scale books exist among the enormous mass of unpublished materials. (His relationship to the history of philosophy intensified in the latter part of his career.)While he had planned on a second part to *Being and Time* that would have examined the work of Kant, Descartes, and Aristotle, this was to have been separate from the first part's laying out of the topic. In his later works, he generally intertwines his own thought with a dialogue with earlier thinkers, much as Derrida, greatly influenced by Heidegger, does. My book will follow this division, devoting the first half to *Being and Time* and the second half to the later Heidegger. Since these later topics are drawn from a variety of texts, at the end of each chapter I will indicate the texts that I believe treat the topics best, and use endnotes to point the interested reader to other works discussing the same subjects. I will also use endnotes and a section at the end of each chapter to indicate connections with other philosophers and relevant secondary literature for readers who want to follow up topics in greater detail.

Part I

Being and Time

1

Introduction to Being and Time

Being and Time Introduction I

Being and Time opens with a quote from one of Plato's late dialogues where the speaker admits that he no longer understands what being means. Interestingly, rather than invoking Plato as one of the great metaphysicians and making some kind of connection with his views on the nature of being, this quote praises him for his *lack* of understanding about it. By the end of many of Plato's dialogues, Socrates brings his conversation partners to the realization that they didn't know what they thought they knew, which opens the way for them to learn. So, before answering the question of being can even be a possibility, Heidegger wants us to pause and fully realize our profound perplexity before this question that dominates his thought from one end of his career to the other: what is the meaning of being? What does it mean to be?

Let's stop and think about this question for a minute – how would you go about answering it? Where should we travel to in order to find being? What instruments might we use to bring it into focus – are there things that could function as ontoloscopes or ontometers? What kinds of experiments or surveys or meditations could uncover being? After just a brief consideration, we should see that not only do we not know how to *answer* the question, we don't really even know how to *ask* it, and this is what the Introduction tries to prepare us for. Be warned: the Introduction is probably the hardest part of the book. It is thorny, abstract, and it throws term after term at you with little to no explanation. It's rough

going, but once we get to the body of the book, we will find concrete experiences to anchor our understanding of the text. This is
the great advantage of phenomenology (which I will define in just
a minute): no matter how difficult the writing, if you can find the
experience it's trying to describe, that can serve as a life-line in
interpreting the text.

In fact, Heidegger gives us the answer to "the being-question"
(this question is so important to him that it gets a name!) on this first
unnumbered page of the book: time is the meaning of being. Not
very helpful, is it? As Douglas Adams showed us, if we don't understand the question then we won't be able to make much sense of the
answer. *Being and Time* begins by quoting a great philosophical
authority not for his knowledge but for his perplexity, then tells us
that we don't understand the question, and demonstrates this by
giving us the answer which means nothing to us at this point. Just
to add a flourish to the peculiarity of these opening moves, the very
last sentence of the book puts this answer into question (488/437).[1]

In fact, there's a well-known problem lurking in the bushes here.
It's called Meno's Paradox since it first arose in the Platonic dialogue titled "Meno" for the main character talking to Socrates in
the text. When Socrates demolishes Meno's attempts to define
virtue, Meno responds with a dilemma, that is, two exhaustive
choices, both of which appear to be unacceptable: either we know
what virtue is or we don't. If we do know it then our inquiry is
obviously unnecessary, but if we don't our inquiry is impossible
since we won't know when and if we run across the right answer.
In other words, if we genuinely don't know what virtue is, then
we won't be able to recognize its correct definition if we find it.
Plato's solution to the dilemma is his theory of recollection that
proposes a third alternative between the dilemma's options of
either complete knowledge or absolute ignorance. He suggests that
we have had knowledge of what he calls the Forms, which provide
definitions of the highly abstract notions his dialogues examine
such as beauty or justice, but we have forgotten them. This means
that we do in fact need to search for them since at present we don't
have an explicit grasp of them, but when we come across the truth
we will recognize it by its distant familiarity.

Heidegger adapts a version of Plato's theory, albeit stripped of
its mythological trappings. "Inquiry, as a kind of seeking, must be
guided beforehand by what is sought. So the meaning of Being
must already be available to us in some way" (25/5). The very fact
that we can ask the question at all, even in a confused way, means

that we have *some* understanding of being, at least that it exists and can be questioned. But pay attention to the qualification: "in some way." We do have an understanding of being, but not in the way we usually think of understanding. Philosophy has traditionally been dominated by the demand Socrates puts to those he questions – define the topic in a fully articulate way that can be defended from objections, or else you don't really know it. Philosophers have traditionally conceived of knowledge in terms of explicit thoughts you can explain and argue for. One of the more radical innovations of the first division of *Being and Time* is its proposal of a different kind of knowledge, one sometimes called "know-how" rather than "knowing-that."[2] I know how to walk or have a conversation or what honey tastes like but I'm not sure I could explain any of these, at least not to anyone who didn't already know them.

Surprisingly, Heidegger wants to spell out something as seemingly abstract and esoteric as the meaning of being in terms of these mundane know-hows. This is why he continues the quote above: "we always conduct our activities in an understanding of Being." He locates this understanding more in our actions than our thoughts, though it's there too. At the most general level, we must have some sense of what it means to be, just to pick out real entities to interact with. By picking up this book, you have demonstrated that you can tell a real object from all the non-existing things you might have reached for. In fact, everything you interact with has to be some kind of being; even a daydream of imaginary scenes is a being of some sort. Every second you're awake you're dealing with something or other, even if only in your thoughts, and all of these interactions successfully pick out things that are. Therefore, your actions must be guided by an understanding of what it means to be, if a tacit one.

But that's not all. Not only do you recognize real beings, but you recognize differences among them. I don't ask my wallet for permission when I take money out of it, the way I would ask permission to get money from you. I don't worry about whether my coffee cup is lonely when I lock it in my office at night, nor do I try to discover and nurture its ambitions. We're constantly differentiating types of beings by treating particular beings differently, which means that we have an understanding of a number of different ways to be. This is what Husserl, Heidegger's teacher, calls "regional ontology," meaning that reality contains profoundly heterogeneous types of things. This understanding of being that we have is turning out to be rather sophisticated.

It isn't explicit, however. We rarely think about the fact that people and objects are completely different kinds of things which call for diverse actions because it's so self-evident. Heidegger calls this kind of understanding "pre-ontological," which just means that it's not an express theory (32/12). It can become explicit when people undertake specialized studies of particular topics because each discipline carves out a particular type of being for its subject: language or historical events or atoms or arguments, for example. But even these disciplines take place on the basis of a pre-ontological understanding, what Heidegger calls here "productive logic" (30/10). One has to start off with a basic, rough and ready sense of what, say, historical events are in order to go about the business of studying them. After a detailed examination, we gain a deeper understanding that can enrich and refine our initial definition, which can then enable us to do a better job examining the topic, and so on. I will be calling this the Hermeneutic Spiral, and the movement of the book as a whole is to continue turning it, going back over material already covered but at a deeper level, with greater focus and understanding. Thus, the vicious circle that Meno had posed as an obstacle that prevents inquiry is actually a virtuous spiral that enables us to learn at all. "What is decisive is not to get out of the circle but to come into it in the right way" (195/153). What Heidegger calls the ontological priority of the question of being in ¶3 means that any empirical inquiry into beings rests on more fundamental notions of what it means to be that kind of being, and ultimately what it means to be at all. Sciences are "naive" or "dogmatic" in that they presuppose these deeper understandings of being without subjecting them to investigation. That they do not do this deeper investigation is not a criticism; that isn't their job. It is the task of philosophy.

Now there are two things you need to know about being right off the bat. First is what Heidegger calls the ontological difference, which is the difference between being and beings or entities or things that are. Beings are just the things and people around us – this book, that cup, Marlon Brando, toenails, etc. Being (at least at this point in Heidegger's thought) is the *way* they are, the different kinds of behavior we can expect from them. These "levels" are not separate or separable, but are fundamentally different *kinds* of phenomena, which he calls "ontic" and "ontological," respectively (note: don't confuse this sense of "ontological" as referring to being in contrast to beings with the other sense of "ontological" as an explicit theory in contrast to pre-ontological understanding;

Heidegger really should have come up with different terms). Claims like, "the Being of entities 'is' not itself an entity" (26/6) mean that the *way* a thing exists is not itself a thing. People, for example, have a distinctive way of existing that is very different from the way inanimate objects are, but this way of existing is plainly not itself a person or a thing or any other entity. It is a way of being – making it ontological – rather than a being itself – which would make it ontic. Confusing the two – treating being as a being – forms one of the most common mistakes in philosophy, what he comes to call onto-theology. This is encouraged by capitalizing "Being," which makes it sound like the great being in the sky, so I will leave it uncapitalized, though I will preserve its original expression in quotations (Heidegger encouraged Joan Stambaugh to translate the German "Sein" by "be-ing" in English in order to capture its dynamism). Once you understand what Heidegger means by being the point is rather obvious, so hopefully it will become clearer as we become familiar with the three kinds of being that appear in *Being and Time*. The second preparatory point is that "Being is always the Being of an entity" (29/9). You can never find a way of being just floating around. It's only particular beings that are in specific ways, so we only encounter being by seeing how entities are. We learn about their being by watching them be, so to speak.

And this starts to ease our initial perplexity about how to answer the being-question. If we only find being among beings, then that's where we should look for it: we need to question beings about their being (26/6). Of course, this solution immediately creates a new problem: *which* beings should we examine? Everything we encounter is a being so taking a survey of them all would be an infinite labor. Heidegger narrows our search in ¶4 The Ontical Priority of the Question of Being where, remember, ontic just means having to do with particular beings as opposed to ontological which pertains to being.

Where should we look for the meaning of being? Happily, we already have the answer to this. The mere fact that we are asking the question of being means that we ourselves have some understanding of its meaning, so we should look for it in us. Metaphysicians have looked far and wide for what it means to be but, like Dorothy's slippers, they had it with them all along. It's initially pre-ontological, as we have seen, but the book as a whole attempts to make it ontological in the sense of an explicitly stated theory.

"Dasein," an ordinary word for existence in German, is used as a technical term for beings like us in the book, specifically beings with the ability to be aware. Another potential terminological land-mine appears here: Heidegger uses the term "existence" exclu-sively for our way of being so, technically, only Dasein exists; other things have their own ways of being. Heidegger initially defines Dasein as the entity for whom, "in its very Being, that Being is an issue for it" (32/12). This means that "we cannot define Dasein's essence by citing a 'what' of the kind that pertains to a subject-matter . . . its essence lies rather in the fact that in each case it has its Being to be, and has it as its own" (32–3/12). Our essence is to have no essence in the sense of specific features or tasks or activities assigned to us by our nature. Rocks have a definite essence that cannot be changed; animals are guided by instinct and cannot reflect on what they ought to do. But we are to some degree unformed, which means that it is up to us to form our selves. We become a particular kind of person by living a particular life, making what Heidegger calls "existentiell" decisions, which means that they pertain to specific Dasein, as opposed to "existential" features that all Dasein have (33/12). To connect this distinction with a previous one, existentiell qualities are ontic ones that pertain to particular Dasein, whereas existential features pertain to our ontological way of being that is common to all Dasein.

As we will see in the next two chapters, we can only live a life within the context of a community and by using a whole bunch of tools. In order to be a professor, I need to have specific kinds of relationships with students, colleagues, and administrators, and use a loose collection of tools such as books, classrooms, chalk-boards, and so on. I cannot *be* a professor by simply willing it or believing that I am; I have to be involved in certain ways with others and things. Unlike the traditional definition of substance, we are essentially *not* self-sufficient; we are inescapably amid the world and among others. But, as we have seen, this means that we must understand their ways of being in order to be able to pick them out and interact with them appropriately (33/13).

And this closes the circle opened on the first page, thus ending the first part of the Introduction. We started off completely befud-dled about how to answer, or even ask the question of the meaning of being. Now we have the first step – we will find that meaning in the entity who possesses an understanding of being as part of its basic make-up: us. A pre-ontological understanding lives in our activities because we act in the world in our attempts to become a particular kind of person, trying to settle the issue of our being. This requires an understanding of our own way of being, because we must realize that it is up to us to live out our lives, and of the ways of being of the entities we need to do so: objects, tools, and other people. An understanding of these three ways of being is built into our way of being, what Heidegger calls existence, so this is what we must analyze as the foundation for understanding all of these ways of being. Or, as Heidegger densely summarizes the conclusion of the first part of the Introduction, "therefore, *fundamental ontology*, from which alone all other ontologies can take their rise, must be sought in the *existential analytic of Dasein*" (34/13). The analysis of existence, Dasein's way of being, forms the foundation for the study of being, ontology.

Being and Time Introduction II

If Part I of the Introduction addresses the why and the what of the inquiry – why it's important and what to study – Part II looks at how to conduct it. We now know that we have to examine Dasein's way of being, what he calls the existential analytic, but how do we do this? This may seem easy – after all, every second of our life gives us data since we are always with ourselves. But ¶5 introduces one of the guiding ideas of Heidegger's thought: that which is most familiar is, *for that very reason,* especially hard to grasp (36/15). Although this sounds paradoxical, you can see it at work in your daily life. Think about some of the features in your room – your desk, or posters on the wall, or the position of the bed. These are things you see every day but, because they're constantly in view, you take them for granted and they become, if not exactly invisible, then unseen, rarely noticed unless something changes. If that's true of your closet door which you often see, how much more does it apply to your self which is *always* there?

It will take work to analyze ourselves, then, and for more than one reason. Heidegger thinks that philosophers have typically started their examination of the self with a presupposition about which activities are essential to our nature. Ever since the Greeks defined humans as the rational animal these presuppositions have usually focused on our ability to think, but this concentration is just an artifact of the way philosophers approach the subject. Think about how Descartes begins his *Meditations*, for instance. He says that he must cease all normal activities and retreat to a cabin where he can just sit in a chair by the fire and think. And lo and behold, what he finds there is that he is really just a thinking thing! Well no wonder – all he's doing while he's examining himself is thinking (85/59). This method prejudices the investigation by intentionally screening out the kinds of things we do the vast majority of the time, just the kinds of things Descartes makes sure to stop doing before he starts studying himself. Plato similarly praises the activity of philosophizing *because* it takes us away from the mundane flotsam and jetsam of life, the insignificant and rather distasteful bodily processes that take up so much of our time.

Heidegger asks an intentionally naive question: if these activities are what we do most of the time, why filter them out when we want to understand ourselves? We spend vastly more time eating cereal and walking to the store and talking with our friends than we do contemplating triangles or ruminating on the nature of justice. Instead of screening them out, we should come up with an understanding of the self starting with these kinds of activities, what he calls our "average *everydayness*" (38/16). These common, daily actions and interactions should not be shunned since it is here that our understanding of being happens. This is one way in which, as he announced on the first page, he conducts the inquiry into being "concretely" (19/1).

Just as he gave us time as the answer to the being-question right away, so Heidegger solves the existential analytic at the start by telling us that the meaning of Dasein is temporality as well (38/17). And, once again, we are not yet able to understand this. We can see one thing right away, however. Part of what it means for Dasein to be temporal is that it is historical. As we will see in 1.IV,[3] the roles we take up in order to settle the issue of our being come from our community, and these roles have been passed down. I can only be a professor because my society has the relevant institutions which have themselves come from medieval universities, ultimately going back to Plato's Academy. It's not just roles that are historical; our most basic ways of thinking and seeing the world are also passed down. We are rarely aware of the fact that they are historical – they usually simply seem to be the way the world is – but that just shows how deeply they determine our ways of experiencing things (41/20).

One of the features of the being-question is how incredibly disorienting it is; as we have seen, we have no ready-made way to pursue it. So one possible way to orient our inquiry, which ¶6 takes up, is to look at how others have gone about it, looking to the great works of metaphysics for clues to the way explorers examine the maps of previous expeditions. Even for those who haven't actually read the canonical texts, Heidegger thinks that ideas from the history of philosophy have surreptitiously infiltrated our ways of thinking so that we employ diluted versions of Platonic or Aristotelian notions without even knowing it. When we think, we typically do so with other people's thoughts, prosthetic limbs for the brain so to speak (42–3/21). When this happens, however, we are not finding things out for ourselves, not having the experiences that originally inspired and informed these ideas when they were first formed. Over time, these traditional ideas have "hardened" (44/22) into clichéd thoughts that students can recite by rote; rather than helping us think, they now hinder it. They cover over instead of uncovering, so that we see what we expect to see, what we think we will see rather than what actually shows up.

If we are to see what appears for itself, we must loosen up these hardened ideas in what Heidegger calls a "destruction" of the tradition, though this isn't as violent as it sounds. Rather than smashing them, we need to dismantle these traditional ideas carefully, studying how they were put together so that we can take them apart and understand the original experiences that gave rise to them in the first place. This is a laborious and, for Heidegger, a deeply respectful, almost reverential activity, even though it is continuously criticizing what it takes apart. This task was originally to take up the entire second part of the book, with chapters on Kant, Descartes, and Aristotle in reverse chronological order.[4]

Heidegger thinks that the flaw common to virtually all metaphysicians is that they didn't ask the question of being rigorously enough. In particular, they ignored the *varieties* of ways to be, fixating instead on a single way of being which they applied to every thing that is. This is especially problematic when it comes to the subject of the foundation of all ontology – the existential analytic which studies us. The dominant thesis of *Being and Time* as we have it (we don't know where Division 3 would have taken us) is that Dasein's way of being is utterly unlike that of anything else, and the two divisions we have are an extended analysis of existence by constant contrast with two other modes of being. Heidegger repeatedly exhorts us to understand Dasein on and in its own terms rather than those borrowed from another kind of being. Let us call this demand the Existential Imperative.[5] Metaphysicians have been seduced by a single idea and ideal of what it means to be – to participate in Forms, to be created by God, to be a substance, etc. – which they then force onto everything. Heidegger argues that the very fact that we treat, say, people differently from hammers or rocks shows that we have at least a vague, pre-ontological appreciation of multiple ways to be.

Turning back to the history of philosophy, one thing that Heidegger finds striking is the prominent role time has played "as a criterion for distinguishing realms of Being" (39/18). For instance, Plato distinguishes the things of this world that we sense and use and that are in time from the Forms that transcend this world as perfect and unchanging outside of time. One of the features that makes the former not fully real and the latter really real is that the latter are not temporal. Thus time plays a decisive role in this analysis of being and yet, Heidegger argues, no one asked *why* time gets to play this part. Why is it time that determines ontological status as opposed to all the other ways reality could have been divided up? His answer is that Dasein is itself, at bottom, temporal so we understand being in temporal ways.

In fact, these two early answers are connected: time is the meaning of being *because* Dasein is ultimately temporal. Heidegger is using a Kantian argument here that I will call The Law of Transcendental Transitivity. Kant argued, in what he called "the highest principle of all synthetic judgments," that the features we use to structure experience will necessarily be found in everything we experience, my Law of Transcendental Transitivity (Kant 1965, A158/B197). Since our minds organize our experience of the world in spatial relations, for example, everything we will ever encounter through the senses will be in space.

Heidegger takes over this argument, with three specific changes. First, he broadens out the kinds of experience to include our mundane interactions with the world, limiting scientific experience (which Kant focused on exclusively) to only one kind of being: presence-at-hand. Second, Heidegger wants to show how time alone can account for all the ways we experience and understand the world and ourselves, as he starts to do in the second half of Division 2 (38/17). Whereas Kant has a wide assortment of forms, concepts, and ideas structuring experience, Heidegger thinks they can all be reduced to different forms of temporality. Third, as we will see in just a minute, Heidegger rejects Kant's belief that behind the phenomena we experience there lies a noumenal realm of reality-in-itself which therefore limits features like space to just phenomena. For Heidegger, the world we experience is the world as it really is, so the features we "impose" on it are really there, rather than just subjective projections.[6] We will examine this idea in more depth in the next chapter.

Now that we have realized that we are unduly guided by traditional theories, we must figure out how to fight this influence and see what the world is actually like. Heidegger's answer is phenomenology, the method invented by his teacher, Edmund Husserl. ¶7 goes into a long etymological examination of the two Greek roots of the word, *phainomena* and *logos*, concluding that their meanings are strikingly overlapping (58/34). Phenomena means those things that come into the light (51/28), metaphorically speaking – that manifest themselves to us. He also goes into another long and rather confusing discussion of a constellation of terms that mean different ways of appearing.[7] The gist of it is that he understands that which appears to us as true reality rather than a sign of something that does not appear, like Plato's Forms or Locke's substance or Kant's noumena: "least of all can the Being of entities ever be anything such that 'behind it' stands something else 'which does not appear'" (60/35).

This means that when we study reality, we don't have to treat what we experience as second best, as a paltry substitute for real reality, or a mask we have to decipher in order to figure out what the real thing behind it is. If you want to know what the world is like, open up your eyes and take a look – *that's* the world. This is why he proclaims that, *"only as phenomenology, is ontology possible"* (60/35). Rather than sitting in a chair and logically reasoning out how the world must be, we should simply go "to the things themselves," as Husserl said, and see what they're like. We no longer have to demote what appears to *mere* appearance, as the long tradition of metaphysics has taught us to do. Ultimately, for Heidegger, to be is to appear to us, so the study of experience is the study of reality. Phenomenology is ontology.

However, as was true of ourselves, the study of experience is not completely straightforward. Although we are to study what appears, things can appear in lots of different ways. In particular, our topic – being – paradoxically shows up as hidden (59/35). This apparent contradiction clears up when we remember what Heidegger means by being, namely, the way that things are. When we drive a car, we are only thinking about the car or, as we will see in 1.III, we often aren't thinking about much of anything but just enjoying the breeze or a song on the radio. The fact that the car is an instrument I am using to get to somewhere is not something that occurs to me, even though I have to pre-ontologically understand this in order to use it for this purpose. We primarily focus on beings; their being informs our interactions with them but while remaining in the background. This is one reason why we lack the grammar and vocabulary to properly talk about being – language is ontically oriented (63/39). While we don't have to go beyond the mundane things of daily life to find the true truth, neither is being a prominent, easily grasped feature of experience. Bringing it into focus will take work.

The second complication in studying experience is that we have a built-in tendency to misunderstand ourselves and the world. Division 1 gives us one reason for this tendency to misinterpret, and Division 2 gives us another, as we will see. Part II was to give us a third, historical one – that we use inappropriate views inherited from the tradition to understand ourselves – though that reason presupposes the other two as explanations for why philosophers have so consistently gotten it wrong in the first place.

These two reasons mean that we can't just take experience as it is; we have to do some work interpreting it to find its true significance. This is why Heidegger calls his phenomenology "hermeneutic" (62/37), which refers to a school of philosophy founded by Friedrich Schleiermacher in the eighteenth century. In traditional Catholicism, people depended on their priest to explain what God wants of them and what the Bible means. Initially this didn't pose a problem since so few people were literate and there were so few copies of the Bible to be read; peasants just looked at the pretty stained glass windows while the priest droned on in Latin. But the Protestant Revolution made the idea that individuals should forge their own personal relationships with God popular, and the invention of the printing press made books cheaper and more plentiful, so people started reading it on their own to figure out how to live and worship. The problem is that the Bible is not an easy book, and misunderstanding it may have rather serious consequences for one's soul. So hermeneutics was founded as the analysis of how interpretation works. Originally it focused on reading texts, but Wilhelm Dilthey expanded its subject matter to psychological and historical understanding, investigating how we understand other people and especially people from different time periods who think and speak differently from us. Heidegger, the next important figure in the history of the movement (the fourth one was his student, Hans-Georg Gadamer), expands interpretation into a constantly operating process in all of our experience. We will see this especially in 1.V.¶32.

Thus for Heidegger, phenomenology is the way to study being, which means that we study it as it appears to us. But phenomenology must be existential, which means that it begins by analyzing our way of being (existence). This fits with phenomenology since the fundamental feature that defines us is our ability to be aware. It must also be hermeneutic in that it interprets experience rather than just accepting it at face value. Furthermore, it must be accompanied by a historical destruction to clear away theories that may block or distort what we see. And finally, it is ontological in that what we experience is reality as it really is. All of these disparate streams of thought are united in Heidegger's form of phenomenology.

Further readings

There is a vast literature on tacit knowledge or know-how (as opposed to knowing-that). Classics include Gilbert Ryle's *The Concept of Mind* and Michael Polanyi's *The Tacit Dimension*, although it can all be traced to Aristotle's discussion of *phronēsis* in *Nicomachean Ethics*. I argue in *Groundless Grounds: A Study of Wittgenstein and Heidegger* that both Heidegger and Wittgenstein offer sophisticated accounts of tacit knowledge, and this idea runs throughout much of Hubert Dreyfus' work, e.g. *What Computers Still Can't Do*.

For further information on phenomenology, one can go to the source – Husserl's *Ideas: General Introduction to Pure Phenomenology* and *Cartesian Meditations* both offer good overviews, while Heidegger's *History of the Concept of Time* goes into detail on certain issues. Dermot Moran's *Introduction to Phenomenology*, on the other hand, gives a more accessible introduction to the movement. One of the great works of hermeneutics is Hans-Georg Gadamer's *Truth and Method*, though once again more introductory works abound. For an insightful discussion of the basic strategy of *Being and Time*, take a look at Jacques Taminiaux's *Heidegger and the Project of Fundamental Ontology*.

2

Being and Time *1.I–IV: Being-in and the World*

Now that we have finished the thorny and rather abstract Introduction, things get a bit smoother. The writing in the book proper is still very hard, but Heidegger slows down and takes more time explaining each new term instead of piling them up one after another as in the Introduction. Another advantage is that he starts using the method of phenomenology instead of just talking about it. The key to practicing phenomenology is that "everything about [the topic in question] which is up for discussion must be treated by exhibiting it directly" (59/35). A phenomenological proof is not a logical argument where premises lead rationally to a conclusion, but a description that lets you see what the author is talking about. Heidegger's descriptions are correct if you find the same structures and phenomena in your experience, and wrong if you don't, although sometimes seeing them aright takes considerable effort (this need for interpretation is why he considers his work "hermeneutic," as briefly discussed in Chapter 1 and further explained in Chapter 3).

This means that no matter how difficult the writing and how thick the terms, Heidegger is always trying to get at something you are already familiar with, albeit only tacitly. As with Plato's recollection, this pre-ontological familiarity allows us to recognize these phenomena when our attention is drawn to them (85/58). Furthermore, the experiences he is describing are from our normal, average everyday lives rather than any kind of exceptional state that you might not have encountered. So whenever you find yourself lost – and this will happen many times, believe me – try to figure out what experience he's trying to describe. If you can chop through the thick verbiage to get to the relevant experience, it can anchor your interpretation of the text.

Heidegger loves coining new words or using common words in new, technical ways, which accounts for a large degree of the difficulty of his writing. But remember – he's trying to describe phenomena that are so close to us that we never pay explicit attention to them, which means that we generally lack a vocabulary for them. We come up with words for what is prominent in our attention when we think about things, but Heidegger is after that which escapes notice. Ironically, phenomenology – the study of what appears – seeks out that which does not appear, at least not explicitly, prominently, plainly) (59/35). It is in the very nature of his project that (the subject will be difficult to understand) since he is fighting against the grain of our normal ways of thinking and speaking.) Thus, we should forgive him a certain amount of neologisms and strange, hard to understand ways of writing if he succeeds in capturing phenomena that have eluded the conceptual and linguistic net of twenty-five centuries of philosophy.) Let us see whether he does.

Being and Time 1.I **Mineness and authenticity**

We still have to get through two more points that Heidegger simply asserts without much explanation or justification. These are still the preliminaries, helping to initially orient our examination of Dasein's way of being – the existential analytic that takes up the book as we have it. We have already seen in ¶4 that Dasein's being is at issue for it (32/12), which really sets the stage for all that follows. Briefly, attempting to settle this issue by being a certain kind of person by interacting with other entities is why Dasein must have an understanding of being) which is why we are studying Dasein as the foundation of the study of being or ontology. This will make more sense as we go along.

Now Heidegger adds that Dasein is *"in each case mine"* (67/41). A human life doesn't just happen; it is owned. This is *my* life; I have an intimate connection with it in a way that I don't have with yours and that a rock doesn't with its. I can be my own man but a rock isn't its own rock; its "survival" doesn't matter to it because it has no relationship to itself. It doesn't know that it is, so it can't strive to perpetuate itself or prosper. It is, but it can't take a stand

or position on its own being. This idea reaches back to the fact that
my being is an issue, in that it is an issue *for me*. *I* have to take up
my projects and live my life in an inescapably personal way.
Streams of awareness and action don't just occur – they are people's lives. Dasein is personal. This also reaches forward to one of
the most important topics of the book, authenticity.

Authenticity translates the German word "*Eigentlichkeit*," which
is built on the root "*eigen*" for "own," as in something that is one's
own. Heidegger says that I can only be authentic because my life
is already mine or, with more jargon, authenticity is founded on
Dasein's in-each-case-mineness (68/43). At first sight this seems
strange – if our lives are always our own, then how could we not
have them and thus be inauthentic? We will get a much more
detailed discussion of authenticity in 2.II, but we can get a first
approximation by saying that authenticity is a kind of full actualization of the always present mineness. My life is automatically
mine, but I don't always own it or own up to it in the sense of
explicitly laying claim to it, taking responsibility for it, truly making
it my own. We will see more of this kind of inauthenticity in 1.IV
and 2.I.

There is an expression, "become who you are," first said by
Pindar and later adopted by Hegel and Nietzsche (quoted at
186/145), that captures some of what authenticity means. At first
glance, the command makes no sense – if I already am who I am,
how can I become it? But we can start to see the point when we
distinguish between a passive way of being who you are and an
active appropriation of your way of being. Certainly, we are all
already Dasein, but without really realizing this in both senses of
the word: understanding it and intentionally trying to live in a
Daseinish way. In fact, Heidegger thinks that most of the time we
live in ways that are inappropriate to the kinds of beings that we
are, so we need to appropriate our lives, which are already our
"property," to do what is proper to our way of being (this is another
family of words that capture some of what "*eigen*" means). To
become what we are is to grasp the nature of our existence and
deliberately live in harmony with it. This gives the Existential
Imperative an ethical dimension, in the broad sense of the word:
we uncover our distinct nature in order to live lives more appropriate to it. Note, however, that living appropriately or authentically
does not mean taking up specific activities, the way many philosophers have singled out particular tasks we need to do in order to
live good lives. Heidegger insists that he is not recommending a

concrete ideal (69/43). Authenticity is a way of living whatever kind of life we choose; it functions as an adverb rather than a verb or a noun.

The second important point of 1.I is that the essence of Dasein is its existence (67/42). This was famously interpreted by Sartre to mean that existence precedes essence, that is, that we just show up totally free and unformed, and create our essence through the decisions we make. Now, we can find some of this in Heidegger – our being is essentially at issue rather than set, requiring us to decide what kind of person to be. However, there are limits on these decisions. When Heidegger says that our essence is *existence*, he doesn't mean just being there in reality; that's what he means by presence-at-hand which is precisely what he is contrasting existence with in the preceding paragraph. Existence is a technical term here which denotes Dasein's kind of being which has very specific features; indeed, it is the whole point of the existential analytic to find and lay these out. "There are certain structures which we shall exhibit – not just any accidental structures, but essential ones which, in every kind of Being that factical Dasein may possess, persist as determinative for the character of its Being" (38/17). Where Sartre opposes existence to any kind of essence, Heidegger believes that existence has an essential, defining structure. That's precisely what he's after.

The important point here, however, is that this way of being is fundamentally unlike other ways of being. As we saw in ¶6, ignoring this distinction is the original sin of all previous metaphysics, so Heidegger emphasizes over and over again the utter heterogeneity between these modes of being in what I'm calling the Existential Imperative. In fact, to prevent any blurring here he coins a new term for Dasein's structures – existentialia – as opposed to characteristics of non-Dasein entities which he calls categories (70/44).

Being and Time 1.II Being-in-the-world and being-in

The beginning of Chapter II of Division 1 gives us our last provisional definition of Dasein – as being-in-the-world – which will inform the rest of this Division (78/53). It is crucial to understand being-in-the-world as a holistic totality, which means that each element can only be and can only be understood in the context of the others. Just as Heidegger says that "and" is the most important word in the title *Being and Time*, so here the hyphens are absolutely crucial to understanding being-in-the-world. However, it's impossible to grasp them all at one gulp so we have to go through them one at a time, and this serial explanation organizes the rest of Division 1: Chapter II explains being-in, Chapter III the world, Chapter IV the being who is in the world, Chapter V returns to discuss being-in at greater depth, and Chapter VI ends the first Division by showing what underlies and unifies all of these aspects. Throughout this discussion of the various aspects, we need constantly to keep the holistic interconnections in mind. Starting from separate pieces can never give us this deep unity, in what I call the Humpty-Dumpty Thesis (170/132).

Heidegger uses the distinction between existentialia and categories to frame his treatment of being-in. Thought of as a category, that is, in terms of non-Dasein things (specifically, present-at-hand objects), being-in means to be located within another object in space, the way a milk jug is *in* the refrigerator. Now, if existentialia and categories are as radically different as Heidegger says, then whatever our being-in is, it *can't* be this common-sense notion. "Being-in, on the other hand, is a state of Dasein's Being; it is an *existentiale*. So one cannot think of it as the Being-present-at-hand of some corporeal Thing (such as a human body) 'in' an entity which is present-at-hand" (79/54).

Heidegger examines the deep structure of the *existentiale* being-in by means of a slightly more superficial one that is closer to our daily lives, *Sein-bei*. Now, as you can imagine, *Being and Time* is a tremendously difficult book to translate. Heidegger is constantly making up words or using them in strange ways and playing on all kinds of word associations that don't carry over to English, and by and large Macquarrie and Robinson do a remarkable job. But translating *Sein-bei* as "being alongside" is just dumb. It suggests *exactly* what Heidegger is explicitly trying to distinguish it from, "the side-by-side-ness of an entity called 'Dasein' with another entity called 'world'" (81/55). The whole point of the analysis of being-in is that we are *not* alongside the world; we're in it, amid things and among people. So wherever the book has "being alongside," we will instead say "being-amid," which I think is much closer to what Heidegger has in mind.

One of the features of our being temporal creatures is that we have a past. At any time that we start thinking about what kind of person to be, we inevitably have a record of already having been a certain kind of person for a period of time. There is no way to start absolutely afresh for beings like us; all acting and thinking is done *in medias res*, already underway. Heidegger captures this in his famous phrase, "always already." We are always already a certain kind of person and any changes we might want to make necessarily start from a context of choices that have already been made that influence what I can do now. This is what he calls our "facticity" (82/56).

Facticity means that we have always already made a bunch of existentiell (that is, pertaining to a particular Dasein) choices, entangling us with the set of people and things involved in those actions.

> Dasein's facticity is such that its Being-in-the-world has always dispersed itself or even split itself up into definite ways of Being-in. The multiplicity of these is indicated by the following examples: having to do with something, producing something, attending to something and looking after it, making use of something. . . . All these ways of Being-in have *concern* as their kind of Being. (83/56)

I am always already a certain kind of person by having led a certain kind of life, and this is composed of performing actions with the relevant tools and people. You are a student by showing up for classes with books and notebooks, asking teachers questions, paying tuition, taking tests, and so on. You are not a student simply by studying, but by doing a number of the kinds of things that students do with basically the right kinds of people, places, and things. Here we see the first turn of the Hermeneutic Spiral mentioned in Chapter I which reinterprets one of Dasein's most basic features in terms of its definition as being-in-the-world to try to settle the issue of our being means to take care of tasks, to do things in the world.

Notice how pedestrian these activities are. They're mundane tasks like watering plants, filling the tank of your car, showing up for class. This is in keeping with Heidegger's insistence that we study Dasein in its average everydayness rather than starting off favoring special actions or states such as contemplation. They are also practical – they're things we *do* in the world. This is what he means when he says that they all are matters of what he calls concern, "*Besorgen*." Don't think of this as sentimental as in being concerned about an elderly family member's well-being. He means something closer to business concerns, dealing with problems that arise by taking appropriate steps. One way to translate it is as taking care of business, which also nicely foreshadows the connection to care ("*Sorge*") that we will see in 1.VI.

We are in the world not by being spatially located within this level of reality or the atmosphere of the earth, but by taking care of things. I must do this because my being is at issue and so I have to perform activities in order to be a certain kind of person, and because this life is mine it is my concern to deal with. The existentiale being-in is more like being in a club or a band or love than being in a building. I am in a club by engaging in common activities with other members, paying dues, coming to meetings, and so on, and this can take place at great spatial distances, on-line for example. The difference between the category being-in and the existentiale, we might say, is the difference between being in a classroom and being in a class. Fully understanding this will require a new understanding of the world as what we are in, which is coming in Chapter III.

The standard metaphysical model portrays us and the world as objects, as self-sufficient substances that may or may not come into contact with other things. This view is most plausible when we disengage from our normal activities in the world in order to contemplate. This is Descartes' moment of setting aside his daily concerns so that he can fully concentrate on the philosophical examination of himself and the world. Husserl, Heidegger's teacher and a great fan of Descartes, built this detachment into phenomenology's method with the phenomenological bracketing or reduction. But Heidegger believes that this apparently innocent first step ruins the entire investigation before it even gets started. For one thing, it filters out what goes on 99 percent of the time in our lives – our average everydayness. How often do you stop and stare at something or just sit in a chair contemplating the idea of knowledge or the number 3, as opposed to putting on your shoes or having a sandwich or playing tennis? By ceasing all the activities that make up our daily lives, we allow them to fall away from our gaze when we try to examine ourselves.

What is left then is precisely what Descartes found: thinking. That's all we're doing when we look at ourselves so we naturally conclude that what we are in essence is a thinking thing, that all the other stuff we put to the side is superficial claptrap, mere accidents. And the world then shows up as inert objects, as we will see in more detail in Chapter III. We are disengaged, without concerns, and at a distance from the things we're looking at. And now that we're at a distance, we feel the need to create some kind of connection. We seem to need to *make* a connection because our artificial stance has *removed* the connection that had been there and that is always there. And what resources do we have to make this connection? The one feature that apparently defines us: thinking. Our initial contact with the world then seems to be made by knowing it (85/59), which raises the question of how we can be certain of this knowledge. All we have are thoughts and sense perceptions that merely purport to be of external objects, which means that we're never in direct contact with these objects, only their representations. So how can we ever be sure if these representations inside our minds match up with the external world?

Heidegger is trying to show that these ideas progress according to an internal logic. Descartes wasn't stupid for getting things so completely wrong; it was the first fateful step of stopping and staring at things that locked him onto this train of thought. Once he took that step, all the other parts of his system follow naturally. We are isolated thinking things who must build a bridge to the world and this connection is intrinsically susceptible to skeptical doubts. All of this, with minor variations, is contained in embryo in the seemingly innocuous preparations of sitting by the fire to start to think.

The good news is that if we can avoid taking this first step, if we can somehow go around it and recover all that it leaves out, an incredibly rich field for philosophical analysis awaits us. We have the chance to create a radically new system that will be far truer to our daily experience, and this is the project of *Being and Time.*

Descartes argues that epistemology must come before metaphysics: we have to be sure of our ways of gathering information before we can trust them to tell us anything about the world. This marks a significant departure from traditional philosophy since Aristotle made ontology first philosophy, and many thinkers over the next couple of centuries follow Descartes' lead. Heidegger wants to turn this revolution back, to make the question of being primary again. Whereas Descartes sets up the problem of skepticism as a natural, even inevitable worry which must be settled before we can say anything about reality, Heidegger argues that this very problem rests on metaphysical assumptions. The only way the question of how we can make a reliable cognitive connection to the world is important, even unavoidable, is if (1) we start off isolated from the world and (2) our primary relationship to it is cognitive. This metaphysical picture treats self and world as distinct entities with no intrinsic connection. Not only is this an assumption – a metaphysical assumption that must be in place before Descartes can begin his epistemological inquiries – but it's wrong. This conception only appears plausible once we have disengaged from our normal activities.

If we have the right understanding of Dasein and world, which is what Division 1 is trying to give us, Descartes' system won't even be able to get off the ground. Heidegger doesn't want to refute it so much as stop it before it starts. On Heidegger's picture, "it is not the case that man 'is' and then has, by way of an extra, a relationship-of-Being towards the 'world' – a world with which he provides himself occasionally. Dasein is never 'proximally' an entity which is, so to speak, free from Being-in, but which sometimes has the inclination to take up a 'relationship' towards the world" (84/57). Knowing is essentially a secondary relationship that derives from our usual being-amid the world. *First*, we deal with things and take care of business. Once we have done this for a long time, we can *then* on occasion temporarily cease these activities and simply stare in "the mode of just tarrying alongside." Heidegger has not yet proven that this is so, but he has at least loosened the grip that this intellectualist picture has on us, and especially on philosophers. Now his task is to show why his account is right.

Being and Time 1.III The world

Being and Time *1.III.A Worldly equipment*

Now that we have seen what it means for Dasein to be-in (the existentiale) as opposed to the way objects are spatially located within a container (the category), we need a new concept of the world which we can be-in in this distinctive way. We are in-the-world through concern through carrying out tasks and pursuing goals, so the world must be the context for these concerns and tasks, that wherein we carry out our daily business. Just as Heidegger approached being-in through its more concrete version of being-amid, so here he starts examining the world by looking at "that world of everyday Dasein which is closest to it . . . the *environment*" (94/66). "Environment" translates "*Umwelt*," the world (*Welt*) around (*um*) us. The word "environment" captures this meaning etymologically but with misleading connotations – Heidegger is not talking about nature or climate change or anything like that. He means the organizations and events like a class or a club or a religious service that we're in by participating in its relevant activities.

In keeping with his commitment to average everydayness, we will focus on how Dasein usually is. In the first place and for the most part we don't stare or contemplate but use and interact with things. Heidegger calls these actions "dealings," which translates "*Umgang*" (95/66–7). Throughout this chapter he weaves together a number of words with the prefix "*um*" to talk about the world "around" us where we go "about" our business, which gets lost in translation. When he turns to the beings that make up the world we reside in, we should start not with special entities like minds or atoms or Forms, but with the most common things we're around all the time – the stuff we use for various purposes. At almost every moment you're employing a vast array of things to be-in the world, that is, to take care of your concerns – you're reading a book, wearing clothes, sitting on a chair, using light to read by, etc.

So let's do a quick phenomenological examination of something at hand that you use. We're studying Heidegger not to memorize what Heidegger thinks, but to learn to see what he's showing us. This is what Husserl meant when he said that we should go to the things themselves instead of going back to Kant, or any thinker. We'll take this book as our subject. Now, set it in front of you and look at it; *really* look at it. Normally we barely take it in since immediate recognition relieves us of the need to take our time deliberately examining things, but now take a hard, careful look. What is it like? What do you actually see? Take a few moments to jot down a description of it before you read on – I'll wait for you.

Got it? How did you describe it? A rectangular object, occupying space, positioned on a table in front of you, containing thin pieces of paper covered with ink markings . . . something like that? Now let me ask you this: is this how you are experiencing the book right now? As an object with certain spatial dimensions containing ink squiggles? Or is it rather that while you're reading, the physical object-book kind of shimmers out of your explicit awareness, and words just enter your mind immediately, almost telepathically? Or what about the pen you used to write down your description? That's another tool – was it present in your experience as a physical object of certain dimensions – or at all – as you were writing with it?

Heidegger thinks that we suffer from a persistent tendency to misunderstand our own experience (96/67). Although we had a genuine experience of the book or pen while using them which was informed by a pre-ontological understanding of their being, this "becomes *invisible* if one interprets it in a way which is ontologically inappropriate" (86/59). The way we actually experienced it during use vanishes when we look directly at it, like a dim star at night. This is another sense in which phenomenology studies that which is hidden (59/35), although here hidden means *too* obvious rather than removed from sight. The problem, as we saw in Chapter II, lies in the stance we take up. In order to describe the book you stopped using it and just stared at it, "tarrying alongside" it (88/61). Now staring at a book is certainly something we're capable of doing and it may at times be worthwhile, but compare the number of times you've just passively observed a book as an object as opposed to picking it up and reading it, or tossing it into your book bag. The ratio is absurdly tilted towards use as our normal mode of interaction and yet, when we tried to understand what the book was, we stopped these activities just to look, something we almost never do. Heidegger wants to avoid this prejudicing preparatory step in order to rediscover what the book was like *while we read it,* what pens are like *as we write with them* (98/69). He calls this mode of being of equipment, the second mode of being discussed after Dasein's existence, readiness-to-hand (*Zuhandenheit*). The rest of Part A of Chapter III explains the characteristics or categories of this mode of being, so let's take these up one at a time.

(1) Equipment is holistic. No single tool can exist without an "ecosystem" of other tools within which it does its work (97–8/68–9). A pen can't be a pen except in relation to something that can be written on, such as paper. It is most itself when it takes its place within a system of implements for writing: paper, but also tables to put the paper on in order to write, chairs to sit on at the table, lights to let us see what we're writing, notebooks to hold the paper written on, backpacks for the notebooks, and so on. Each item in this system is an "in-order-to" ("*Um-zu*") that refers to other pieces of equipment which all come together to form a circuit of use unified by the goal of producing something or bringing something about, its "towards which" (99/70).

Experientially, it is the whole that is first, as the Gestalt psychologists discovered. You walk into a restaurant, not a collection of individual items that you then piece together into a whole which you determine to be a restaurant; it presents itself as a place-for-eating from the start. Out of this totality, individual items such as your chair or a menu can emerge when activities such as sitting down or ordering temporarily bring them forward, but the whole comes first (98/69). Indeed, it is this initial whole that makes the individual items meaningful: I see the menu *as* a list of things I can order from the waiter to eat rather than encountering it as a thin object with squiggles whose purpose I must discern from environmental clues because I know I'm in a restaurant.[2]

(2) As we saw in our phenomenological exercise, we get at tools not by examining them but by using them. However, this access is problematic because while I'm using it, I'm generally not thinking about the thing at all. The tool dissolves into the project at hand rather than standing out as a discrete object with notable characteristics. As long as it's functioning properly I pay no attention to my car, just driving on autopilot as it were. Tools "withdraw" from thematic attention during use (99/69), as they must for us to use them fluidly and competently. Try writing the sentence "I am now writing this sentence with my pen" while concentrating on the pen you're holding in your hand. A lot harder than when you stop paying attention to it and just let your hand take care of things, isn't it? Obviously, we must understand the tools in order to use them, but this pre-ontological understanding is more of a know-how. Heidegger calls it *Umsicht* (seeing around or perhaps taking it all in, having a sense of your surroundings), translated here as "circumspection" (98/69) which again is etymologically correct but decidedly odd in English. When we stop and stare, we only think of knowledge as knowing-that, which is why philosophers have traditionally missed this other far more common variety.

(3) When we make something, it is usually itself another tool, such as a cobbler making shoes (Heidegger favors old-timey, craft examples). Furthermore, it's meant for people, either a specific individual or just the generic shoe-wearer. Even if I'm making an item for myself, it will generally be something that others could use, an example of a general kind of tool. This means that even if I am completely alone in the *Umwelt* of my workshop, toiling away in

the dead of night, I'm still occupying and working within a public world (100/71). Others bleed into these apparently private moments in that the tools being made are to-be-used-by-someone in relatively standard ways set by society. This resolves the concern Heidegger briefly mentioned earlier (92/64) about our being locked away into private, solipsistic worlds, a topic he will address in more detail in Chapter IV.

(4) Recall from the Introduction that Heidegger believes that phenomenology is ontology (60/35): to be means to appear to us in some way, to become manifest. This means that rather than being a misleading "mere" appearance which we have to surpass in order to grasp true reality, the way things appear to us is the way they are, although they often need to be interpreted. Heidegger now applies this ontological view to readiness-to-hand. A tool's usability is not some subjective idea we project onto the physical object that is what's really there. We experience the hammer as a ready-to-hand tool so that's how it is. "*Readiness-to-hand is the way in which entities as they are 'in-themselves' are defined ontologico-categorially*" (101/71). The "in-themselves" is a rejection of Kant's distinction between things as they are for-us (phenomena) and as they are in-themselves (noumena) without any interference from us. Heidegger's phenomenological ontology is meant to collapse the two.[3]

This is a little confusing since, if hammers are only really hammers when someone is hammering with them, their being depends on our using them. This makes readiness-to-hand Dasein-dependent, which would seem to make it merely subjective as opposed to what the world is really like. But Heidegger's not interested in what things are like completely independent of us; how could we ever find that out? No matter where or how we look it will always be us looking, so we will always bring whatever interference we produce along with us to any attempt to investigate how things are independent of our interference. We are *essentially* in-the-world so we can never get to a world-without-Dasein. All we can study is the world-as-it-appears-to-us, so this is what we should think of as true reality. "If we are inquiring about the meaning of Being, our investigation does not then become a 'deep' one, nor does it puzzle out what stands behind Being. It asks about Being itself insofar as Being enters into the intelligibility of Dasein" (193/152). Readiness-to-hand may only characterize beings-for-us, but everything we encounter and can talk or think about is necessarily something for-us, so the qualification falls away as meaningless. This anti-realism is a common response to Kant's system among continental thinkers, shared by figures such as Hegel, Nietzsche, and Husserl.

(5) As we saw in no. 2, tools withdraw during use, a property Heidegger calls "inconspicuousness." But if they're so elusive, the question arises of how we ever become explicitly aware of them. Well, although they are inconspicuous while they're functioning properly, they become conspicuous when a problem arises. While I'm driving along the road I don't think about the steering wheel and pedals, or the car at all, but if the engine sputters and stops, the car suddenly pops back into focus, squeezing out everything else. At this point, the book's third way of being – presence-at-hand – "announces itself" (103/73). This is the kind of being that things have when we just stare at them. They're inert, possessing physical properties, just lying around, as we'll discuss more in a moment.

Now this state of disrepair is really a transitional stage between readiness-to-hand and full presence-at-hand. The tool still retains its in-order-to references to other tools and to the goal I am using it for. In fact, these become prominent for the first time. I was driving to the store in order to get a loaf of bread to make a sandwich to take for lunch tomorrow when I go hiking with the Outdoors Club. I am in-the-club by participating in its activities such as hiking and these activities require various pieces of equipment – shoes, clothes, transportation, etc. Although I of course "knew" all this – I didn't just get into the car and randomly drive off – I may very well have not given it any thought, simply carrying out the tasks while humming a happy little tune or thinking about something wholly unrelated.

When my car breaks down, however, I become exceedingly, even painfully aware of this whole web-work of interconnected tools, tasks, and goals precisely because I now need to figure out how to repair the broken tool or come up with another way to carry out my task. "When an assignment has been disturbed . . . the context of equipment is lit up, not as something never seen before, but as a totality constantly sighted beforehand in circumspection. With this totality, however, the world announces itself" (105/75). These chains of use were already there but I had been navigating them without conscious control or thought. When an obstacle arises, that is when the paths I had been following shimmer into visibility, at least long enough to repair the damage and get back onto a path, at which point I can relax again and let my hands and feet take

over getting me where I need to go. The links of in-order-tos sink
silently beneath the surface once more as I resume my humming.
This web of instrumental connections is the world.

Heidegger summarizes all of these ideas in a single dense sentence: "being-in-the-world, according to our Interpretation hith-
erto, amounts to a non-thematic circumspective absorption in
references or assignments constitutive for the readiness-to-hand of
a totality of equipment" (107/76). Normally, we are in-the-world
by dealing with our concerns and this is a non-thematic absorption.
We rarely give explicit thought to our tasks, the tools we use to
accomplish them, or even ourselves. We are absorbed in our work
and absorbed into the world. When you're driving to the store, you
are *in* that activity of doing what you need to do in order to be-in
the Outdoors Club. *That* is where your self is "located," rather than
pulling the levers of the body from a separated mental interiority.
"Dasein finds 'itself' proximally in *what* it does, uses, expects,
avoids – in those things environmentally ready-to-hand with which
it is proximally *concerned*" (155/119). We are in-the-world in being
absorbed into these circulating circuits of use that make up what
Heidegger calls a world.

(6) A world is a fluid dynamic circulation of activity that sucks me
in when I "get into" what we're doing, as we say in English. Each
tool I use indicates or points towards other tools in its equipmental
ecosystem and towards the general purpose the tools as a whole
are meant to bring about, the towards-which. This feature is translated here as "significance," but the German "*Bedeutung*" also contains a sense of pointing or indicating (120/87). Thus the pen
deflects my attention away from it towards the paper on which I
need to jot something down, which itself indicates the goal I have
in writing – the test I'm taking notes for or the trip to the store I'm
writing a list for. But the end of the activity itself also signifies; it
too points towards further ends *it* serves. A product like the shoes
the cobbler makes is the towards-which for her, but the person who
buys them uses them as a means in-order-to go about her business
– looking smart at work or running a marathon. It's important to
remember that Heidegger is talking about modes of being rather
than groups of entities, which means that a particular entity can
change its mode of being under different conditions. I'm using the
pen in-order-to take the notes (the immediate towards-which), but
I'm taking notes in turn in-order-to do well on the test, which I'm
doing in-order-to pass the class, and so on.

(7) Taking a page from Aristotle, Heidegger points out that this chain of instrumental goods can't go on forever. There has to be a reason why we engage in the series of activities at all and this can't be in-order-to do something else because that would just perpetuate the regress; we must anchor the chain of actions on something that itself doesn't derive its meaning from something further. Whereas Aristotle makes happiness the non-instrumental good – the thing that is good in itself rather than good for something else – Heidegger (in his early work) is an existentialist, so he doesn't have a high opinion of happiness. Instead, he returns to the very first thing he said about Dasein – that our being is an issue for us (32/12). We come into the world without a pre-set personality or instincts about what to do, which is rather unsettling. We go about our business in an attempt to settle this issue, to become a certain kind of person by taking up specific roles like student or friend or daughter. Heidegger calls this role our "for-the-sake-of-which" (116–17/84). This is the point that unifies and anchors all the instrumental chains of in-order-tos that we live in by being in-the-world. The reason why you do all of the tasks of taking notes and trying to pass the class and so on is that you want to be a student, and being a student is made up of doing the right kinds of activities, dealing with the right kinds of equipment in a particular *Umwelt* like a classroom or a college campus.

It is only in light of these roles that we are in-a-world at all, which lets us encounter individual items as meaningful. This is what Heidegger means when he says that our involvement in our roles "frees" beings (117–18/85). Depending on what role we take up and which particular activities we do in order to fulfill it, different things are going to detach themselves from the unnoticed background to stand out and call for attention. For instance, if you come to class with a laptop you might notice the electrical outlets for the first time whereas before they had simply been fused into the general, nondescript background. When you enter the room the chair you usually sit on will be highlighted, so to speak, attracting you to it while the other chairs remain washed out surroundings. When an electrician on the other hand enters the room, the outlets and the lights stand out to her while the chairs and blackboards will withdraw.

To understand this tool here and now, this pen for example, I must grasp its place horizontally in its circulating system of accompanying equipment and vertically in its chains of in-order-tos. These chains collectively point to a towards-which that takes its

place within other instrumental chains but ultimately these lines
gather together to lead up to a for-the-sake-of-which, a way of
understanding myself through the world that I live in. The world
in Heidegger's sense is this inconspicuous web-work of interconnections that are unified in an overarching goal, like lines of longitude meeting at the poles of a globe. These lines of significance are
where we live, where we make a life for ourselves and make a self
from our lives. The world is significant in the sense of being meaningful, too. This pen has meaning by having a position in my activities aimed at being a certain kind of person. The world makes sense
to me, and makes sense for me, and gives sense to me. It is the
necessary condition for the possibility of encountering particular
items of use (119–20/86) This aligns Heidegger's work with Kant's,
who also seeks the necessary conditions for experience. The difference, as we noted above, is that whereas Kant limits this to
scientific experience, Heidegger broadens the question to our non-
scientific, average everyday lives as well, as we will see in sections
B and C of Chapter III.

Being and Time 1.III.B *The contrast with Descartes*

In order to clarify his notion of worldhood, Heidegger contrasts it
with "the most extreme" (122/89) *mis*interpretation he can find:
Descartes'. Recall the analysis of equipment. The virtually unbro-
ken tradition of overlooking such a common feature of our lives is
not due to a millennia-long run of philosophers' stupidity. Rather,
it is in the nature of equipment to be overlooked both because tools
are inconspicuous (they withdraw from attention when working
well) and because they signify (they deflect attention away from
themselves towards other equipment and their purpose). We typically become aware of a tool when it doesn't work well – when it
breaks or is missing or not in the right place. Then it becomes conspicuous and partially transforms into a present-at-hand object by
just sitting there and not doing what we want it to do. This is a
transitional stage which partakes in both modes of being: it's
present-at-hand because it is no longer disappearing into the activity it's used for, but it still retains links of significance to other tools
and actions. Indeed, this is when the world or "the context of
equipment is lit up" (105/75) because we are now extremely,
uncomfortably conscious of what we were using the tool for. My
car's breaking down makes me painfully aware of the fact that I

was using it to drive to the store because I now see that I will fail to do so, or I look around for another tool that can accomplish the same ends, such as a bus. If I repair the tool or find a successful replacement, I can submerge once again into the action and allow the equipment and its world to fade back into pre-ontological familiarity.

However, I can also turn this pause in my activities into a full stop, cutting off the signifying connections in order just to stare at the tool in front of me. This completes its transformation into a purely present-at-hand object I am simply beholding, which forms the basis for science and for virtually all previous metaphysics. Descartes' basic metaphysical view is that to be is to be a substance and this section of *Being and Time* walks us through the being of substances, that is, what it means to be a substance. First, the essential features that characterize a particular substance are those that remain constant across changes in the object and across variation of perceivers; this is the conclusion Descartes draws from his examination of melting wax and it explains why he privileges mathematical properties (128/95–6). Second, a substance is self-sufficient: it needs nothing else in order to be (125/92). Third, our best access to a substance is through merely beholding it, which is why Descartes clears his schedule of concerns before starting to meditate (129/96).

The fundamental problem with Descartes' approach is – you guessed it: he doesn't ask about the being of beings deeply enough. Heidegger is somewhat outraged at the fact that Descartes stretches the notion of substance so far as to encompass not just thinking things and extended material things, but even the infinitely separated God (125/92). They all are and, since to be is to be a substance, they all are substances, just with some variations.

What's happening here is that Descartes starts with a specific conception of being which he then forces onto everything that is, a metaphysical Procrustes' bed (128–9/96). Note that this is the exact opposite of phenomenology which tries to be as open-minded as possible when approaching experience, allowing it to tell us what it is like rather than the other way around. Descartes' approach is especially problematic because it makes us into basically the same kind of entity as everything else (131/98), whereas Heidegger's guiding Existential Imperative is to differentiate our being from others. In particular, the present-at-hand way substances are is about as far as you can get from Dasein's existence. Where substances are inert and persist through change, we are dynamic and, as temporal creatures, open to profound change; where substances are self-sufficient things that may, but need not, enter into relations with external things, Dasein is essentially dependent on and intertwined with the world, equipment, and others. Thus, not only is presence-at-hand not the same as existence, they are diametrically opposed in many ways, making the traditional conception of us as substance deeply wrong.

Being and Time *1.III.C Lived space*

Now that we have the contrast with Descartes out of the way, we can turn to Heidegger's account of space as we live it, as we experience it on a daily basis. Whereas present-at-hand space is the space of Newton – a homogeneous, inert container of whatever happens to be located within it – the space we live in is made up of places. These are distinct areas that are not just located at different coordinates but have their own spatiality, their own feel. Think of how differently your bedroom at home feels from your classroom, or a cathedral, or a forest, or even other rooms in the house like the kitchen or den. Because we are in-the-world by concernful dealing or purposeful acting, places are organized around different towards-whichs. A classroom is for-learning, while a restaurant is for-eating, and the place's purpose organizes its set of equipment around that goal (145/111). The classroom has tables and chairs and chalkboards, not fenced in sheep or trays of silverware; if you walked into a classroom with silverware set up in the corner it would immediately strike you as *out of place*, as not appropriate for this place.

Taking up a particular purpose allows me to be-in-the-room as a localized environment or *Umwelt*. People with different towards-whichs can be in different environments even if they're located in the same objective space. Entering the classroom as a student highlights the chairs as to-be-sat-upon, the tables or desks as to-put-your-notebooks-on, the lectern and chalkboard as to-look-at-and-take-notes-from. By sharing this aim students inhabit the same place; the professor will be in the same place though from a somewhat different perspective since she must teach what the students learn, presenting items in a slightly different light or from a different angle, such as the chalkboard now being to-write-upon rather than to-read-from. For an electrician, on the other hand, most of that will remain fused together in the unnoticed background while lights-to-be-checked-and-kept-in-repair or frayed-wires-to-be-fixed will call out to her.

Because we are at bottom spatial creatures, one of the few correct insights Heidegger credits Descartes with (134/101), the pursuit of our tasks is itself spatial by the Law of Transcendental Transitivity mentioned in Chapter 1. We go about our business around and through the various places our tasks lay out. As environments (*Umwelten*), these places are made up of the signifying links between unified groups of equipment set up around specific goals. We enter a place by taking up its goal through using its equipment. Heidegger is now adding that these groups of equipment are usually laid out in space; they have what we might call an arrangement. This word captures the idea that each piece has its own place in an ordered totality and that these equipmental relationships have spatial connotations. The tools in the cobbler's workshop are arranged so that he can make shoes, with the table at the right height and the needed tools within reach.[5]

This also determines the nature of the "measurements" of lived space. Present-at-hand space is measured with neutral quantified units of feet or meters, but we only encounter these under specific circumstances (136/103). The space we move through in our average everyday taking care of business is measured circumspectively (*Umsicht*), in terms of tasks. Dasein has an intrinsic preference for closeness over distance because equipment must literally be ready-to-our-hands in order to be available for use. When you sit at your desk you arrange your own personal ecosystem of tools – notebooks, pen, coffee, laptop – all to be within-reach. Although "within-reach" does not meet Descartes' rigid standards of quantifiability and non-variance across circumstances and observers, it's perhaps the most important and common unit of measurement employed in our daily lives. Beyond it lie farther regions such as graspable-if-I-stretch or beyond-my-reach-without-getting-out-of-my-chair or back-in-my-room-so-inaccessible-for-the-present. "Though these estimates may be imprecise and variable if we try to compute them, in the everydayness of Dasein they have their own definiteness which is thoroughly intelligible" (140/105). Interestingly, neuroscientists have actually found that different neurons fire when monkeys look at something desirable that is within-reach as opposed to things that are out-of-reach.[6]

Thus circumspective closeness is not the same thing as objectively measured closeness. Heidegger uses circumspective closeness in two different ways without explicitly differentiating them.

First, there is pragmatic closeness or availability: a tool is close when I can use it easily (141–2/107). The clock across the room can be closer to me than a book in my book-bag right next to me because I can use the clock easily and quickly by glancing at it while it would take time and effort to dig around in my book-bag to get the book out. This kind of closeness can easily change. The store may be close as long as my car is functioning fine but if it sputters and dies on the way, the store suddenly stretches far away. What was "an easy drive" away becomes "a long, hot walk" away, even though the objective distance hasn't changed. The second form concerns where my attention is focused. My glasses are right next to my face but I almost never pay attention to them; I look through them. The friend I'm waving at twenty feet away is much closer to me in this sense than the glasses, although the glasses are both objectively closer and closer in the first pragmatic sense. They're fulfilling their purpose well whereas I cannot talk to my friend yet.

Another way lived space differs from present-at-hand space is that objective locations are separated from each other; this is almost the definition of space. Dasein, however, "de-severs;" we leap across the intervening space between us and what we're dealing with. My primary location is rarely at the zero-point of my body – normally I'm over there, at the object of my concern. When I get up to leave, I'm already there at the door, perhaps even at my room or the dining hall where I'm heading (142/107). This is one reason why Heidegger dismisses any notion of our being "inside" ourselves and then having to exit an inner sphere to make contact with the outside world. I am always already outside myself, out there with the things that I'm interacting with (89/62). When I'm talking with you, I'm right there at your face eight feet away, or I'm with you even though we're talking on the phone and you're half-way across the world.

Of course, all of this meaningfulness drains out once I cease my activities simply to observe objectively (147/112). Then we're left with the emptied-out husk of neutral homogeneous space that Descartes begins with. Heidegger's incessant talk about being can become rather annoying at times, but he's absolutely right to insist on it because what kinds of beings we take things to be guides how we will experience and think about them. Thus, "if one is oriented by Thinghood [i.e., presence-at-hand], these latter quali-ties [like beautiful or useful] must be taken as non-quantifiable value-predicates by which what is in the first instance just a material Thing, gets stamped" (132/99). In other words, if we start off with the ontological assumption that reality is made up of inert material objects, then any qualitative features we experience will inevitably appear to be merely subjective projections of our minds. They can't be really real because we've already pre-judged what is real to be quantifiable, invariant features such as weight or length. Heidegger's phenomenological ontology, on the other hand, attempts to return us to the world we actually live in and to restore philosophical respectability to it.

Being and Time 1.IV The who

Chapter IV turns to the question of the who of the being who is-in-the-world. In a sense, of course, that's what we've been studying all along in the existential analytic – what it is to be Dasein – but this chapter asks about the selfhood of Dasein, what it means to be a self. At first, this doesn't seem like it could be a question. We know what it is for things to be themselves – one of the most fundamental laws of logic is the law of identity: A=A. Things simply are what they are – what else could they be? – so Dasein is just itself. But of course Heidegger thinks that in this conception "Dasein is tacitly conceived in advance as something present-at-hand" (150/114) and, in accordance with the Existential Imperative, we must understand Dasein in its own way. In general, "traditional logic fails us when confronted with these phenomena . . . it has its foundation in an ontology of the present-at-hand" (166–7/129). In fact, as paradoxical as it sounds, Heidegger argues that for the most part Dasein is *not* itself (151/116, 167/129). In order to understand what this means, we need to understand what he means by others and to examine our experience of others phenomenologically.

  Heidegger's initial definition of others is equally paradoxical: "by 'Others' we do not mean everyone else but me – those over against whom the 'I' stands out. They are rather those from whom, for the most part, one does *not* distinguish oneself – those among whom one is too" (154/118). Recall his first discussion of the presence of others in our environment as those for whom we're making things or from whom we've bought the tools we're using (163/125). This shows that from the beginning, our environment is a public world, always already permeated by others. So if we find ourselves in our tasks and these essentially involve others, then our selves

have built-in – and are built out of – connections with others. Being
a teacher for example involves, in addition to using equipment,
having certain relations with students and administrators. Profes-
sorial tasks don't just refer to or signify other pieces of equipment,
but other people as well. Without them, these activities can't have
that meaning so I can't be that self. Although our lives are in each
case our own, they are also always public and interconnected.
Calling them others is misleading because they're not usually
experienced as set apart from me, no more than the world is a set
of objects facing me across a chasm. In my average everyday going
about my business I don't experience myself as a distinct separate
entity, cut off from others with whom I need to establish some kind
of contact. Certain events can introduce a separation, but this is just
a temporary suspension of the usually ongoing flow of direct
contact. Normally we are a part of the group, among and amid
our friends or class or family. Holistically, it is only out of these
masses that we can then individuate and find ourselves as distinct
individuals.[7]

Although Heidegger's analysis is not a developmental one, I
think it applies here and looking at it in this light may be illuminating. Babies do not differentiate between themselves and their
mothers. As we grow up, we find ourselves more of a "we" than
an "I," one of the pack rather than a lone wolf. We are *in* our group
of friends or *in* a conversation in a similar way to how we're
absorbed in our tasks. And just as this inconspicuous absorption
stops when a malfunction interrupts its smooth flow, so we fall out
of the group and into an individual self when we find ourselves
different from them. As an existentialist, Heidegger thinks that
instead of priding ourselves on our individuality we find it uncomfortable to be suddenly thrown out of the warm embrace of our
peers. Humans are, as Nietzsche put it, herd animals who find
blending in to be reassuring, despite all of our talk about being
your own person. Throughout our behavior, "there is constant care
as to the way one differs from" others (163/126). Think back to the
burning embarrassment of childhood experiences like showing up
to the first day of school not wearing what everyone else is. This
is when sociality breaks down, like the malfunctioning hammer.
Just as you then stare at the hammer as an object, so now your self
sticks out like a sore thumb. Moments of self-consciousness such
as these gradually accumulate into a consciousness of your self.

Heidegger calls this worry about not fitting in "distantiality,"
which is one of the ways we are initially and often not ourselves

(164/126). Throughout our lives we care very much what others think of us, up to and including caring that they know that we don't care what they think of us. Heidegger uses the German term "*das Man*" very interestingly in this discussion. It's translated here as "the they," which does capture some of the meaning – what will they all be talking about around the water cooler tomorrow? What party are they all going to tonight? – though it also misses something. Some translate it as "the one," in the sense that there is a proper, agreed-upon way "one" does things – the way one sets a table or ties a tie. When I just go with the flow of socially accepted ways of doing things I am living my life as "one" is supposed to, and Heidegger says that in this case it is the one who is living my life, not me. This tends to wear away or, in Kierkegaard's phrase, "level down" any unique or extraordinary actions while disburdening us both of the need to deliberately make decisions and of the worry about whether or not we're behaving properly (165/127). After all, everyone is doing it so it can't be that bad. We end up with an "addiction to becoming 'lived'" (240/196).

This represents an "inconspicuous domination by Others" (164/126). We are not actively leading our lives but following what is expected. We are less invested in our decisions and feel less responsible for them because we can always take refuge in the fact that they're all doing the same, that it's just what one does. One of the problems in discussing this is that we have a limited way of talking about it. As Heidegger says, traditional logic is based on presence-at-hand (166–7/129) and, just as this ontology made ready-to-hand equipment and the world "invisible" (86/59), so recognizing only objects like rocks and cups will miss important social phenomena (166/128). As we will see in the second half of this book, Heidegger finds our standard ways of talking about many subjects like freedom and decision-making limited and distortive, despite the fact that they have been prominent topics of philosophy. Obviously no one *forces* us to do the proper things, but neither do we consciously make these decisions. Instead, this public intelligibility allows us to go on autopilot, to ride on the inertia of accepted behavior. Adherence isn't compelled by force, but by the strange looks you get if you diverge too much from standard ways of doing things. Try violating these norms in public – wipe your nose on your sleeve or stand too close to someone when talking to them – and you'll feel the pressure brought to bear on norm-violations.[8]

Now this public intelligibility is absolutely essential to having a public life, to having a world at all. For a hammer to be a hammer, there has to be a way to hammer, and this is a socially determined function. If there weren't a way one hammers then there wouldn't be hammers, even if there were hard, heavy pieces of metal attached to the ends of sticks of wood.[9] They would not occupy a node in a world in Heidegger's sense and so could not be that tool. It is society that lays out these webs by offering the selection of for-the-sake-of-whichs we can take up to enter worlds. It is from my culture that I got the idea of being a professor; I didn't just make the idea of lecturing at and grading young people myself. Even if I did the exact same activities – met with a group of 18–22-year-olds a couple of times a week, told them to read certain books and write essays which I read and wrote comments on – they wouldn't add up to being a professor unless this were an accepted role in my time and place. It is my society that determines what it is to be a professor by laying out its chains of tasks and tools, thus erecting that world. "The 'they' itself articulates the referential context of significance" (167/129, see also 239/194).

Heidegger is playing on two registers of the notion of average-ness without being explicit about it. On the one hand, he values averageness against the tradition's tendency to concentrate on exceptional states of Dasein. Phenomenology seeks the common, the mundane in order to resist the temptation to focus on the ideal or transcendent. On the other hand, he shares the existentialists' general suspicion of the way society tears down the exceptional in the sense of great and extraordinary. Here averageness represents a pressure to conform, to force oneself into the standard, losing what is unique and great.

So we see that we are always already with others, just as much as we are always in-the-world. The problem of other minds is as artificial as the problem of the external world; it is our nature to be social. "Dasein in itself is essentially Being-with" (156/120). This means that our being with others is not a contingent matter that could have been otherwise. It isn't based on the contingent, ontic fact that we happen to live in proximity with other Dasein and encounter them.

This is where the standard proof of the existence of other minds begins. We are first inside our own consciousness and then we bump into other bodies that bear a certain resemblance to ours. These bodies tend to do the same kinds of things that I do in similar circumstances – lick their lips and say "yum" when eating chocolate, yell and hold their thumbs when they hit them with a hammer – so I infer from these similar outward similarities that there are likely to be parallel inner experiences accompanying them – pleasure and pain, respectively) This is known as the Argument from Analogy because I infer analogous mental events from analo-/gous bodily behavior.

Heidegger thinks this gets it exactly backwards: I start off within the crowd long before I can retreat to my own consciousness. But the argument itself is flawed. For me to study these specific kinds of bodies and to find these behaviors analogous I have to already be primed to pay special attention to them. As he often argues, any empirical study rests on a pre-ontological understanding which guides what we examine and how we interpret what we see. As we now know from psychology, babies come into the world already oriented towards people, especially faces, and this forms the basis for any inferences about them. " 'Empathy' does not first constitute Being-with; only on the basis of Being-with does 'empathy' become possible" (162/125).

Like Kant, Heidegger is seeking the conditions for the possibility of having experience at all as well as the specific kind of experience that we have, broadening experience to include our average, everyday lives. Here Heidegger is accommodating the distinction Kant made between treating objects as mere means for our ends and other people as ends-in-themselves. But whereas Kant reasons his way to this conclusion, Heidegger places the fundamental distinction between Dasein and things or tools at the level of an immediate apprehension: we simply experience them as fundamentally different which then forms the basis for the distinctive ways we treat people.[10]

Our primary experience of others is (not) an objective observation of them, but neither are they objects of concern, like equipment. Heidegger gives this kind of awareness its own name: *Fürsorge*, translated as solicitude (157/121). This is not a great translation, though I'm not sure what would be better. One possibility is caring for others because this resonates with concern (*Besorge*) as taking care of business and clearly connects to the root of both, care (*Sorge*), which we will turn to in 1.VI. We just need to avoid the sentimental sense of care in these terms. He briefly mentions two extreme versions of solicitude on pp. 158–9/122. One takes the other's responsibility over from them, whereas the second frees the other to their own lives. This discussion is extremely under-developed but we can see the inauthentic domination of *das Man* in the former while the latter, I believe, is what Heidegger sees his own existential analytic as doing for the reader. And with Chapter IV, we have run through the three facets of being-in-the-world, thus completing its initial interpretation – Heidegger's first approach to laying out Dasein's being, i.e. the existential analytic that is to serve as the foundation of ontology. And now we begin turning the Hermeneutic Spiral by returning to these ideas at a deeper level.

Further readings

Hubert Dreyfus has been one of the most important voices in applying Heidegger's insights to other fields, especially to artificial intelligence. The issue touched on here is called the Frame Argument, discussed in connection with Heidegger in Dreyfus' *Being-in-the-World: A Commentary on Heidegger's Being and Time, Division I* and *What Computers Still Can't Do*, as well as in Kiverstein and Wheeler's *Heidegger and Cognitive Science*. Jeff Malpas has written extensively on the issue of space in Heidegger in *Heidegger's Topology: Being, Place, World* and *Heidegger and the Thinking of Place: Explorations in the Topology of Being*. Two excellent, pioneering books on the contrast between *Being and Time* and Descartes' thought, especially concerning epistemological issues, are Charles Guignon's *Heidegger and the Problem of Knowledge* and John Richardson's *Existential Epistemology: A Heideggerian Critique of the Cartesian Project*.

Merleau-Ponty's *Phenomenology of Perception* serves as the foundation for attempts to connect phenomenology with neuroscience; more recent work includes Gallagher's *How the Body Shapes the Mind* and Gallagher and Zahavi's *The Phenomenological Mind*. Hegel's writings, such as *Science of Logic* or *The Philosophy of Right*, represent the classics on communitarianism or social holism. Charles Taylor and Alasdair MacIntyre have written on this topic more recently in, among other works, *Sources of the Self: The Making of the Modern Identity* and *After Virtue* respectively. One of the key insights informing all of Levinas' work is the idea that we directly perceive others rather than having to infer their existence; *Basic Philosophical Writings* contains a nice selection of his essays. Foucault made the kind of conformism Heidegger describes in 1.IV central to his middle works, especially *The History of Sexuality: An Introduction* and *Discipline and Punish: The Birth of the Prison*.

The Heart of the Book

see p. 77 note 1

3

Being and Time *1.V–VI: The There and Care*

Being and Time is a highly systematic work whose parts interconnect in complex and fascinating ways. The central topic of the book – Dasein's way of being – is itself deeply holistic, with all of its components being "equi-primordial" or equally fundamental. Each facet is defined in terms of the others, each of which in turn has an interdependent definition, so that each part can only be understood in light of the others. Just as each point on a circle can with justification be considered the beginning or the end, so each aspect of Dasein's existential structure can be thought of as the most important, the key that unlocks all the others.

But an especially good case can be made that Chapters V and VI of Division 1 form the true center of the book. Structurally, Chapter V's re-examination of being-in represents the first major turn of the Hermeneutic Spiral, that is, the repetition of a previous analysis at a deeper level, which is the way the book as a whole operates. These chapters also strike me as less focused than those that came before. They're more sprawling, meandering, even containing some tangents that don't fit well into *Being and Time*'s overall architectonic. Finally, some of the topics taken up in Chapter VI will become central to his later career, as we'll see in the second half of this book.

Being and Time 1.V The there

Phenomenology, as defined in the Introduction, describes how things show themselves to us. It studies the way things appear rather than reasoning about realms cut off from us like Kant's noumena. But this method is at the same time oriented towards that which does not show itself proximally and for the most part. It must be accessible in some way if it is to be a subject matter for phenomenology, or for any kind of analysis whatsoever in Heidegger's view (how can we study or even talk about what we cannot have any access to?), but some phenomena don't lie on the surface. They must be coaxed out of hiding or read correctly, which is one reason why phenomenology is hermeneutic: experience needs to be interpreted. Our and equipment's ways of being, as we have seen, vanish when we focus directly on them by stopping and observing. To catch a glimpse of these inconspicuous phenomena, we need to carry out our daily activities while trying to, "so to speak, 'listen in'" on ourselves (179/139).

But while a tool and its way of being withdraw from attention, what is most inconspicuous, what we pay least attention to, is its being at all (59/35). If you don't think about the pen's penness while you write or when you stare at it, how much less do you think about the mere fact that the pen is, that it's real? In fact, have you ever explicitly thought this about anything – just that it is? Heidegger believes that we very rarely if ever attend to this most basic possible fact, a state he later calls the oblivion or forgetfulness of being. Along with the pen's being, we also don't notice the correlative fact that we are aware of it. Awareness also is always there – when it's not, neither are we, to paraphrase Epicurus – but, for just that fact, we don't pay explicit attention to it. I never stop in the middle of grocery shopping to stare at a can of beans and say to myself, "This can of beans is. And I, I am. I am here, being aware of this can of beans." Just think of the funny looks one would get.

This is what Heidegger is trying to get at with the there or the clearing. He takes the term "Dasein" which is a common word for plain old existence in German and puts a hyphen in it to indicate that it literally means being ("Sein") the there ("Da"). We are the there that spaces things out, similar to the way Kant attributes the existence of space to the transcendental subject, which is what allows any and all heres and theres to be (171/132). What is especially disorienting about this idea is that we're not in the there; we are the there. Remember, Heidegger is struggling to get beyond the standard ontology organized around present-at-hand things or objects, self-sufficient substances that stand around and occasionally bump into each other. He hints at this ontological innovation when he says that if you frame the topic in terms of subject and world, then Dasein would be neither of these but rather the between (170/132). This characterization is inadequate because it still holds onto subject and world as objects separated by a gap, but it does help limber up our ontological imaginations to start thinking of ourselves as a profoundly different *kind* of thing than things, whether skin-bag or disembodied mind.

The other phrase, the clearing, comes from Heidegger's beloved walks in the woods, especially the Black Forest where he spent a lot of time. As one walks through a thick wood the trees press in, blocking out much of the light, until suddenly one comes out into a clearing where the trees are sparse, light streams in and everything is bright and open. The clearing ("*Lichtung*") is where there is light ("*Licht*") and a kind of airy lightness. This, according to Heidegger, is what we are. Throughout this unimaginably enormous universe, as far as we know, all kinds of cataclysmic and banal things are taking place all the time, but unseen, unheard, unwitnessed. Here, in this tiny corner of the universe, for this brief moment, a clearing has opened up in the dark woods of the real. We are here, and we are the there in which things can appear. Beings manifest themselves by appearing to us; witnessing them allows them to come into the light. We are reality's act of becoming aware of itself, a truly awesome, humbling privilege even though we ignore it and take it for granted in grocery shopping and TV watching.

Heidegger wants to make us aware of this most basic possible fact of our awareness. At one point, he even suggests that letting being show itself is the one for-the-sake-of-which that all Dasein share simply by being Dasein (186/146), an idea he will explicitly propose in his later talk about our role as the shepherd or care-taker of being, as we will see. However, he isn't just noting this fact; he wants to explore and understand it. What is our awareness like? What structures does it have? What makes our clearing the way it is? This is Heidegger's version of Kant's examination of the ways the mind in a sense "creates" phenomenal reality by giving shape to the sensory input it gets from the outside and Husserl's analysis of the transcendental subject's constitution of experience. However, where Kant thought the particular forms and concepts built into the transcendental subject are ultimately inexplicable, a lack that many German Idealists took him to task for, Heidegger wants to find out why our world is the way it is rather than some other way.

In Chapter V, Heidegger explains the three features that shape the there: state-of-mind, understanding, and discourse. These are equi-primordial which means that they're all equally fundamental. None forms the basis for the others, nor can any be derived from the others, nor can any be fully understood independently of the others. In Part A he explains how these three structure the basic there while Part B describes their everyday "fallen" versions.

Being and Time 1.V.A The trifold constitution of the there

¶¶29–30 State-of-mind

As with the components of being-in-the-world, although the three facets of the there are inextricably interconnected, we can only take them up one at a time. We will start with "Befindlichkeit." This is translated here as "state-of-mind," which is generally regarded as a lousy translation because it conjures up a static mental quality within us, precisely the idea Heidegger is trying to get rid of. However, there is no good translation since Heidegger made the word up. As footnote 2 on p. 172 says, he derives it from the common German phrase, "Wie befinden Sie sich?" This means something like "How are you?" or "How's it going?," but notice that this last phrase taken literally speaks of the motion ("going") of something ("it"), even though we're not really talking about something moving. The German phrase also says something that usually gets passed over, which could be more literally translated as "How do you find yourself?" Heidegger makes the quality in question here a noun – the how-one-finds-oneself-ness.

Befindlichkeit certainly means what the question "How are you?" asks about – your general well-being, how life is treating you, your general karmic thermostat reading. As we have seen him do before, Heidegger approaches this basic feature through the more concrete, ontic version of it, which is mood (172/134). This translates "Stimmung," which does mean mood but also carries the more literal connotation of the tuning of a musical instrument. This is important because all of these aspects are about how we become aware of or disclose things. Moods aren't so much internal feelings for Heidegger as ways of showing us features of the world. Things show up differently depending on our mood, a bit like the way the same note can sound different depending on how an instrument is tuned, or a radio can tune into different stations. The example he gives in ¶30 is the mood of fear which lets things show up as threatening or scary (180/141). Someone who felt confident about their ability to handle a situation would not see it as a threat, nor would pure, cold cognition (173/134, 391/341). Not only do moods color how things show up, we will see in Chapter VI that we *need* to have some mood or other in which things matter to us if we are to have a world at all (176/137). It is only if you are in a class that the equipment necessary to accomplish the relevant goal can show up in its chains of significance, and the way it shows up changes with the way that goal matters to you. When you're feeling sick of being a student, the books and tests feel like a burden to be endured while if you're enthusiastically engaged, they feel eagerly tantalizing.

One of the reasons Heidegger likes the phrase *"Befindlichkeit"* is that it emphasizes our passivity. We *find* ourselves in a mood not of our making or of our choice, and we can't change our mood simply by deciding to do so. Sometimes we can affect it indirectly, by putting ourselves into a context that reminds us of the reasons why we should be happy instead of sad, for example. But this is pitting one mood against another, trying to get a "counter-mood" going to battle and replace the one we're in rather than simply controlling it from above (175/136). Although we can sometimes figure out the cause of our moods, they often just happen to us for no discernible reason and can persist despite countervailing events. We cannot explain our mood entirely in terms of what happens to us because the mood we're in plays a large role in determining how we react to these things. If I'm feeling good, I can take pretty serious problems in my stride ("Oh well, that kind of thing happens"), whereas when I'm down even a minor setback can plummet me into depression and make me abandon what I was trying to do ("Now I'll *never* be able to finish this! Oh, forget the whole thing!").

Heidegger thinks that this reveals significant limits to our autonomy, to our ability to control the kind of person we are, despite traditional philosophy's great confidence in our ability to control our selves and our actions. This passivity goes all the way to the mere fact that we exist at all: "the mood brings Dasein before the that-it-is' of its 'there', which, as such, stares it in the face with the inexorability of an enigma" (175/136). We find ourselves in a clearing we didn't create and which we cannot control. We didn't choose to be born; we were, in Heidegger's term, thrown into being alive at all as well as into our facticity, that is, the particular facts of our lives – when and where and to whom we were born, what kind of personality we have, etc. (174/135). This fact is inescapably mysterious. Any answer we give – God created us, for example – would itself be inexplicable – why did God do this? Why is there a God at all and why did He pick that purpose and me for it? There are inescapable limits to the kinds of answers we can get to traditional philosophical questions about why we're here and to traditional philosophical goals like autonomy, and these facts are revealed by moods, not reason. Heidegger often points out discoveries that can only be made by other facets of our being than reason.

¶¶31–3 *Understanding, interpretation, and assertions*

The second basic component of the there after *Befindlichkeit* is understanding, though Heidegger emphasizes that both understanding and state-of-mind are always present and determine each other. By understanding, he means knowing-how to do things, a competence at appropriately interacting with different kinds of entities (183/143). When we are in-the-world we know how to move along its lines of significance: we understand how to be a student by knowing how to use pens and paper and desks and chairs properly. Heidegger explains this understanding as projecting things onto their possibilities. Etymologically, "projection" translates "*Entwurf*," which literally means to throw forward, which we can see in the word "projectile." It also connects *Entwurf*'s throwing-forward with *Geworfenheit*'s being-thrown as revealed in states-of-mind.

When we understand a tool, our know-how is of what it can-do. This hammer is not experienced as a stable, inert thing but as hammerable, or can-drive-in-nails. It is in terms of its ability rather than its physical properties that we encounter it first and for the most part (184/144). I "free" it for its possibilities when I take up a relevant goal (the "towards-which"), say, building a bookcase. Although I had a pre-ontological understanding of the hammer's connections to other equipment (wood and nails) and tasks (putting wood together) when I ran my eyes over it upon entering the room, all of that remained coiled up within the thing which was itself fused into the smooth background. It's when I project myself onto the possibility of hammering that I then free or pry the hammer loose from the background and project it onto its possibility, pulling out that chain of equipment and actions and tying it to my for-the-sake-of-which of being a carpenter.

The for-the-sake-of-which is the self-defining possibility I project my self onto when I take it up as an attempt to settle the issue of my being: I will *be* a carpenter. But we mustn't think of this possibility in the traditional sense as a potential which is not actualized, a possible thing or state I could be in but which I am not at present. That's a present-at-hand kind of possibility while we must obey the Existential Imperative and think of Dasein's distinctive form of possibility. A possibility isn't something a Dasein is not; no, we *are* our possibilities (185/145). Just as we always find ourselves already in a kind of life with certain projects underway rather than ever starting with a clean slate – we are thrown into a context of facticity – so we never reach a climactic moment of decisive completion of our for-the-sake-of-which, the moment in a movie when the music hits a crescendo and the credits start to roll. It's a horizon that recedes as we approach it – continually throwing it forward from where we are – until it is suddenly behind us. My being a professor constantly involves new tasks to be done; the moment all of that stops, so does my being a professor in anything more than a merely nominal or honorific sense. When I have no more possibilities that doesn't mean that I've fully actualized that role; that is precisely when I am no longer it. Being a student means to constantly have more classes to take, more assignments to complete, all with the goal of graduating. But the moment of graduation is not when you are a fully actualized student; that's precisely when you stop being a student.

As we said, thrownness and projection are equi-primordial, braided together in complex and deep ways. Projection is the more active aspect, meaning what I chose to do, whereas thrownness indicates those facts which I simply find to be the case, but rather than being in conflict, the two can only exist together. I find myself at present in this environment (*Umwelt*) of a classroom because of the choices I have already made. However, I have to continue to maintain this project; if I suddenly drop this for-the-sake-of-which, I will find myself out of the class (even if I'm still spatially located within the four walls of the classroom). But then whether I keep it up and how I keep at it is informed by the way I find it at present – is it tiresome and frustrating or fun and rewarding? I can decide to remain committed to the project despite my present mood, but only because I find my commitment as to-be-maintained-regardless-of-how-I-feel, which itself is a kind of feeling. "Dasein is Being-possible which has been delivered over to itself – *thrown possibility through and through*" (183/144).

Now, it is because I am in my world through projecting my for-the-sake-of-which that I find the world intelligible, understandable, meaningful (192/151). It is through significance – the lines of in-order-tos that I press into when I perform my tasks – that beings are significant – I understand what they can do, what they're for. We don't encounter bare meaningless things, except when disengaged observation renders them mute and inert (190/149). Normally things show up *as* specific things – as a rake or a towel or a chair (189/149). Most of the time we take this in by using it as a rake or a towel, but we can also develop this understanding into an explicit thought of what it is we're taking it to be. This is what Heidegger calls "interpretation." This translates "*Auslegung*" which literally means laying something out so that it can be looked over. When we use the hammer, we pull out that interlinked chain of in-order-tos and tie it to our for-the-sake-of-which, forming an intelligible context within which to locate it: it's the thing that drives the nails into the wood in order to fasten them together towards making the bookcase for the sake of being a carpenter. It is this context of significance – this *Umwelt* – that gives the hammer meaning.

Normally, of course, the hammer withdraws and we give no conscious thought to any of this. "In the mere encountering of something, it is understood in terms of a totality of involvements; and such seeing hides in itself the explicitness of the assignment-relations (of the in-order-to) which belong to that totality" (189/149). Interpretation, however, pulls these coiled up chains out of things to lay them out for us to see, rendering explicit what had been implicit in our actions. This is, Heidegger says, projecting the possibility inherent in understanding by developing its intrinsic nature: "in it the understanding appropriates understandingly that which is understood by it" (188/148). His overall project is precisely to interpret the existential structure of Dasein that we all understand implicitly by just living in the world.

Heidegger introduces a very important concept here that develops the hermeneutic aspects of *Being and Time*. He rejects the possibility of attaining an immediate, "presuppositionless apprehending of something presented to us" (191–2/150). Philosophers have always been wary of presumptions, even defining the discipline as the critical examination of assumptions. It has always sought to strip away the accidental views our particular society happened to give us, for they may be false, and the perspective that the specific make-up of our body and senses forces upon us, for it is limited, that we may look upon the very face of reality. Husserl believed that phenomenology finally succeeded in giving us this long sought after innocent intuition but Heidegger has shown that these supposedly purified perceptions contain and perpetuate deep prejudices. Stilling our engagement in the world to mere observation ends up producing just the kind of distortions the method was designed to avoid.

Paragraph ¶32 lays out his view of interpretation. Although there is a form of interpretation that is an explicit act, we are always interpreting in another sense in that we always understand entities *as* particular kinds of entities. Nothing enters our awareness except through one or another pre-ontological understanding of being, rendering entities tools or objects or other Dasein but never mere meaningless things. The closest we get to this is turning something into a present-at-hand object but this is still a meaning, just one set at some distance from human or social concerns. Heidegger lays out three fore-structures of interpretation though we won't worry about the differences among them. The important point is that every time we see or think about or encounter entities in any way, these fore-structures have already prepared our experience of them. Much like Kant and Husserl, Heidegger is arguing that we never encounter raw data that is just given to us and which our thought or senses passively mirror. By the time we can perceive or think about it, experience has been structured in specific ways. For Heidegger these concepts can evolve in time (this is the significance of the discussion of scientific revolutions in ¶3 of the Introduction, and it becomes prominent in his later work), unlike Kant's, and we have the ability to switch from one to another, but we can never remove them entirely to see what things are "really" like independently of all interpretation. We can only access the world through some interpretive scheme or other.

Interpretation can become assertions. Explicitly laying these implicit meanings out allows me to capture them in language and state them outright. However, Heidegger believes that this is, as the title of ¶33 states, "a derivative mode of interpretation." First, it depends on interpretation because we can only state the meanings that we find there. If I didn't understand what the hammer was for, I couldn't say that the hammer was too heavy for the job. But he means more than this. Although assertions purport to merely state what is the case, as so often happens in *Being and Time*, these apparently innocent descriptions actually distort what had been going on.

Assertions do three things: (1) They point out something, which Heidegger connects to the Greek word "*apophansis.*" They train our attention onto their subjects which lets them appear to us, bringing them into the there. Even if the entity in question is not present for immediate perception, if I say "My dog is brown," I've created a tiny clearing in which he appears to us, a tele-clearing if you will. Language opens up wormholes through which things both present and not present can present themselves to us. (2) Assertions predicate. They attribute a quality to an entity although this unification of subject and predicate (S is P) also separates them, indeed it separates them *in* combining them. In what had been an interconnected whole – a brown-dog – the brownness of the dog now stands out from the other qualities and from the dog himself. The other features have dimmed down as the spotlight brings his brownness forth. (3) Assertions communicate, that is, they highlight the predicate for other people. Saying "My dog is brown" brings his brownness forward for you too so that we now share a clearing focused on his color (196–9/154–7).

Due to its subject–predicate grammar, our language tacitly endorses and reinforces the tradition's substance–accident ontology (199/157). We think in terms of self-contained entities that possess properties because our grammar divides the world into subjects with predicates. This is the fore-structure that language imposes on us, as philosophers as diverse as Nietzsche and Bertrand Russell have noted.[1]

Making assertions about items is also derivative because it can take us out of the ongoing flow of concernful dealing that makes up our usual way of being-in-the-world.

> Something *ready-to-hand with which* we have to do or perform something, turns into something '*about which*' the assertion that points it out is made. Our fore-sight is aimed at something present-at-hand in what is ready-to-hand. Both *by* and *for* this way of looking at it, the ready-to-hand becomes veiled as ready-to-hand. . . . It has been cut off from that significance which, as such, constitutes environmentality. (200/158)

Making assertions forms part of the detached, observational stance that changes ready-to-hand equipment into present-at-hand objects. When we try to put it into words, what we put into words has been altered by this very attempt. Experience in the wild, as phenomenology shows, is very different from the domesticated world we speak of.

Assertions point out or highlight aspects of the world, making them apophantical, but within a different context from their usual everyday use. Usage also interprets in the sense of experiencing entities as particular kinds of entities, but this is what Heidegger calls the "existential-*hermeneutical* 'as'" that governs how we go about our daily business (201/158). If we find the hammer we're using too heavy, this need not come to words at all – we can simply lay it aside and take up a different one with little or no conscious thought. "Interpretation is carried out primordially not in a theoretical statement but in an action of circumspective concern" (200/157). Or it may arise as a non-grammatical muttering "too heavy." The mere fact of expressing the group of words "This hammer is too heavy" doesn't automatically put us onto the derivative apophantical as of assertions; the point is how we say it and thereby how we experience the hammer. The theoretical apophantical assertion, when its fore-structure of understanding has been unpacked or explicitly interpreted, means "This Thing – a hammer – has the property of heaviness" (200/157). The existential-hermeneutic experience doesn't find a thing there at all, as we saw when we examined the way equipment withdraws in ¶16. Tools are more like tunnels or pathways to get to a goal than discretely bounded objects. The hammer doesn't come across as a spatially extended body but as a way to get to the fastened wood of the bird house. If a problem arises, this tunnel caves in or meets resistance, so I back out and look for an alternate route.

¶34 *Discourse and language*

Like many Heidegger scholars, I find *Being and Time*'s discussion of discourse and language rather confusing and possibly confused. Discourse represents the third equi-primordial aspect of the there, though apparently it had already been playing a "suppressed" role in his earlier discussions, most obviously in assertions (203/160). Briefly, discourse is the articulation of the world in its significance. The word "articulation" has a helpful double meaning. On the one hand, it means to express something in words so that language is the more concrete manifestation of discourse. But it also means finding and distinguishing something's inherent divisions the way one articulates a skeleton by separating out the bones at the joints. When we understand the world, it is as an interconnected context of groups of tools united towards accomplishing goals.

Although this is holistic, that does (not) mean that it's a solid mono-
lith without parts. I can only understand my pen in terms of something to write on and a reason to remember or communicate what
I'm writing, but I still need to know which item to grasp in my
hand and what to place on top of what. My use of the writing-
ensemble does take it in as a whole but it also articulates it into
separate items. This comes alive in our use and it can then be
articulated into words (204/161) Language can only take place
on the basis of a pre-linguistic articulation of the world into name-
able and speakable entities and events. Discourse is part of the
there because it discloses the world as intelligibly interconnected
links.

Discourse and language are also important parts of our being-
with other Dasein. Listening to others is an essential and primordial way of being open to people, which we experience as an
immediate contact with them (206–7/163–4). Rather than commu-
nicating by means of passing words out from our minds through
the external medium of sounds and scribbles which then get taken
in and decoded by another mind, we find ourselves out there in
the world, with others. Their words are immediately intelligible
rather than in need of a separate act of interpretation, as some theories of language have it.

Being and Time 1.V.B The everyday there and falling

Now that Heidegger has explained the basic structures of the there
– state-of-mind, understanding, and discourse – he turns to the
way we are our there in our everyday lives. This, however, is the
existential sense of everydayness rather than the phenomenological one. Whereas phenomenology is interested in what goes on in
the first place and most of the time, rather than passing over the
ordinary for the extraordinary, existentialism views this state with
suspicion. Heidegger denies that his analyses have anything "mor-
alizing" about them (211/167), and it is true that these are intrinsic
features of Dasein that form permanent possibilities rather than an
unfortunate state that humanity ended up in because of the Fall,
or that contemporary Europeans are in because of historical events
(which is closer to his later view). However, it's pretty clear that
these analyses, even their names, have strong negative connotations. In general, they represent the there that is ruled by the they
(*das Man*).

¶35 Idle talk

Idle talk appears to be the fallen version of discourse; in German the etymological connection between the former (*Gerede*) and the latter (*Rede*) is clear. Idle talk is the consequence of two basic facts about Dasein that we have already covered: when we gain a facility with using equipment, we can stop paying attention to our use of it (1.II), and we are intrinsically social creatures (1.IV). When combined, they mean that we can disengage from a conversation and let our mouths run on autopilot, just blathering on with little attention to our own or our interlocutor's words. Moreover, we can simply pass on what we have heard without examining the meaning for ourselves. I can tell you what I was told about my computer's problems without understanding a word of it. In Heidegger's terms, I do not genuinely bring the phenomenon in question to show itself in my clearing, even while speaking of it accurately (213/169). Husserl speaks of this in his late essay, "The Origin of Geometry," when he distinguishes between the absent-minded way most of us do math and the way someone like Descartes did it with a clear and distinct perception focused on each step.

Idle talk represents almost the exact inversion of discourse: it "amounts to perverting the act of disclosing into an act of closing off" (213/169). Whereas discourse is part of the clearing because it opens things up to us, showing us the world, idle talk keeps us from having vivid, explicit experiences. We pass along what "they" say about problems in the Middle East or engine troubles with nary a thought or insight into the matters ourselves. Idle talk contains and perpetuates the they's fore-structures of understanding so that we automatically think and see the way one does: "the 'they' prescribes one's state-of-mind, and determines what and how one 'sees'" (213/170).

¶36 Curiosity

Curiosity, the second facet of the fallen there, contributes to the traditional privileging of disengaged observation over engaged interaction. Instead of following out what concerns us, we withdraw from our immediate interests and just follow up stray questions that happen to pop into our heads and seem mildly interesting. Think of web-surfing. You might start off with a focused, definite goal – you need to find out the answer to a question for class, say

– but as you search, your gaze strays to links or pictures in the margins that beckon seductively. They have nothing to do with what you're trying to find out, or really with your life at all. How does the latest celebrity scandal really affect you? Why should you be interested? But you click just for the sake of looking and, to paraphrase Robert Frost, click leads on to click until you wake up two hours later having rummaged through a lot of other people's dirty laundry or just random bits of information, none of which actually matters to you and none of which you'll retain the moment you get up from your computer. Idle talk informs curiosity since we're particularly interested in what everyone is talking about this week (217/173).

¶37 Ambiguity

Ambiguity is the effect of accumulated idle talk and curiosity. We get so loaded up with these non-genuine ways of awareness that "it soon becomes impossible to decide what is disclosed in a genuine understanding, and what is not" (217/173). This also contributes to the Kierkegaardian leveling down of publicness that Heidegger discusses in 1.IV (165/127). No matter how new or original something appears, soon idle talk gets a line on it – "oh, that's that thing where people do x or y" – allowing you to pass over it without paying the attention needed to come to grips with something truly innovative. At most, it becomes an item of curiosity, covered in the light moments of news programs or websites that tame everything distinctive.

¶38 Falling and thrownness

Together, these three – idle talk, curiosity, and ambiguity – constitute the everyday form of our there, the way we usually disclose the world, and it is fallen in the sense that we become absorbed, lost even, in the public way "one" understands matters (220/175). We have fallen into the world such that we are inauthentic or not our own. Now, Dasein is essentially in-the-world; we have to be. Fallenness concerns the *way* we are in-the-world, such that the they has taken over the way we are there.

This is *tranquilizing*, as we saw in 1.IV's discussion of disburdening (165/127). "They" reassure us that we're leading the right kind of life by doing what "one" does – one becomes a lawyer or a doctor, one keeps up with the latest developments, one talks about these subjects. This reassurance is *tempting* precisely because our being is an issue for us (224/179). We want to settle this issue definitively and know that we've done a good job, and seeing what everyone else is doing is the most obvious and easiest clue to determining this. However, all of this is *alienating* because we leave it up to others to tell us how to live rather than living our own lives (221–2/177–8). Ultimately all of this reinforces the fact that we are thrown since we are delivered over to these public ways of understanding things long before we can come up with our own.

Being and Time 1.VI Anxiety, care, reality, and truth

Chapter VI is an interesting amalgam in the overall structure of *Being and Time*. Its first two sections, on anxiety and care, are tremendously important in the book's ongoing examination of Dasein's way of being, that is, the existential analytic. Anxiety turns out to be an important tool for understanding ourselves and care is revealed as the deep meaning that unifies the different aspects of being-in-the-world. This makes the discussion of care a natural ending point for Division 1 since we can now understand the facets of being-in-the-world both on their own and in combination, preparing us for the next turn of the Hermeneutic Spiral when we go back through these aspects at a deeper level in Division 2.

But Heidegger doesn't leave it there. Instead, he tacks on a section about the notion of reality and the idea of proving the external world, and another on a new definition of truth. These are extremely big ideas, reality and truth, with long philosophical histories to them and Heidegger says some very interesting, innovative things about them, but they don't really fit here. They both need considerably more discussion and their specific contribution to the existential analytic is far from clear, including their placement at this particular point in the book. If I had to guess, I would say that they were meant for Division 3 where he was going to turn to being itself rather than focusing on Dasein, as he suggests at one point (227–8/183). These topics, especially truth, become very important in his later work, as we will see in the second half of this book.

¶40 *Anxiety as a distinctive way to disclose Dasein*

Our job in the portions of *Being and Time* that we have is to under-stand existence, Dasein's way of being. This means developing a fourth kind of sight (*Sicht*) alongside circumspection (*Umsicht*) of ready-to-hand equipment, considerateness (*Rücksicht*) of other existing Dasein, and theoretical (also etymologically related to sight in its roots which connect it to words like "theater" or "specu-lation" to "spectacles") observation of present-at-hand objects: now we also have transparency (*Durchsichtigkeit*) (186/146). However, a number of obstacles hinder our "seeing-through" ourselves. For one thing, like equipment we are inconspicuous: going about our daily tasks involves virtually no attention to ourselves. We are absorbed into our world in that all of our attention is on the tasks at hand rather than on ourselves doing those tasks. As Wittgenstein said, the eye that takes in the visual field is not itself within the field; if anything, it *is* the field the way Dasein is the clearing.

Heidegger now explains a second difficulty we have in getting a good look at ourselves. Due to a number of uncomfortable fea-tures about our existence which we will discuss in Division 2, we actively avoid an honest examination of our way of being. As he now puts it, "Dasein's absorption in the 'they' and its absorption in the 'world' of its concern, make manifest something like a *fleeing* of Dasein in the face of itself" (229/184). Our falling has already been discussed in Part A of 1.V, but he now says that it was already there in the concernful absorption in our tasks of 1.II and III and the public reassurances of 1.IV. We seek to lose ourselves in the world by becoming absorbed in our activities, looking for distrac-tions that kill time and relieve us of the burden of actively leading our lives. He now says that these features lead us away from our-selves, a new spin on what he called their alienating nature (222/178).

Paradoxically, this obstacle turns out to aid our investigation. We can only flee from that which we have some knowledge of just to be able to avoid it or to know that we want to (229/185). Just as we have a pre-ontological understanding of readiness-to-hand and presence-at-hand, our fleeing falling indicates that we may hope to find "an understanding state-of-mind in which Dasein has been disclosed to itself in some distinctive way" (226/182): anxiety.

Heidegger illuminates anxiety by contrasting it with the state-of-mind fear as covered in ¶30. Fear is definite: I know what it is

that frightens me, roughly where it does or can come from. I pin-
point the threat as that snarling dog, which also gives me activities
to do – I can run away – and equipment to use – I can throw him
a bone – to neutralize the threat. Fear still allows me to absorb
myself into the world, using equipment in order to accomplish
goals.

Anxiety, on the other hand, is amorphous, a stultifying fog that
comes from nothing and nowhere specific. We saw earlier that
moods often come on independently or even in spite of external
events. Anxiety extends this idea to the point that part of what
makes it anxiety is that nothing specific triggers it. If someone asks
me what was bothering me once the mood has passed I might very
well say "Oh, it was nothing," which contains more truth than we
realize for Heidegger (see BW 101). "*Angst*," as the footnote on
p. 227 mentions, could also be translated as "dread," "uneasiness,"
or "*malaise*," all of which capture part of the meaning.

If nothing specific has set it off, then neither is there anything for
me to do to neutralize it. Anxiety gives me nothing to do; it closes
off activities rather than disclosing them. Like the similar states-of-
mind of extreme depression and boredom, when I am struck by
malaise I find myself repelled from the equipment I normally use
for entertainment and enjoyment. I can't lose myself in a movie, I
find web-surfing dull, I toss away a book because the words just
sit there on the page instead of drawing me into the story. In the
sense Heidegger gives it, I'm not *in* my world anymore since I'm
not concerned with any of its goals or activities, leaving me unable
to press forward into its possibilities. "That in the face of which one
is anxious is completely indefinite. . . . Entities within-the-world
are not 'relevant' at all. . . . Here the totality of involvements of the
ready-to-hand or present-at-hand discovered within-the-world, is,
as such, of no consequence; it collapses into itself; the world has
the character of completely lacking significance" (231/186). The
world's chains of significance collapse in anxiety, when I can no
longer thoughtlessly press forward and absorb myself into my
activities. And if significance collapses then the world as a whole
does so, since that is what worldhood is made of.

And here Heidegger brings back his analysis of equipment
breakdown but at a deeper level since we've now turned the
Hermeneutic Spiral. Recall that it is only when a tool breaks down
that it gets lit up instead of remaining inconspicuous, as it does
while functioning properly (105/75). But the world as a whole and
my being in the world also remain inconspicuous while I'm

absorbed into my daily concerns. I only become aware of this when I have been ejected from my world and remain outside, repelled from entering it by my lack of caring: "the *world as world* is disclosed first and foremost by anxiety" (232/187). The wholesale collapse of significance marks a breakdown of worldhood itself by preventing me from unthinkingly sinking into the business I usually busy myself with.

Heidegger says that this experience "individualizes" Dasein because it separates us from our world which is what normally defines us. For the most part one is what one does, but in full-blown anxiety you can't really *do* anything – you just flail about, trying to find some activity to occupy yourself with. This shows us that we can't be exhaustively defined by worldly things and activities since we're still ourselves even while all of that is on hold. This marks an important difference from the inauthentic self-understanding we normally operate on. "Anxiety thus takes away from Dasein the possibility of understanding itself, as it falls, in terms of the 'world' and the way things have been publicly interpreted" (232/187). Anxiety removes us from our daily routine and prevents our simply defining ourselves in terms of our occupations and preoccupations.

This state-of-mind finds expression in the mood of uncanniness, where the German "*Unheimlichkeit*" literally means "not-at-home-ness." Whereas *das Man* reassures us and makes us feel at home in the world, "anxiety brings [Dasein] back from its absorption in the 'world'. Everyday familiarity collapses" (233/189). We recognize our surroundings, of course, but it all seems strange somehow – alien and alienated from us. The equipment that usually fuses seamlessly with our body now feels rubbery, stiff, and awkward. We flee from this horribly uncomfortable *malaise*, which forms the topic of Sartre's work *Nausea*, back into the world which is why Heidegger calls fear a fallen form of anxiety (234/189). This doesn't mean that an authentic person can never be afraid. It just means that the inauthentic flight from anxiety is always into the world, to keep ourselves busy with some form of business, preoccupied with our occupation, and it is this flight into the world – shared by fearful attempts to neutralize a threat – that marks inauthenticity.

With all content drained out of the self by the collapse of the world, we can now see the structure that it had filled in. Anxiety "induces the slipping away of beings as a whole. . . . Where there is nothing to hold onto, pure Da-sein is all that is still there" (BW 101). Not being in any particular world makes us realize that normally we are in some world or other. When we are not engaging in action, we realize that we never just sit around like this normally, uncomfortably indolent. When we do not define ourselves in terms of what we do, we see that we usually are absorbed into our normal routines. Just as circumspection (*Umsicht*) frees tools from the background when we need to use them in-order-to do something (117/85), and considerateness (*Rücksicht*) frees other Dasein for personal relationships (160/123), so anxious transparency (*Durchsichtigkeit*) frees us from our usual fusion with our world and routines. This allows us to "see through" all the specifics of our life to its underlying structure, "undisguised by entities within-the-world, to which, proximally and for the most part, Dasein clings" (235/191). Clearing out the contents lets us see the form of existence clearly. "What it does is precisely to bring Dasein face to face with its world as world, and thus bring it face to face with itself as Being-in-the-world" (233/188). If a tool's breakdown makes the world light up, the breakdown of our lives in anxiety lights up being-in-the-world.

¶41 Care as the meaning of being-in-the-world

Instead of the localized breakdown of specific tools, anxiety marks the collapse of the significance of worldhood as a whole. But, as the Chinese language has it, this crisis is also an opportunity, a phenomenological opportunity in this case. Just as breakdowns let us see the equipment that had been inconspicuous, so anxiety's individualization of Dasein, by separating us from our normal absorption into worlds, lets us see the structure of existence, precisely what we have been looking for from the start of the book. *Not*-being-in-a-world gives us the perspective we need to see our usual being-in-the-world. A general rule of Heideggerian phenomenology is that "everything positive becomes particularly clear when seen from the side of the privative" (BP 309).

Now that we have gone through the individual parts of being-in-the-world – Being-in in 1.II and 1.V, worldhood in 1.III, and the self that is in-the-world in 1.IV – and now that anxiety has placed us outside this entire structure and temporarily drained it of content so that we can see it on its own, we are in a position to truly understand it. This means grasping its meaning, which Heidegger defines as that which explains why something is the way it is and why it has the particular features that it does (370–1/324). For a holistic but complex phenomenon like being-in-the-world, grasping its meaning entails seeing what makes it possible and unifies it.

Heidegger finds this meaning in care. This word, "*Sorge*," forms the base for both concern (*Besorge*) for equipment and solicitude (*Fürsorge*) of others, which we can now see as types of care: taking care of business and caring for others. All of the features of being-in-the-world are now revealed as ways that we care about ourselves, and in two densely packed pages (236–7/191–2), Heidegger takes us on a whirlwind tour of the facets he has already covered but now from the perspective of care. This completes the first turning of the Hermeneutic Spiral: 1.II–V gave us a basic sense of these aspects individually, which enables us now to come back and achieve a deeper understanding of them.

First is the very first, and in many ways the most important, thing we learned about Dasein – the fact that its being is an issue for it (32/12). Our being can only be an issue for us if we care what happens to us. This issue has to matter to us for us to pursue ways of settling it. Were we wholly indifferent to our selves the way a rock is, we could never find that our being needed to be settled and would not be motivated to attempt to do so. We try to settle it by projecting ourselves onto possibilities, that is, onto specific for-the-sake-of-whichs. As we saw in ¶31's discussion of understanding, we *are* these possibilities even though they never become fully actualized (185/145). Being a student means taking care of the tasks one must do to be a student. Thus Dasein is always "*ahead of itself. . . 'beyond itself'*" (236/191), all of which Heidegger groups under the heading of existentiality, drawing on the roots of "ek-sist" as standing outside oneself. Just as when I cross the room I'm already at the door, so every time a student shows up for class or takes a test she is doing this towards graduating.

However, we are also always *already* in a world, always in a world that we *find* ourselves in, as revealed in states-of-mind (*Befindlichkeit*) as explained in ¶29. This world already has a great many features defined, either by our past choices (to attend this school, to take this class), facts about our personality that account for these decisions (a desire to be either near to or far from home, an enjoyment of a particular kind of thinking or professor), or our society (that it has institutions of higher learning), all of which Heidegger collectively names our facticity.

It is crucial to grasp the deep interdependence of these facets. Heidegger repeatedly insists that they're not just stuck together but belong together such that none could exist without the others.

"Existing is always factical. Existentiality is essentially determined by facticity" (236/192), and vice versa. I can only project myself onto the possibilities that I find available in the world I find myself in although, conversely, one of the reasons I find myself in this environment is because of earlier projections, themselves organized and limited by facts I was thrown into. I can only find myself limited by restrictions if I try to surpass or actualize them in choices I make and I can only make choices if I find a limited selection of choices available and myself inclined towards some options over others.

Together, factical existence (or existential facticity) lets me be-in-a-world. I can only find facts about myself and my options and choose from among these options within the public arena which supplies the equipmental lines of significance for me to project myself onto. Without these tasks and their correlative groups of equipment, I could not be a student or a husband or a factory worker. Proximally and for the most part, of course, I simply take over the world as it is presented to me by society, meaning that normally I am in my world by being fallen into it.

And this is how I care about myself, how I try to settle the issue of my being, how I live out a life. Care is the reason why I do any of it: an indifferent being could not have a world because it would not care about settling its being by taking up possibilities in a world it was thrown into. Care is the "a priori" of being-in-the-world in that it is the necessary condition for these components to exist and for them to do so in this united, meaningful fashion. In Heidegger's sense, care is the meaning of being-in-the-world.

¶¶43–4 Reality and truth

Heidegger now switches gears. After successfully bringing Division 1 to a climactic close by showing care to be the united meaning of existence (Dasein's being) as being-in-the-world, he takes up two broader issues: the question of independent reality and the nature of truth. These are obviously very big, important philosophical topics though, as I said above, their placement sticks out from the overall structure of the book like a sore thumb to me. Division 2 will begin by ignoring these ruminations, picking up where ¶42 left off, as if they were simply pasted in here. This could be evidence of the fact that Heidegger rushed the completion of the book.

He reminds us once again that the tradition's disengaged contemplation of presence-at-hand – which is how he is using the term "reality" here – passes over the inconspicuous ready-to-hand. One of his goals throughout the book is to show that "among the modes of Being of entities within-the-world, Reality has no priority" (254–5/211). He has been focusing on the other modes of being – equipment's readiness-to-hand and Dasein's existence – because these have gotten so little attention and because they are extremely important in our everyday lives, much more prevalent and significant than presence-at-hand. He makes two specific points about present-at-hand reality, one of which has already been covered while the other is rather confusing and given too little explanation here.

The first topic, covered in (a), is the proof of the external world, the lack of which Kant called "the scandal of philosophy." Heidegger rather famously turns this phrase back on Kant, arguing that the true scandal is that anyone finds it scandalous, indeed that anyone thinks the world needs proving in the first place (249/205). Proofs of the external world are not self-evidently and inescapably necessary for us to complete in order to be responsible thinkers in our attempts to understand the world, the way Descartes presents the issue. The very idea that such a proof is intelligible, much less necessary, rests on a bed of assumptions about what kind of being the world is, what kind of being we are, and what the relationship between the two is like. It treats world and self as present-at-hand objects which are self-enclosed entities that may or may not come into contact with each other. It is treating this connection as contingent that makes it necessary to connect the two, traditionally by means of knowledge, and simultaneously renders any connection forever insecure (246/202).

If these assumptions are wrong then the need for a proof that follows from them falls away, and we know by this point in the book that Heidegger considers them deeply wrong. The world is made up of ready-to-hand equipment in sequences of in-order-tos that dangle from a for-the-sake-of-which projected by a Dasein. No Dasein, no for-the-sake-of-which, and thus no world. And, as we just learned from the holistic interconnections of care in ¶42, this works the other way too. Dasein can only be a Dasein by taking up some for-the-sake-of-which or other and these only exist in our carrying out of the tasks that make them up with the appropriate tools. Thus we can only be ourselves, indeed we can only be a self, by being-in-the-world. This is what Heidegger meant when he first introduced the term: "worldhood itself is an *existentiale*. . . . Ontologically, 'world' is not a way of characterizing those entities which Dasein essentially is *not*; it is rather a characteristic of Dasein itself" (92/64). Unlike substances, Dasein is an essentially porous entity, intermingling with others and worldly entities in its very being. We aren't first ourselves and then emerge from this interior into an outside, but are in-a-world from the beginning. We are, in ourselves, in the world. This is why "if Dasein is understood correctly, it defies such proofs, because, in its Being, it already *is* what subsequent proofs deem necessary to demonstrate for it" (249/205). We are walking, talking proofs of the external world because actions such as walking and talking show that the world isn't external at all. Attempts to prove the external world are the true scandal of philosophy because they betray the deep misconceptions that make such an idea seem intelligible and pressing.

The second major topic (after some scuffling with Dilthey and Scheler in (b)) is the idea that when we talk of reality we mean the world as it is in itself. The ultimate level of reality, the really real (*ontos on*, as Plato has it) according to a long tradition of realism, is what is there independently of us. Our interactions and perceptions may affect the way we experience things but any such features are secondary qualities, not true reality but a subjective layer projected onto what's really there. We encountered this idea when Heidegger rejected the idea that readiness-to-hand was "merely a way of taking [entities] . . . as if some world-stuff which is proximally present-at-hand in itself were 'given subjective colouring'" (101/71). The subjective coloring – the way we take up and use things – is due to our interactions, so if all Dasein disappeared, the thought goes, everything would revert back to just present-at-hand things, which demonstrates that that is what is really real.

Heidegger's commitment to phenomenological ontology rejects this line of thought. What we experience is what is real and it is as we experience it, so "*readiness-to-hand is the way in which entities as they are 'in themselves' are defined*" (101/71). It's certainly true that without Dasein there can be no ready-to-hand equipment. To be a piece of equipment is to fit into a series of in-order-tos anchored on a for-the-sake-of-which taken up by Dasein in an attempt to settle the issue of her being. But why should we conclude from this that readiness-to-hand is a less real form of being? Making Dasein-dependence an ontological flaw or weakness, the sign of a lower level of reality, is an assumption, one that only seems self-evident if one takes presence-at-hand to be the paradigm of reality. It is then that "the other modes of Being become defined negatively and privatively with regard to Reality" (245/201).

Not only is presence-at-hand not the legitimate trustworthy form of reality, but it is actually deceptive. One of the reasons philosophers have favored it is that it appears to be independent of us: presence-at-hand is what remains when the lines of signification that integrate it into Dasein's world have been cut. But we know that isn't true. To be is to become manifest in the clearing, and this happens in three fundamental ways: as ready-to-hand, present-at-hand, and existing. Each of these is a way for things to appear to us. This is a bit confusing when it comes to presence-at-hand because it appears to us precisely as something that doesn't need to appear at all. In other words, part of the way we experience presence-at-hand is as something wholly independent of experience, what is there anyway, as Bernard Williams puts it.[4] But remember that this is hermeneutic phenomenology: we need to interpret our experience. And we know that all three are meanings, that is, ways to understand being which only exist in relation to an understanding, which means that "Reality is possible only in the understanding of Being" (251/207).

Heidegger's paradoxical conclusion is that Dasein-independence is itself a meaning, a feature of a way of being that is itself Dasein-dependent. Only as long as Dasein is around to understand and experience present-at-hand objects can they appear as not needing Dasein in order to be. They need Dasein to be there in order not to need Dasein.

> Only as long as Dasein is (that is, only as long as an understanding of Being is ontically possible), "is there" Being. When Dasein does not exist, "independence" "is" not either, nor "is" the "in-itself". . . . In such a case it cannot be said that entities are, nor can it be said that they are not. But now, as long as there is an understanding of Being and therefore an understanding of presence-at-hand, it can indeed be said that in this case entities will still continue to be. (255/212)

As long as there are Dasein around understanding present-at-hand objects, we understand them to pre-exist Dasein and to be around long after we're all gone. But if there are no Dasein then neither can there be presence-at-hand, and thus no reality. It's not that everything vanishes if we're gone; rather, we lose the ability to apply terms meaningfully to that scenario, up to and including the claim that things would still be. All the terms we use in understanding the world are our terms, even the ones we use to try to escape the limitations of our experience and knowledge.

There is a common interpretation of these passages that reads Heidegger as saying that while beings are Dasein-independent, being is not. This would presumably allow him to say that things will still exist after we're gone but that they would not have a mode of being. He comes closest to saying this here: "Being (not entities) is dependent upon the understanding of Being; that is to say, Reality (not the Real) is dependent upon care" (255/212). I disagree with this reading, however. This statement directly follows the discussion of independence as only making sense if there are Dasein around. Beings cannot be without a way of being, and still being there after we're gone is a feature of presence-at-hand or Reality. You can't have Real things without the mode of being of Reality which is explicitly Dasein-dependent.[5]

This also ties into the discussion of truth. Heidegger begins in ¶44(a) with the traditional conception of truth as the correspondence between a sentence or thought and the world. If I think that "The cat is on the mat" and Mr. Whiskers is in fact located there, then my thought is true. As you might expect by now, Heidegger sees this as a present-at-hand way of viewing the situation. There are these entities – a cat and a mat – that are sitting out there in this relationship to each other, and my thought is another object – something like a picture – that bears a relationship of similarity to them, all of which takes place primarily in the derivative form of assertions (267/225).

As a phenomenologist, Heidegger is interested in the way we encounter truth, the way it enters our experience (260/217). First, following Husserl's lead, he gets rid of the idea that we have two entities – thought/sentence and state of affairs – which we bring together to compare. Rather, he sees the whole process of formulating a thought or statement and checking its accuracy as one continuous process of uncovering. As we saw in ¶33, assertions let things be seen by pointing them out; they highlight features of the world and bring them into the clearing. Thus the statement "The cat is on the mat" brings Mr. Whiskers in his on-the-matness into my clearing by prying him free from the rest of the world to become my focus. Looking at the actual cat to check the truth of the statement is an extension of the focus already begun by the statement, not a separate step (261/218).

In (b), Heidegger traces this notion of truth as uncovering to the Greek word for truth, ά–λήθεια or a-lētheia. As so often happens, a well-placed hyphen brings out truths etymologically stored in the roots of the word. The "a-" is privative, as in "asexual" or "amoral." Here it indicates the un-hiddenness or dis-covering of features in the world, which indicates that things are initially hidden or covered until we remove them from their concealment by bringing them into the light or clearing (*Lichtung*) (265/222). It also indicates, as we have seen many times, that Dasein has an intrinsic tendency to cover over and disguise matters. Although it is our nature as the clearing to reveal reality, we constantly *fall* back into dissembling and superficial ways of doing so. Thus Dasein is essentially in both the truth and the untruth, an idea Heidegger develops in his later work. We are in the truth in that we have a pre-ontological understanding of all the matters dealt with here; we are in untruth because we do not naturally have overt access to this understanding and we fall into all kinds of misconceptions about it.

If truth is uncovering and it is Dasein who uncovers, then truth is Dasein-dependent, as we see in (c). Without Dasein there can be no truth, though neither can there be falsity; like reality, the concept as a whole is only applicable in the clearing. Truth is not decided by our personal whims, of course; we cannot control how things appear to us. But without us, no appearing, and so no truth. Here too the paradox of appearing to us as not needing to appear to us reappears: "through Newton the laws became true and with them, entities became accessible in themselves to Dasein. Once entities have been uncovered, they show themselves as entities which beforehand already were" (269/227). Once Newton revealed material objects as obeying the laws of thermodynamics, they manifest themselves as having always obeyed them; previous scientists and philosophers had just misunderstood them. But this itself is a revelation, an event of truth as Heidegger will call it in his later work, and so essentially dependent on Dasein.

Further readings

Antonio Damasio has written extensively on the role emotion plays in cognition, perhaps most famously in *Descartes' Error: Emotion, Reason, and the Human Brain.* For a closer connection with Heidegger, see Guignon's "The Body, Bodily Feelings, and Existential Feelings: A Heideggerian Perspective." The essays collected in François Raffoul and Eric Nelson's *Rethinking Facticity* address the issue of facticity. Look for Mark Wrathall's recent collection, *Heidegger and*

Unconcealment: Truth, Language, and History, for an illuminating discussion of language and truth, although much of it deals with the later Heidegger. I recommend Heidegger's own 1929 lecture "What Is Metaphysics?" (in BW) for a helpful discussion of anxiety. A number of scholars have taken up the issue of realism: Taylor Carman in _Heidegger's Analytic: Interpretation, Discourse and Authenticity in Being and Time_; Graham Harman in _Tool-Being: Heidegger and the Metaphysics of Objects_; Quentin Meillassoux in _After Finitude: An Essay on the Necessity of Contingency_; and myself in _A Thing of This World: A History of Continental Anti-Realism_. Finally, Ernst Tugendhat's "Heidegger's Idea of Truth" (in Wolin's _The Heidegger Controversy: A Critical Reader_) remains one of the classic discussions of Heidegger's treatment of truth.

4

Being and Time 2.I–III.¶64: *Authenticity*

Heidegger begins Division 2 with a dense but helpful review of the overarching strategy of the book. We are after the meaning of being which is "the horizon within which something like Being in general becomes intelligible" (274/231). "Horizon" is a term from Husserl's phenomenology which means the way we understand something, the concepts that apply to it, rather like Heidegger's own fore-structures of understanding which he refers to on the next page. Care, for example, is the meaning of being-in-the-world: it shows us that and how Dasein is-in-a-world, and the facets of being-in-the-world all turn out to be concrete manifestations of care, as we saw in 1.VI.¶41. Once we understand that what it means to be Dasein is to care what happens to ourselves, we can understand why it takes the form of pursuing projects in a world we've been thrown into. Care makes these facets intelligible, both individually and as modes of a single deep fact about us.

Being and Time seeks the meaning of being in general which will explain how the various ways of being are united and why it has these modes. This is a daunting task – it asks how anything whatsoever is intelligible in any way whatsoever. Intelligibility, however, isn't an objective fact about reality; it's not a molecular constitution of things or an object that just sits around somewhere waiting for us to run across it. Intelligible means intelligible to us, understandable by creatures like us, and when we're dealing with so vast a topic, this almost trivial fact can help us get a purchase on it. We can get a grip on the intelligibility of being in general, on what it means for anything to make sense to us, by understanding our own understanding. As a metaphor, imagine that we're investigating the visibility of being, not of this or that particular entity but of anything at all. This isn't an intrinsic property of being that exists independently of us but something that refers to us, specifically to our ability to see; visibility is a direct index of seeing. We discover the visibility of being by studying human sight, which we get at by examining our optic anatomy – the structure of the eyeball, the optic nerve, the visual part of the brain, etc. – and this correlates to the existential analytic. We are analyzing existence – Dasein's way of being – in order to fully grasp our understanding which will show us what it means for anything to be understandable, that is, the meaning of being.[1]

It is crucial, therefore, to fully understand existence in order to understand understanding in order to get at the understandability of being, and Heidegger now questions whether we have succeeded in doing so. In particular, studying Dasein in our average everydayness leaves out our authentic way of being since we are usually fallen and inauthentic (275–6/232–3). Here Heidegger switches from the neutral phenomenological notion of average everydayness as simply what we do proximally and for the most part to the existential judgment of this state as inauthentic. Whereas this approach to examining ourselves mundanely was initially praised for avoiding traditional prejudicial emphases on unusual states or activities (37–8/16–17), now he finds fault with it as itself prejudiced towards our inauthentic selves.[2]

As long as we do not have Dasein's authentic way of being in view, our analysis remains incomplete since we have not uncovered Dasein as a whole. Capturing this side of existence therefore forms one of the two goals of Division 2, especially 2.I–III which I will discuss in this chapter. Heidegger also finds the unity of existence that he has achieved so far to be lacking, which strikes me as a rather forced criticism. Care showed how the three facets of being-in-the-world were aspects of a single characteristic quite satisfactorily for me. But now he wants a further elaboration of this unity and a greater intelligibility of the structure as a whole. He gives the Hermeneutic Spiral another turn by going a level deeper into Dasein's being, to temporality as "the primordial meaning of Dasein's Being" (278/235). This is what care rests upon, similar to the way being-in-the-world is unified and made intelligible by care. Just as we revisited the three aspects of being-in-the-world and understood them anew in terms of care in 1.VI.¶41, so we will now go through them one more time as aspects or forms of temporality in 2.IV–VI, as we will see in the next chapter. Unfortunately, Heidegger does not finish this project, nor does he give us a very clear sense of authenticity, making Division 2 generally less satisfying than Division 1 for me. Still, it contains some brilliant and fascinating ideas, so let us begin.

Being and Time 2.I Being-a-whole and death

To get at the meaning of being in general we have to understand what meaning itself is, which is to be meaningful to beings that can understand or grasp meaning, i.e., Dasein. So to understand meaning in general or what it means for anything to be meaningful, we have to understand understanding itself which, like all the equi-primordial facets of Dasein, is holistically integrated into our entire way of being. Thus, the next step in the reasoning goes, understanding our understanding requires us to understand ourselves, our way of being in its entirety, which requires that we get Dasein's being as a whole into view. The key to the strategy of the entire book is that the existential analytic is the foundation for ontology (34/13).

But this presents us with a problem, for Dasein never is a whole. It is part of our nature always to have something outstanding; part of being-there is always still not yet here (279/236). Being a Dasein means to pursue projects by taking up tasks and taking care of them in a world. We are-in-a-world by maintaining a certain identity, our for-the-sake-of-which, that tries to settle the issue of our being, and these roles are woven out of tasks to be done. The point at which there is nothing left to be done is the point at which one is no longer being that role. Not doing those kinds of things means not being that kind of person. As long as one is a student, there are still more things to do – classes to take, books to read, tests to take. Once there are no more studenty things to do, one is not a fully realized student, but a graduate – an ex-student. One is only complete when one has completed the relevant tasks and so is no longer engaged in that activity.

Not only is this true of particular ways of making a living, but it is true of life itself. When I have run out of tasks to do, I am done; my jobs have been executed. I am not a fully actualized person when I have no more responsibilities to work on; at this point I am no longer a Dasein at all. This is death (281/237). If this is true, however, then it seems that our attempt to grasp Dasein as a whole is ruined from the start.

Here we must remind ourselves of the Existential Imperative: are we thinking about our not-yet and death as existentialia, that is, appropriate to Dasein's distinctive way of being, or do "substructures of entities with another kind of Being (presence-at-hand or life) thrust themselves to the fore unnoticed, and threaten to bring confusion to the interpretation of this phenomenon" (285/241)? In fact, Heidegger argues, our worry had been inadvertently thinking of Dasein's not-yet either in ready-to-hand terms, as something that is not presently available for use (286–7/242), or in present-at-hand terms, as something that is a whole but not presented as such to us at present, like the shadowed last quarter of the moon (287/243).

But this is not our not-yet. Rather, "any Dasein always exists in just such a manner that its 'not-yet' *belongs* to it" (287/243). What is still outstanding for us is not simply separated from our present state of being; instead, we live our present in the light of the not-yet finished goals we pursue. The situation of students sitting in a class cannot be comprehended simply by listing all the facts that are presently true about it. These facts only make sense in relation to the goals of understanding the material, doing well on tests, and ultimately graduating. None of the students have yet graduated – if they had, they would no longer be students – but all of their present actions – taking down notes, listening, showing up for class at all – are intelligible *as* steps towards this goal, just as a hammer gets its significance from its position in the world's web of instrumental relations. The end of all activities is present in their beginning, because we start to act in order to reach the goal. We act purposefully and conceive our actions full with their purpose. This is a temporal version of what we saw in Dasein's spatiality. Dasein is never inside itself but out in the world, with the object of its focus (89/62, 142/107–8, 156/120). When I get up to open the window I am already at the window, and it is only in light of this goal that my present state of getting up or taking a step makes sense. We can now see that this is not just a spatial leap to the object of concern, but also a jump ahead in time to the final aim as already there in my present action.

When all of my possibilities have come to an end, so has my being-in-the-world because it always involves projecting myself onto some possibilities or others. This is death, which relates to our projecting ourselves onto possibilities in general the way specific ends relate to particular acts. "Just as Dasein *is* already its 'not-yet', and is its 'not-yet' constantly as long as it is, it *is* already its end too" (289/245). Heidegger is less interested in the moment we breathe our last breath – what he calls "Being-at-an-end" – than in the way our lives are permeated with the sense that we are always heading towards this moment – "*being-towards-the-end*;" it is in this sense that "death is a way to be" rather than the finishing off of our being (289/245). Studying the final moment of life phenomenologically would be rather difficult after all since none of us has yet experienced it, so we must find another way to examine it.

¶47 rejects the possibility of vicariously experiencing death through others' dying because, no matter how close we are to the dying, no matter how upsetting another's death is, it still is unavoidably they who die, not us. We're just there, along with the dying (282/239).[3] The fact that people can generally substitute for or "be represented by" others is an important fact about public everydayness (283/239). The subway train that approaches was not built or summoned specially for me, but for anyone to ride; these shoes belong to me, but they were made for the generic size 9.5 foot-owner, and anyone else with similar feet could have bought and worn them. Ironically, even the for-the-sake-of-whichs that I use to become my own person are themselves generic slots that anyone with the proper credentials could fulfill – someone else could teach my classes; if my wife had met someone else, he would have been her husband, and so on.

This substitutability, however, breaks down when it comes to death. No one can die for me; at most they can sacrifice themselves to postpone my death. Although Dasein's *life* is in-each-case-mine, our death is even more so: we live our lives the way one lives, but each of us must die our own death. *Das Man* tries to distract us from this unsettling fact, as Heidegger explains in ¶51. We all know that "one dies," but paradoxically this very certainty allows me to avoid the realization that *I* will die (297/253). Furthermore, idle talk presents death as a present-at-hand actual event rather than a possibility. This might sound like it would force us to confront our mortality but in fact it lets us suppress the knowledge. Death will happen, of course, but at some point in the future, which means that it has nothing to do with what's happening right now so I can safely ignore it. Indeed, we are often chided not to dwell on such gloomy facts but to concentrate on seizing the day and living in the present. Just as that which one is anxious about "is completely indefinite" (231/186), so death *"is possible at any moment.* Along with the certainty of death goes the *indefiniteness* of its 'when'" (302/258).

This attitude towards death bears all the features of fallenness, as covered in 1.V.B. It tranquilizes us by letting us think happy thoughts. It turns anxiety about death into fear which gives us things to busy ourselves with so we don't have to think about the inevitability of death. But, since we all will in fact die, this distraction alienates us from our true nature (298/253–4). However, as we saw earlier (229/184), the very fact that we flee from it means that we somehow know it, which holds out the promise that we can turn to face and understand it (299/255).

The fact that we normally experience death in a fallen way is not just a contingent fact about us, but an essential clue to the nature of our existence. Since existing means always being ahead-of-ourselves as fallen into the world we've been thrown into, death must share these characteristics (293/249–50). We have just seen how death is fallen. We disclose that we have been thrown into a mortal life through the state-of-mind of anxiety (295/251). Since it is inevitable there is nothing for us to do about it unless we transform this into a fallen state of fear which motivates us to exercise, eat right, etc. (not that these activities are shameful, but we cannot let them distract us from the iron-clad necessity of death). Moreover, like anxiety, death is about and reveals my being-in-the-world as a whole because it refers to the final collapse of my being-there at all. This is most fully shown in death's relation to projecting possibilities since it represents the end of such activities. "Death, as possibility, gives Dasein nothing to be 'actualized', nothing which Dasein, as actual, could itself *be*. It is the possibility of the impossibility of every way of comporting oneself towards anything, of every way of existing" (307/262). Death is the possibility of there being no more possibilities and so no world and no self to be-there. Being-towards-the-end has an ultimacy to it as the end of working towards ends, which is what he means when he calls it "not to be outstripped."

Heidegger calls the authentic attitude towards it anticipation (306/262), which does **not** mean that you're looking forward to dying but that you acknowledge its inevitability and allow it to exert its full force on your whole way of living. It is less about how you prepare for the moment of death than how you live as a mortal; I think that "being-mortal" might capture more of what Heidegger means since this is a constant fact about us rather than a future event. As he writes a little later, Dasein "does not have an end at which it just stops, but it *exists finitely*" (378/329).

Anticipation also shows us that death is "non-relational" because in it, Dasein "has been wrenched away from the 'they'" (307/263). For one thing, as we have seen, each of us must die for ourselves, so it breaks down the communal substitutability that marks publicness. But "non-relational" means more than this: "it makes manifest that all Being-amid the things with which we concern ourselves, and all Being-with-Others, will fail us when our ownmost potentiality-for-Being is the issue" (308/263). These are the two forms of care (*Sorge*) – concern (*Besorge*) for dealing with equipment and solicitude (*Fürsorge*) of others – and they will break down because care as a whole breaks down when my projecting onto possibilities gets rebuffed by this ultimate impossibility.

As always, breakdowns enable us to see what had been inconspicuous and taken for granted. When we're talking about our possibilities, however, we're talking about the choices we make, down to the most fundamental ones concerning what kind of person we want to be. Average everyday life has the property of taking over and living our lives for us as we simply go along with the flow of what one does. I know what students do so I can let my routine lead me through my daily life – wake up at a certain time, go to classes, write my papers. I can fulfill the vast majority of my obligations with minimal thought or attention, culminating in "the oblivious passing of our lives" (BP 264). Once again, Heidegger switches valence mid-analysis. Our facility with tools in Division 1 is what allows us to use them in unthinking absorption, guided by circumspection rather than explicit thought. Now, however, this fact is what keeps us inauthentic, what prevents us from examining our beliefs and lives the way Socrates deplored so long ago.

The anticipation of death – the blood-pounding-in-your-ears, bone-deep realization that you will die (300/256) – as awful as it is, brings with it the opportunity to become authentic by provoking a crisis in our everyday lives. Authenticity involves taking up roles and making choices because you have decided to rather than because they are just what one does. Dasein is authentically itself only to the extent that, *as* concernful Being-amid and solicitous Being-with, it projects itself upon its ownmost potentiality-for-Being rather than upon the possibility of the they-self. The entity which anticipates its non-relational possibility, is thus forced by that very anticipation into the possibility of taking over from itself its ownmost Being" (308/263). Numberless decisions made in particular situations have gradually accreted around and behind us to form a person that we are and a life that we lead. Normally the demands of the tasks we're absorbed in keep us from looking at this life as a whole but the realization of mortality interrupts this ongoing process, forcing us into a new perspective. "When, by anticipation, one becomes free *for* one's own death, one is liberated from one's lostness in those possibilities which may accidentally thrust themselves upon one; and one is liberated in such a way that for the first time one can authentically understand and choose among the factical possibilities. . . . It shatters all one's tenaciousness to whatever existence one has reached" (308/264).

Think of someone in a stale marriage. It may have started well but, over the years, minor insults and omissions have taken their toll and there is little love left. She continues more out of inertia than actual decision. She has become habituated to this life and it leads her on through the activities one does, the routine she is used to. At some point, however, something shakes her out of her complacency – as Heidegger has shown us about moods, it can be something very minor – and suddenly she sees her life explicitly, almost for the first time, and now she can actively decide whether she wants to remain in the marriage, perhaps to re-engage in it with new energy, or leave it. This represents an active taking up of one's life, awakening from the passive inertia of everydayness. This is, as I understand it, authenticity.

Being and Time 2.II Conscience and resoluteness

Heidegger begins 2.II looking for an "attestation" of Dasein's authenticity, the mode of existing that was missing from Division 1 (312/267). This demand is due to the nature of phenomenology: if he wants to claim that we have another way of existing that doesn't appear in average everydayness, he has to find evidence of it rather than simply arguing that it must exist, and we can only find this evidence within our own lives. Thus the "witness" that he calls to the stand to testify about authenticity is us. As we have seen, Dasein is always in both truth and untruth which means that we have the knowledge we're seeking but we can't directly access it right away. And when we try to make this pre-ontological understanding explicit we tend to misconstrue it, veering off into inappropriate ontological interpretations. However, we must have some access to this way of being in order to talk about it and we can only find the clue to it within ourselves.

Of course, it isn't our everyday selves that call us to authenticity because this self is ensconced in inauthenticity. In our everydayness we listen to the noisy hubbub of what "they" say about matters which covers over another voice that we could hear were we to quiet the they's incessant idle talk: the call of conscience. As we have seen, anxiety and the anticipation of death function as large-scale breakdowns of our world that deflate the significance of our normal concerns, individualizing us by temporarily cutting us off from the substitutable roles of the they. The call of conscience also functions like anxiety and death, isolating us to produce moments of bell jar silence in which it can be heard (316–17/271–3).

In this post-Nietzschean world, it is not a transcendent authority but we ourselves who call, but it is the self in anxious uncanniness, the self that is not at home in the world, the self that, ejected from a broken-down world, sees through to the "lit up" structure of being-in-the-world (322/277). Conscience discloses our true nature and in so doing summons us to become what we are, that is, to appropriate our selves by living in a way that is appropriate to the kind of beings that we are. A little like Kant's noumenal self issuing ethical orders to the phenomenal self under the influence of inclinations, the call of conscience "comes *from* me and yet *from beyond me and over me*" and, also as in Kant, the conscience "calls, against our expectations and even against our will" (320/275). This fits with the common meaning of conscience as something that tells us what we don't want to hear, usually that we're behaving badly in trying to get what we want. We fall into inauthentic average everydayness in order to flee from dreadful existential features, so the call to acknowledge and take up these features goes against our ontological inclinations. We want to be at home in the world, to be tranquilized or reassured that the life we have chosen is good and right, that it is how one ought to live. But Heidegger argues that uncanniness, literally "not-being-at-homeness," "is the basic kind of Being-in-the-world, even though in an everyday way it has been covered up" (322/277). We are fundamentally not at home in the world, thrown and abandoned in it, and the they's attempts to settle in and settle down by settling the issue of our being make it inauthentic.

Although the conscience is a form of discourse, it says nothing, which ties into his earlier discussion of silence (208/165). It is not concerned with specific misdeeds – that would be a fallen and ontic (or existentiell) way of interpreting conscience which, like fear, gives us things to do in order to disarm it. That view of conscience allows us to treat life as a ready-to-hand affair that can be calculated and managed by piling up enough good deeds to offset the bad on one's moral spreadsheet (336–8/289–92). Instead, the call says that "*Dasein as such is guilty*" (331/285), regardless of particular deeds or misdeeds. In order to understand this ontological or existential guilt we must examine what Heidegger means by it more closely.

He gives an obscure discussion of the meaning of guilt which involves responsibility and, in his terms, being the basis for a lack or a "nullity," a translation of the neologism "*Nichtigkeit*" or, more literally, "notness" (329/283). Doing something bad often involves depriving someone of something – of possessions in theft, of freedom in enslaving, of comfort or life in harming or killing. Such actions make us responsible for reducing the victims in some way which means that we owe them something, which ties into the literal meaning of the German word for guilt, "*Schuldig*" as a debt. However, as usual we must be careful to understand this lack in existential rather than present-at-hand terms (329/283). As we have seen, Dasein has or is that which it lacks; it is its not-yet. Similarly, its nullity is not something that isn't there, the way that I am simply not a horse, but rather something that pervades our very being, the way a student is, *in* being a student, not a graduate. Thus, being guilty means that we are permeated with a notness, shot through with holes that mean that we can never simply be a whole. Another way to think about this is to say that Dasein is finite. Whereas philosophy has traditionally sought ways to overcome our limitations, Heidegger believes that we must accept and live out our finitude rather than live and think in denial of it. Since Dasein's being is care our ontological guilt – that is, the fact that we are defined by nullity – should inform and manifest itself in all three facets of care, facticity (thrownness), existence (projection), and falling (329/284), so Heidegger shows the distinct form nullity takes in each.

First, and I think most important here, is our thrownness. This means that Dasein "has been brought into its 'there', but *not* of its own accord. . . . It never comes back behind its thrownness in such a way that it might first release this 'that-it-is-and-has-to-be' from *its Being*-its-Self and lead it into the 'there'" (329–30/284). This is actually a fairly clear explanation of what Heidegger means by thrownness: we were born, "thrown" into this life and a host of particular features about our particular life (collectively called facticity), but not of our doing and not by our choice. We did not decide to be born, or where or when or as what, nor did we enact our own creation. We are, before our first breath, beneficiaries of people and events that we had no part in, even though we owe our very existence to them. This inescapable indebtedness is the "not" or nullity that lies at the very basis of our being anything at all.

Furthermore, this isn't just about birth as a past event that took place and now is over. It continues to inform the way we live throughout our lives. "In existing as thrown – Dasein constantly lags behind its possibilities. . . . 'Being-a-basis' means *never* to have power over one's ownmost Being from the ground up" (330/284). Our lives and our selves are always already underway, always partially formed by the decisions we have made and the kind of person we are in the process of becoming. Although the possibility Heidegger is ruling out here – "having power over one's ownmost Being from the ground up" – may sound rather extravagant, I think this ideal has guided much of the history of philosophy. Philosophers have always resented their own past, the fact that they lived a great deal of their lives without keeping strict control over their actions, thoughts, and beliefs. Think of Descartes' admonishing himself for having accepted what he had been taught without challenging it in his youth, or Socrates' scolding the supposedly wise men of Athens for simply taking on societally accepted beliefs. For these philosophers – and I think they are emblematic of the discipline as a whole – swallowing down an idea without genuinely examining it and deliberately deciding whether one assents to it means that you don't really believe it, that you are being lived as Heidegger puts it.

And both thinkers look to philosophy to overcome this past passivity. By emptying himself of beliefs through methodological doubt, Descartes attempts to bring himself into his (epistemological) there of his own accord, in Heidegger's terminology. He proposes to, in a sense, reboot his mind from scratch, only this time in total control. The same goes for Socrates' *elenchus* or examination of beliefs, as well as for Kant's absolute autonomy over the phenomenal self, and the Stoics, and Spinoza, and Hegel, and many others. The quest to actively take charge of one's life and one's beliefs has in many ways defined philosophy.

We witness here, in this chapter of *Being and Time*, the end of this dream. Heidegger argues that the enterprise as a whole is misconceived. We will always "lag behind" our selves because we must rely on something given just in order to examine our beliefs. However, even though we didn't create our selves, this doesn't mean that they're not really us. We are these selves that we partially inherit and we are responsible for them. This self with all its quirks, with its tastes and preferences, is the only me there is since there is no noumenal self beyond what exists in this world. Therefore, my very self is pervaded by a "not" from the ground up, but still it is who I am.[5] Heidegger expands this idea in his later work, as we will see when we examine Descartes and Nietzsche in the second half of this book.

In keeping with the Existential Imperative we must understand how we are this thrownness existentially. It's not simply a fact about our origin that sits in the past the way the creation of a painting at a certain date by a certain painter is just a set fact about it; we live our thrownness. Dasein is its thrown basis by projecting itself "upon possibilities into which it has been thrown" (330/284), which means that the range of possibilities open to us is limited by the facts we were thrown into. No matter how much I may want to, I cannot be a samurai because I was born into late twentieth-century America which does not offer that as a for-the-sake-of-which. Nor can I be a professional football player because of the body I was born into as well as the preferences for reading and not getting injured that I find in myself. Thus, the second facet of being-in-the-world, projection, is also fundamentally determined by nots in that there are many, many things that I cannot do and many ways of living that I cannot partake of either they are not open to me given my society or not live options in William James' phrase because of my Befindlichkeit. As we saw above, projection and thrownness are deeply interconnected.

Projection is further informed by nullity in that each choice I make is in itself a choosing not to do countless other things. If I sit down to read a book, by that very action I am not practicing football or learning how to play a musical instrument or mowing the yard. And, as these actions are what add up to being a particular for-the-sake-of-which, I am constantly making myself not into myriad kinds of people by making myself into one type. This is just the nature of choice, at least for finite, temporal creatures like us: freedom, however, is only in the choice of one possibility – that is, in tolerating one's not having chosen the others" (331/285). Acting (in certain ways) intrinsically entails not acting (in others).

Fallenness, the third facet of care, is the most obviously notful. In being fallen, we are proximally and for the most part not ourselves) as Heidegger said in 1.IV (151/116). Inauthentic everyday life has fallen away from our true self, which is precisely what our conscience tells us. Confronting us with our being-in-the-world temporarily drained of content, conscience summons us "to one's own Self. Not to what Dasein counts for, can do, or concerns itself with in being with one another publicly. . . . *In passing over* the 'they' . . . the call pushes it into insignificance. But the Self, which the appeal has robbed of this lodgment and hiding-place, gets brought to itself by the call" (317/273). The conscience does not allow us to define ourselves in terms of what we do and what we concern ourselves with in our daily affairs or with what "they" tell us "one" ought to do. In these uncanny moments of dread and anxiety, we are inescapably faced with the question of whether we are leading the right kind of life, a life that is genuine and worthy, a life that we want. A life is made up of the accretion of countless minor and seemingly trivial decisions going on all the time, most of which occur as we coast through on inertia, and it's only when there is a breakdown that temporarily kicks us out of our world and our lives that we can see these and actually decide whether they are what we truly want or not. In this sense, these breakdown experiences resemble Nietzsche's eternal recurrence thought experiment.

Hearing this call and understanding what it says does not come out in a theoretical grasp of facts but in taking appropriate actions, the way the circumspective understanding of equipment lives in the use of tools or the genuine acknowledgment of mortality consists in acting in the certainty that I will die. We hear and understand the call when we are summoned to our true self and choose that self (333–4/287). The existential conscience, unlike the common-sense existentiell conscience, does not give us specific ontic actions to take or avoid; doing that would turn decisions into mere obedience (340/294). As Kierkegaard argues, one of the truths we must accept is that there is no way to be sure that we are living a good life, that we must make choices in the dark about their ultimate worth. What is essential for authenticity is that they are *our* choices.

In my reading (which is by no means universally shared), this is Heidegger at his most voluntaristic, meaning accepting and praising a notion of free will as not determined by external factors. This comes out clearly at the beginning of the chapter:

The "they" even hides the manner in which it has tacitly relieved Dasein of the burden of explicitly *choosing* these possibilities. It remains indefinite who has "really" done the choosing. Dasein makes no choices, gets carried along by the nobody, and thus ensnares itself in inauthenticity. This process can be reversed only if Dasein specifically brings itself back to itself from its lostness in the "they"] . . . "Making up" for not choosing signifies *choosing to make this choice* – deciding for a potentiality-for-Being, and making this decision from one's own Self. (312–13/268)

Inauthentic everyday Dasein is absorbed into the they and its mundane activities. We usually coast on auto-pilot, simply following our usual routine of what one does with little to no thought. But my being is an issue which means that my being a certain kind of person, my adherence to a particular for-the-sake-of-which, is never a settled fact but something that requires continual commitment. At any moment I can break off from my present trajectory and take up an entirely new one, as Sartre emphasizes.

However, proximally and for the most part we don't feel this freedom, this unsettledness. In fact, we think very little about our choices, going with the flow of society and the inertia of our past. No one is forcing me to do the things I do but neither am I explicitly choosing them, which shows that our usual understanding of freedom and action is too simplistic. It is the one who chooses and acts most of the time. In order to reverse this I have to start making my decisions for myself, to "live deliberately . . . and not, when I came to die, discover that I had not lived," in Thoreau's words.[6] This is the opportunity offered by these moments of crisis – anxiety, anticipation of death, and the call of conscience. They remove me from the flow of life by causing a breakdown in my for-the-sake-of-which and world so that I can see them afresh, almost from the outside, and intentionally decide if this is how I want to live. This choosing to make choices is what Heidegger calls resoluteness (343/296–7), which changes the there that I'm in into what he calls the situation (346–7/299–300), which involves seeing my possibilities as possibilities rather than foregone conclusions. The things that I am acting on are not absolute actualities but can always be put aside (355/308), and many of the things I've put aside are still possibilities in that they can always be taken back up. Resoluteness removes the blinders our routine places on our choices, showing us that our being is an unresolved and unresolvable issue made up of a tissue of possibilities rather than a wall of actualities.

Now there are two important qualifications to make to this voluntaristic notion of authenticity as explicitly making choices. First, we never overcome our thrownness. In order to be a self at all we have to be-in-a-world which means taking up some for-the-sake-of-which or other which is offered by society (344/298). Authenticity doesn't mean escaping the world of the they but inhabiting it in a certain way, what he calls an existentiell modification of it (168/130).

Second, I cannot simply decide to start deciding. This is part of what he means when he says that the call of conscience comes from me but not from me. In a formulation he will come to favor in his later work, Heidegger says that "'it' calls" (320/275). The call doesn't come from anywhere else but me – not from society or God, for instance – but neither can I initiate or control it. This is another way he undermines the traditional notion of autonomy. Even the limited form of autonomy that resoluteness can achieve is not something I can give myself; it must be given by a mood or being called. Even his choice of metaphor – hearing rather than the more traditional sight (186–7/146–7) to hearing – indicates this shift: we direct our visual focus where we will, but sounds befall us. We cannot bring on the call; we can only prepare and wait for it, which he calls wanting to have a conscience (334/288). Thinking that we can produce this call would violate its message of our nullity or finitude. Much of this argument gets developed more fully in his later analysis of technology.

Being and Time 2.III.¶¶61–4 Being-a-whole and selfhood

2.III has two main focuses which I think are better treated separately, so I will discuss being-a-whole and selfhood here, and leave temporality for my next chapter. The flaw with Division 1 which required a second one was that Heidegger did not think that he had gotten Dasein in its entirety into his purview: that portrait lacked authenticity (275/232). Chapters I and II of Division 2 have given us a better sense of authentic existence as anticipatory resoluteness in a situation, thus solving this problem (357/309). However, a new worry arises here about how these features of authenticity interconnect. Throughout the book, Heidegger continually worries about a certain kind of holism. The very first point he made about being-in-the-world was that "it stands for a *unitary* phenomenon. This primary datum must be seen as a whole" (78/53), what I called the Humpty-Dumpty Thesis. It is essential to the understanding of Dasein that we understand how all of its characteristics intermingle and presuppose each other from the start. This was true of being-in-the-world and of the world, and now he applies this requirement to authenticity. Its features must form an organic unity rather than being merely welded together afterwards.

¶62 attempts to show how the facets of authenticity – anticipation, resoluteness, and the situation – all involve each other at a deep level. I must admit that I don't find all of his claims here persuasive, but many of them do make sense. For instance, resoluteness involves guilt and this guilt is ontological or existential, that is, it doesn't result from particular deeds nor can it be assuaged by good deeds. Dasein as such is guilty and is so as long as it lives, so Dasein is guilty up until it dies which brings in the anticipation of death. Guilt, no more than death, can be outstripped (353/305). Conversely, resoluteness means taking over the fact that we are null or shot through with lacks and limitations of power. But death is the ultimate not – it is when our Dasein is not, as Epicurus points out – making it the greatest revealer of our finitude or nullity (354/306). Heidegger's conclusion is that "care harbours in itself both death and guilt equiprimordially" (354/306). These matters are intrinsic to care, Dasein's nature, and they are equiprimordial, which means that they're on the same level ontologically rather than either being the foundation from which the other can be derived. Furthermore, they both reveal the situation by conscience's calling itself to task (355/307).

¶63 revisits hermeneutics, that is, the way interpretation works and, in particular, the way *Being and Time*'s existential analytic works, as previously discussed in ¶32. We see here a turn of the Hermeneutic Spiral as he revises or takes another look at one of the first things he said about Dasein: the fact that we are closest to ourselves means that we are farthest when it comes to achieving a clear understanding of the kinds of beings we are. This was simply stated in the Introduction (36/15), but now he can explain why this is the case. For one thing, as we have seen in Division 1, our selves are inconspicuous; in our normal absorption in our daily activities we take no notice of ourselves. Division 2 has added the existential claim that this fallen absorption is motivated by a fleeing in the face of features of existence we find unsettling, such as death or anxiety. This is another reason why Heidegger's interpretation of existence can seem so strange, along with the basic fact that we have no vocabulary or grammar to capture it since language is typically oriented towards our daily ontic affairs (63/38–9). Part of us actively resists what he's telling us, like a patient in psychoanalysis avoiding the key issue as the therapist approaches it. "The laying-bare of Dasein's primordial Being must rather be *wrested from Dasein*. . . . Existential analysis, therefore, constantly has the character of *doing violence*" (359/311).

Of course, just as in therapy, a part of us – the part that houses the voice of conscience – is an ally in addition to the inauthentic part that resists. ¶44 showed us that Dasein is always in both truth and untruth simultaneously or, as he will say in his later work, every revealing is at the same time a concealing. When we experience the pen as ready-to-hand while writing with it, for example, its potential presence-at-hand is covered over; staring at it on the other hand brings its presence-at-hand to the fore but also covers its previous readiness-to-hand. Like the Gestalt switch of pictures such as the duck-rabbit, we can only see it one way at a time; whichever way we're experiencing it prevents us from seeing it the other way.

Although Dasein is naturally attracted to inauthentic average everyday life "which covers up ontically Dasein's authentic Being, so that the ontology which is directed towards this entity is denied an appropriate basis" (359/311), we also have a pre-ontological understanding of ourselves. Without this we wouldn't know how to act in the world or even that we had to act in a world (360–1/312–13). Our findings can be "attested" by ourselves because, like Socrates' solution to Meno's Paradox, we will recognize the truth when we find it.

This is how Heidegger solves the apparently circular reasoning he seems to find himself in. As he explained in the discussion of the fore-structures of understanding in ¶32, the ways we experience and understand phenomena are shaped by deep presuppositions about what kinds of entities they are. I will only check the mood of my wife because I start off classifying her as a Dasein which is the kind of creature that has moods and for whom moods influence how they will behave and react. I do not check my shoes' mood before putting them on because they are not that kind of being.

Now the goal of *Being and Time* as we have it is to distinguish Dasein's way of being from other ways of being (what I am calling the Existential Imperative) because Dasein is the being who has an understanding of being in general. Thus the existential analytic – that is, the analysis of our way of being, existence – is fundamental ontology – the foundation for understanding the meaning of being in general – since we are the being who already possesses this understanding (34–5/13–15). However, we can only differentiate among these modes of being (existence, readiness-to-hand, and presence-at-hand) if we start off with an understanding of being in general, since this is what we are understanding these three as modes of. We can only understand these as three modes of *being* if we have some sense of what being means, but we were supposed to obtain that from an understanding of one of them, namely, existence, which requires us to distinguish among them as three modes of being (362/314).

As he did in his earlier discussion of interpretation (195/153) and in the Introduction (27–8/7–8), Heidegger criticizes this objection for taking the ideas involved to be steps in a logical proof where circular reasoning would be a problem. These are existential truths, ideas we live rather than grasp intellectually. Just as my understanding of the hammer occurs in my hammering with it, so my understanding of existence comes out in my existing, in acting the way Dasein acts. Since we are always already acting in the world, we are always already enacting our understanding of existence; it is only in light of this that we know that we have to act. We also always understand the other two modes because we are constantly using tools and, less frequently, staring at objects. "Entities can be experienced 'factually' only when Being is already understood, even if it has not been conceptualized" (363/315). Just as our existence refutes external world skepticism (249/205–6), so too does it untie the circle here; our very nature eludes these artificial problems.[7]

It is essential that we get the right fore-understanding of Dasein in place in order to interpret whatever data we find correctly, which requires that we get existence as a whole in our purview, and this is what he thinks he has now accomplished with his account of authenticity. "The authenticity of the potentiality-for-Being-one's-Self guarantees that primordial existentiality is something we see in advance, and this assures us that we are coining the appropriate existential concepts" (364/316). Seeking a guarantee that he has hit on the definitive account and congratulating himself on having achieved it seem to me at odds with his more general emphasis on the finitude of understanding. How can we ever be sure that we've reached bedrock in any inquiry? It has long been the epistemological dream of philosophers to find truths that are so true they cannot be false, beliefs we can know that we'll never change our minds about. This is the nature of Aristotle's self-evident first principles or Descartes' clear and distinct perceptions. But this quest for certainty, as John Dewey calls it, misconstrues the kinds of beings we are. We never get absolute truth, only what seems right given the evidence presently available. Part of being temporal beings is that we can never ensure what we'll think tomorrow, as the closing questioning sentences of *Being and Time* attest.

¶64 then returns to the question of selfhood, first discussed in 1.IV. As the Hermeneutic Spiral has turned, our investigation of the subject now takes place at a deeper level than the previous one since we can now take into account all the facts about existence we have gained in the meantime. As always, the Existential Imperative guides our investigation so that "'I'-hood and Selfhood must be conceived *existentially*" (365/318). Accordingly, the central problem with traditional notions of the self is that they treat it as a present-at-hand substance.

Heidegger focuses primarily on Kant here, reaching a similar conclusion to his 1929 book, *Kant and the Problem of Metaphysics*: Kant made some crucial advances but ultimately retreated before their radical implications to more traditional, flawed ideas. Kant's transcendental subject binds together sensory data into the experience of substantial objects and a coherent world. The forms of the intuition and concepts of the understanding are ultimately just different ways of unifying experience; this partially integrates self and world, thus anticipating some of Heidegger's ideas.[8] But Kant doesn't satisfactorily account for why the subject does this, leaving the connection between self and world contingent and external, precisely the kind of linkage Heidegger criticizes. This problematic arrangement is inevitable, Heidegger thinks, if we start with subject and world as separate present-at-hand entities. Despite Kant's efforts to bring them together, they can never have more than an accidental relationship if each is its own self-sufficient object. Kant's problem is that he overlooks the question of being; had he genuinely asked what being means, he might have been able to construct a conception of existence as a mode of being distinct from present-at-hand which could have formed the foundation for a genuine unity like being-in-the-world (367–8/321). This isn't just bad luck or stupidity; as we have seen, the mistakes philosophers tend to fall into are motivated by the inconspicuousness of the entities involved, the inheritance of traditional ideas, and a flight from troubling ideas (359/311, 368/322).

Now, midway through Chapter III of Division 2, we have arrived at what we have been seeking in this division: a full account of authenticity. Remember, this translates *"Eigentlichkeit"* which is a noun built from the word for own *("eigen")*, as in something that is one's own. Authenticity is the kind of life that is most one's own, that suits the kind of being that we are, and which enables us to own up to our lives rather than being lived by the they. "Dasein becomes 'essentially' Dasein in that authentic existence which constitutes itself as anticipatory resoluteness" (370/323). In being authentic, we become who we are (186/145) in that we live a life of our own, one that we have appropriated and one that is appropriate (another way to translate *"eigentlich"*) to our proper way of being as existing.

This line of argumentation repeats Aristotle's function argument in the *Nicomachean Ethics,* the only book that in my mind rivals *Being and Time* as an accurate account of what it's like to be a human.[9] Aristotle believes that all things possess a distinctive activity that makes them what they are and which constitutes the highest aspect of their nature. In what is sometimes called perfectionist ethics, living well or flourishing means performing that activity with excellence. Since he understands humans to be rational animals, the best form of life for us is that which exercises our highest and most distinctive faculty – reason – as well as possible. Surely it's just a coincidence, as Nietzsche slyly insinuates, that a philosopher happens to conclude that philosophizing represents the best form of life possible for our species.

Heidegger seems to be employing a version of this argument, as captured in the various meanings of *"Eigentlichkeit."* There is a problem when we apply this to Dasein, however, because one of our defining features is that our being is an issue for us; it is fundamentally unsettled and can never be settled. This is how Sartre interprets Heidegger's claim that *"the 'essence' of Dasein lies in existence"* (67/42). Sartre thinks this means that we first just show up or get born as blank slates without essence, and we then make ourselves into something through our choices. This is partially wrong, in that Sartre reads existence here as just being there, a form of presence-at-hand that Heidegger rightly rejects (see BW 229–33). Existence in *Being and Time* stands for a complexly structured way of being distinct from readiness-to-hand and presence-at-hand. Dasein does in fact have a detailed way of being, which is the subject of the book.

However, Sartre is partially right in that Heidegger believes that there is no particular kind of activity that is pre-ordained for us by a deity or the universe or our own natures. While the form of our lives is set in our nature, the content is contingent and derived from the particular culture we happen to be born in. That is how I understand this passage:

> Anxiety discloses an insignificance of the world; and this insignificance reveals the nullity of that with which one can concern oneself – or, in other words, the impossibility of projecting oneself upon a potentiality-for-Being which belongs to existence and which is founded primarily upon one's objects of concern. The revealing of this possibility, however, signifies that one is letting the possibility of an authentic potentiality-for-Being be lit up. (393/343)

A "potentiality-for-Being which belongs to existence" means a particular role like reasoning or worshipping God or bringing about the kingdom of ends or freeing the proletariat that is somehow metaphysically Right. It would be a project that God or the universe smiles upon, a purpose for which we were created, a potential that lies in our very soul, the actualization of which marks the only good kind of life. What we learn from anxiety is that there is no such thing. Anxiety renders all worldly significance, the substance of the roles for the sake of which I live and act, insignificant. I see its nullity in that in the end it just doesn't matter whether or not I lead a happy or important life. Nothing that I can concern myself with is of ultimate metaphysical significance. The deep acknowledgment of mortality indicates the same thing since, no matter how successful or benevolent I am, everyone I've ever known or cared about and everything I do upon this earth will eventually crumble into the dust and be forgotten as time creaks on towards forever. Life as such – not just specific kinds of lives – is null, in the end. This is what anxiety and boredom and the anticipation of death tell me; this is what conscience eloquently tells me in remaining silent. Heidegger had already established that silence can be a profound form of communication (208/164–5). My conscience tells me that there is nothing to be done precisely by not saying anything; it says *nothing*, literally, conveying the message of nullity (369–70/322–3). This is another facet of the fact that my being is unsettled, that I can never settle it in a way that would make my life meaningful. I'm thrown here not of my own volition, I have to exist whether I want to or not, and I can do nothing to escape this. The riddle of life is inexorable: I can never know why I was born, why I will die, and what I should do in between.

The irony is that living in the realization that there is no right way to live *is* the right way to live. "Dasein *is authentically itself* in the primordial individualization of the reticent resoluteness which exacts anxiety of itself" (369/322). We must keep ourselves if not quite in a perpetual state of anxiety then at least open for it, waiting and wanting to have a conscience by acknowledging the deep contingency of what we live for and even that we live at all.

Further readings

For an illuminating account of Heidegger (and Levinas) on death and authenticity, see Simon Critchley's second lecture in Steven Levine's *On Heidegger's Being and Time*, as well as the essays in Volume 1 of Dreyfus and Wrathall's anthology, *Heidegger Reexamined*. Charles Guignon has written extensively on the notion of authenticity, such as in *On Being Authentic*. Michel Haar's *Heidegger and the Essence of Man* is excellent on these subjects, as well as on some topics from later Heidegger. See Richard Rorty's *Contingency, Irony, Solidarity* for a kind of authenticity partially inspired by Heidegger. On autonomy, you can't do much better than Robert Pippin's excellent *Modernism as a Philosophical Problem: On the Dissatisfactions of European High Culture* and *Idealism as Modernism: Hegelian Variations*. There are a number of books on the connections between Heidegger and Aristotle, including Walter Brogan's *Heidegger and Aristotle: The Twofoldness of Being*; William McNeill's *The Glance of the Eye: Heidegger, Aristotle, and the Ends of Theory*; and Ted Sadler's *Heidegger and Aristotle: The Question of Being*.

5

Being and Time 2.III.¶65–VI: *Temporality as the Meaning of Existence*

Having gotten Dasein's being in its entirety into our purview with the discussion of authenticity in the first half of Division 2, we can make another turn of the Hermeneutic Spiral, the last one of the book, to analyze the entire structure of existence at a deeper level. Care gave us the meaning of being-in-the-world in 1.VI and now Heidegger continues his ontological excavation by digging underneath care for its meaning. This will yield "a conception of the *entire phenomenal content of Dasein's basic existential constitution* in the *ultimate foundations of its own ontological intelligibility*" (351/304, all italics added). Authenticity gives us Dasein's constitution in its entirety, and its meaning will be that which underlies it and makes it possible and intelligible with its particular characteristics. Its meaning makes the various facets of the structure possible and shows their unity by showing them to be aspects of something deeper.

The meaning of Dasein is temporality as announced in ¶5 of the Introduction (38/17): this is what underlies, makes possible, and unifies the facets of care as being-in-the-world. Our job now is to understand what temporality is and see how all the structures we have uncovered so far are somehow manifestations of it.

> If we have regard for the possible totality, unity, and development of those fundamental structures of Dasein which we have hitherto exhibited, these structures are all to be conceived as at bottom "temporal" and as modes of the temporalizing of temporality. Thus, when temporality has been laid bare, there arises for the existential

analytic the task of *repeating* our analysis of Dasein in the sense of Interpreting its essential structures with regard to their temporality. (352/304)

This task occupies the rest of *Being and Time*, which makes this discussion a real break in the book even though it occurs in the middle of 2.III. The first job of Division 2 was to complete the analysis of existence by adding an account of authenticity, which was accomplished in 2.I, II, and most of III. With this totality achieved, the second job is to give the Hermeneutic Spiral a final turn to re-examine all of existence in temporal terms. 2.III.¶65 gives us a quick recap of the three facets of authenticity as temporal, while ¶66 lays out the plan for the rest of the division.

Being and Time 2.III.¶65 Temporality as the ontological meaning of care

In Heidegger's usage, the meaning of something is what makes it possible, somewhat like Kant's transcendental inquiry into the conditions for the possibility of science or ethics. Something's meaning explains why it has the particular features that it does by showing them to be forms of an underlying phenomenon which also demonstrates their inner unity (371/324). The argument of 1.VI was that a being who cares must take the form of being-in-the-world since this is the way one carries out caring – by taking up roles that open up worlds we have been thrown into and within which we strive to settle the issue of our being. Thus temporality, if it is the meaning of care, must show us why care takes the specific form it does and consists in the particular aspects it does by showing how they are actually aspects of a single underlying phenomenon.

At this point we are not looking at just any manifestation of care, the way we did earlier, but focusing on authentic care. This is because it is in authenticity that "Dasein becomes 'essentially' Dasein" (370/323). Heidegger gives authenticity an ontological privilege because it reflects the way we truly are, we just usually don't own up to it. Although inauthentic care is certainly a real form of existence and so also rooted in temporality, it is essential that he show how authentic care is temporal because that way of living is a more accurate representation of our own true nature. To understand the temporality of authentic care means seeing its facets as aspects of temporality. These facets are anticipation, resoluteness, and being-in the situation, so we will take them up in turn.

First is anticipation. All projection involves an "ahead-of-itself," that is, projecting goals that one has not yet achieved, which means the future: being a student for instance means working towards graduation. This is of course not a present-at-hand future that is simply not here, but an existential future that I relate to or "am" right now. As a student, I *am* striving *towards* graduation as the goal that organizes and explains my present behavior. I could not take up any for-the-sake-of-which if I were not able to relate myself to the future. This is true of average everyday living, but my relationship becomes authentic or truly my own when I project myself onto my ownmost potentiality, that is, my being-towards-death. Death is the closing off of the future in that I cannot take up any projects beyond it, but by the phenomenological law of breakdowns, it thereby lights up my future by not letting me take it for granted the way I usually do. Living authentically means living in light of my death, living a mortal life. Obviously, we can only anticipate our death if we are "*futural*" (373/325) or can live in light of futural goals and events. Therefore, the future is the condition for the possibility of anticipation, the first aspect of authenticity.

Part of authentic anticipation is taking up resoluteness, as Heidegger tried to show in ¶62. In order to project, I depend on the particular world that I am thrown into and my specific past that both restricts and opens possibilities for me. Once again heeding the Existential Imperative, this is not a present-at-hand past which is simply no longer here and so completely detached from me, but a past that I still am. Heidegger plays on the grammar of "*sein*" as a more common auxiliary verb in German than English's use of "have," so that many expressions literally say that one *is* what (in English) one *has* done. This relationship to the past occurs in every projection – I can only take up for-the-sake-of-whichs that are available to me in the society I find myself in – but the authentic attitude towards this fact is resoluteness, which lives in full awareness of guilt: I am from the start reliant on factors not of my making or choosing in order to make or choose anything. In authentic projecting, I own up to my previous choices and the situation that structures my options and live these, which can only happen if I am intrinsically related to the past.

Resolutely recognizing the limited options available to me and choosing among them in anticipation of death takes place by acting in the situation. This shows me what is actually open to me and what isn't, thus preventing what Sartre calls bad faith. Genuine action is in-the-world by taking up various groups of equipment in order to carry out my daily tasks. I can only take up my past and project towards my future in the present arena of activity, amid the environment and tools of mundane business. This occurs on the basis of our being in the present.

Taken together, we can see that these three directions of authenticity take place on the basis of the three tenses of time. In Chapter IV Heidegger will show that all of Dasein's activity is temporal, but here his focus is to show that authentic behavior presupposes temporality, and that its three facets are forms of temporality (374/326). He also throws in other pieces of the puzzle: projection onto a for-the-sake-of-which and existence have their meaning in the future, finding oneself in a state-of-mind, facticity, and thrownness are aligned with the past, and falling amid the world takes place in the present (375–6/327–8). These will receive more attention in Chapter IV.

Heidegger's early admonition that we lack the vocabulary and grammar to speak properly of being (63/39) also applies to time, the other part of the book's title. Temporality isn't an entity so we shouldn't talk about it the way we talk about beings. Instead, like being, we should see it as a dynamic process, like an event, a term he increasingly relies on in his later work. Instead of saying that "temporality *is*" this or that, we should rather say that "temporality temporalizes" in these ways (377/328). In one sense, of course, this is perfectly empty – if you don't know what temporality is, being told that it temporalizes doesn't really help.

Heidegger likes these tautological phrases, which he uses throughout his career,[1] for a couple of reasons. First, it obeys phenomenology's emphasis on focusing on the phenomenon – "to the things themselves!" as the battle cry goes – rather than trying to explain it in terms borrowed from a different kind of entity. The experience of heat, for example, cannot be encompassed by stating that it is actually molecular motion, even if this is perfectly true and useful in scientific contexts. It just doesn't capture the *hotness* of heat. Second, as we have seen, the objection that such circular statements won't help someone unfamiliar with the topic doesn't apply here since, as Dasein, we already possess a pre-ontological understanding of the relevant phenomena. Our lives are permeated by time; we live in it the way a fish lives in water. We just need some help articulating this unthematic understanding. As Augustine famously said, if no one asks me what time is I know perfectly well what it is but if asked to define it, I'm at a loss. These tautologous statements are meant to be first stabs at drawing this understanding out of us, like the phenomenological device of formal indications.

Heidegger calls the three tenses of temporality "ecstases," which literally means to stand outside of oneself, the way one gets swept up in moments of ecstasy (377/329). The future, past, and present are all ways that we are outside of ourselves, intrinsically open to an externality which makes us what we are. In anticipating the future I am stretched out towards goals and accomplishments not yet achieved. In resolving myself to the past I am open to events that have already taken place. And in the present, as we saw in Division 1, we are absorbed into the world as we press into our environment. Indeed, just calling us being-in-the-world already means that we are not enclosed within a sphere of subjectivity, locked inside the closet of the skull, but always already outside ourselves, out there in the world. Recall what he said about Dasein being like an in-between rather than a substance (170/132). Now he has articulated this outside-of-ourselves into three directions that map onto the three tenses of time. Our clearing is propped open, so to speak, in these three dimensions.

We can even go back behind being-in-the-world to the very first thing Heidegger said about Dasein, that our being is an issue for us. This means that we never coincide with ourselves so that we can just be someone or something. We are pervaded by nullity, by lacks and gaps and cracks which is what lets the light into the clearing. It is being stretched out that opens us up; it is because we are never simply where we are that we can be anywhere – that we can be-there (Da-sein). It is extraordinary how profoundly this contradicts two millennia of metaphysics that focus on self-sufficient, self-contained substances.

Finally, Heidegger says that although the three tenses are intertwined and interdependent, as we will see in Chapter IV, the future does enjoy a priority (378/329). This again is rather unorthodox since most philosophers privilege the present. Augustine, for example, argues that only the present exists: the past is no more and the future is not yet, so neither actually exists except in our minds. Heidegger's phenomenological orientation closes off this line of thought. We are describing the way the world appears to us, so if we experience the future and the past then they are real, they just have a different kind of being from the present. From the perspective of phenomenological ontology, we can't distinguish between the subjective features we project onto the world and the objective qualities that are really there independent of us) Because it is always us examining the world, we will always see it the way we do, with whatever properties we introduce. This is why, according to the Law of Transcendental Transitivity, being is temporal: ⊗ temporality is the meaning of Dasein's being so it determines everything about us/including how we experience reality/But if all reality is experienced as temporal, and we are only talking about reality as it is experienced, then reality is temporal)(38–40/17–18). We don't have the ability to see what the world is like independently of the ways we experience it, so any world we can talk about is the way the world is for us and as Nietzsche argues, without the contrast of the world in-itself, it simply becomes the world.[2] That's why Heidegger doesn't hesitate to call a tool's readiness-to-hand the way it is in-itself (101/71) even though it can only have this way of being in relation to our using it. This is also why he says that temporality is finite (379/330). Our temporality is finite since we are mortal and there is no temporality but ours, so time itself is finite.

The future has a priority because it is in terms of futural projections that the other tenses get their meaning. Depending on what my goal is, different parts of my facticity and different features and portions of my environment will come to the fore as relevant and important, while others will fade into the background as irrelevant. Past facts and present environmental features exert reciprocal forces on what comes into the clearing of course, but Heidegger thinks that even these are filtered through and primarily determined by my for-the-sake-of-which. We saw this earlier in the contrast between how the student and the electrician see the *Umwelt* of the classroom. With this turn of the Hermeneutic Spiral, we can now understand this difference in for-the-sake-of-whichs as different ways of projecting ourselves into the future.

Having explained Dasein's temporality and the way it is the meaning of authentic care, ¶66 then lays out the rest of the book as repeating much of the existential analysis from the perspective of temporality. Chapter IV of Division 2 will show the temporality of inauthenticity to complement the account of authentic temporality just completed (380/331). Then in 2.V we will return to the point touched on in ¶6 of the Introduction (41/19–20), that the concrete form that temporality takes is history (381/332). Finally, since being-in-the-world is temporal, the beings we encounter in-the-world will be temporal as well) 2.VI will examine the particular kind of temporality, called within-timeness, of circumspective concern and its object, tools (381–2/333).

Being and Time 2.IV The temporality of everydayness

This chapter continues the final turn of the Hermeneutic Spiral. We know that temporality is the meaning of care, which is itself the meaning of being-in-the-world (which is in turn the meaning of our being an issue for ourselves) and we have seen how temporality underlies authentic existence in the first three chapters of Division 2. Now Heidegger returns to the topics of Division 1 – the components of average everyday inauthentic being-in-the-world – to show how they too are based on temporality. 2.IV deals with the temporality of disclosedness, the subject matter of 1.V, because we are in-the-world by disclosing it – opening it up and letting it appear. Heidegger also discusses the temporality of our usual way of being-in-the-world – circumspective concernful dealing – and the temporality of the beings we deal with most of the time – equipment. This chapter also takes up two more topics from Division 1 – the way circumspective concern changes into theoretical observation and temporality as the foundation of space – though this gets a rather brief and unhelpful discussion.

We begin with the temporality of disclosedness in ¶68 since disclosedness is what constitutes the there which makes us Da-sein, that is, the being that is there or is the there. We are the there in which the world and beings can appear by becoming aware of them, making this element of existence the most important. Nothing else could happen unless we could become aware of beings or, in Heidegger's terms, bring them into the clearing, making it the ultimate condition for the possibility of anything else. This takes on even greater prominence in the later work where it becomes the sole defining feature of what he will come to term "man." As we saw in 1.V, this disclosive being-in is made up of understanding, state-of-mind, falling, and discourse, so Heidegger now shows how each of these is actually a facet of temporality.

We start with understanding in ¶68(a) since it is first among equals in the components of disclosedness. The relative priority of understanding among the aspects of disclosedness, and of disclosedness itself among the facets of being-in-the-world, align with Heidegger's prioritizing of the future (378/329) since both of these elements are the futural part of their respective contexts. Understanding means projecting oneself on a potentiality-for-being, taking up a for-the-sake-of-which and living in light of that goal-driven self-definition. This is not necessarily a thematic, theoretical understanding; we usually grasp these possibilities by living them. This is clearly a futural form of behavior since we project or "throw-forward" the kind of person we seek to be as an ongoing project that always involves still outstanding tasks and goals up until death. Even though I *am* a student in the present, I am this only by relating myself to the not-yet possibility of graduating, or finishing this class, or this assignment (385/336).

Heidegger uses "the *'ahead-of-itself'*" as "a formally undifferentiated term for the future" (386/337). This is the neutral sense of the future that has not yet become either authentic or inauthentic. The authentic form of the future, as we saw in 2.III, is anticipation, and now he introduces the term "awaiting" for the inauthentic relationship to the future, though "expecting" also slips in and I'm not sure how these terms differ. Awaiting understands itself entirely and exclusively in terms of worldly concerns, holding to the view that one is what one does (283/239, first touched on at 155/119).

This inauthentic future brings in its wake an inauthentic way of being-amid the things one concerns oneself with that he calls "waiting-towards," which occurs on the basis of an inauthentic present called "making present." This also brings in an inauthentic past of "forgetting." I don't know why Heidegger introduces all three tenses here instead of focusing on one at a time as he explains the corresponding ecstasis, nor do I see why he includes contrasts with the authentic ecstases (moment of vision and repetition) that are brief to the point of being unhelpful. Supposedly, he rushed the composition of Division 2 to get it published in time to help him secure a job, and passages like this certainly look rushed. We will postpone looking at these until 2.V, where we get a fuller analysis.

Next is the temporality of state-of-mind. As we know from 1.V, states-of-mind confront us with our thrownness by showing how little control we have over our moods (174–5/135–6). This is only possible on the basis of our being open to the past, that is, being aware of and still affected by what has already happened. His neutral term for the past, like ahead-of-itself for the future, is "having been." We have to live in the wake of our past decisions and of things we didn't choose in order to be able to see that we were thrown into this life.

Now, many moods appear to be directed towards the future, not the past: I fear what *will* happen, not what has already occurred. Heidegger responds to this objection with a rather odd argument. He says that states-of-mind are based on having been because even when they involve a future event, "the existentially basic character of moods lies in *bringing* one *back to* something" (390/340). Since care is intrinsically care about ourselves (237/193), our moods always bring the subject matter back to ourselves. I fear how that event will affect me, which relates the expected event *back* to myself, and this "backness" is a phenomenon of the past. I find this unpersuasive; if anything, I bring the event back to myself in the present and it threatens my ongoing concerns. Furthermore, I don't see why Heidegger needs this argument. There are other, better ways to connect thrownness with the past, as we saw hints of in 1.V and will see more fully in 2.V.

The third ecstasis of everyday being-in is the temporality of falling which is based on the present. It is in the present that I discover ready-to-hand tools and present-at-hand objects in the world by absorbing myself into my tasks (397/346). As 1.V.¶¶35–7 explained, falling consists in idle talk, curiosity, and ambiguity, though he discusses only curiosity here. Curiosity means to flit from topic to topic, never staying with anything long enough to examine it patiently in any depth or make it one's own but leaping away to something new which itself is not really desired for its own sake but only because it is new. Curiosity seeks distractions from where it is and what it is actually open to, forgetting what it just picked up, chasing pipe dreams rather than realistically assessing the situation Dasein is in. It confuses and jumbles up the situation like the panicked bewilderment of a person fleeing their burning house who grabs whatever is near rather than thinking out what is important and should be saved (392/342).

Finally, Heidegger gives a strangely brief discussion of discourse as what articulates the there that has been disclosed by understanding, state-of-mind, and falling. It is temporal in some unexplained sense but it is not aligned with any of the three tenses, though it does have some sympathy with the present since one primarily articulates one's environment. Once again I don't follow Heidegger's logic here, since we articulate the past and future as well. Moreover, the brevity of this analysis (two paragraphs) seems to result from the fact that discourse is something of an "odd man out" in the overall architectonic of *Being and Time*.

He then draws all of ¶68 together in a short paragraph that emphasizes the holism of temporality, the way all of its ecstases participate in each other. We have three neutral terms – ahead-of, having been, and the present – each of which divides into authentic and inauthentic versions: anticipation or awaiting, repetition or having forgotten, and making-present or the moment of vision, respectively. Together, these latter options produce the temporality of inauthentic being-in-the-world which complements the temporality of authentic care covered in ¶65.

As we saw in 1.VI, care is what "clears" the clearing, that is, what opens up a world within which entities can appear. We have since established that temporality is what allows us to care: we need to be open to future, past, and present in order to try to be someone by being-in-a-world. Our clearing, and so our world, is temporal through and through because our ways of experiencing it are temporal, and so are the entities we find in the world. This is Heidegger's version of Kant's highest principle that the subjective facts about the way we experience phenomena will necessarily be true of everything we experience. For Kant, this means that all phenomena will obey the laws of Euclidean geometry and Newtonian physics. Heidegger, on the other hand, includes the mundane parts of our everyday lives which are not captured by science, and the primary feature we impart to experience for him is temporality.

¶69(a) turns to the temporality of the entities we encounter in our worldly circumspective concern. We are in-the-world by dealing with equipment to complete tasks, taking care of business in the form of care (*Sorge*) called concern (*Besorge*) (the other form of care, solicitude of others, is not treated here). If we are at bottom temporal then our dealings are made possible by temporality, and the beings we encounter will bear the stamp of time, as Heidegger now demonstrates.

Being-amid the world means taking up tools and letting them be involved in tasks, what he sometimes calls freeing them. We encounter tools in interrelated groups of equipment as in-order-tos which accomplish towards-whichs, as we saw in some detail in 1.III.¶¶15–18. I find my pen handy to write in its context of table-paper-light when I take notes in a class. Heidegger now shows that the structure of these encounters was surreptitiously temporal. (I project myself futurally onto a towards-which – I need to take these notes – which itself dangles from goals further in the future – so that I can pass the class and graduate. Coming back from this goal, I look around and find myself already in an environment which contains groupings of equipment – I find myself at a desk with pens and paper at-hand and light overhead – due to choices I have made – to go to college, to register for this course, to come to class prepared – which themselves result from certain characteristics I find in myself – I like studying, the family I was born into expected a college education. From this future goal, past choices, and already-present environment, I then discover the pen at-hand and use it in the present (404/353).

Heidegger also repeats another important topic covered in Division 1: the way equipmental breakdowns light up the world (105/74–5). If we were not temporal creatures always living in light of the past and future, if we lived exclusively in the present, we could never discover broken or missing tools. The contents of the present moment, imagined in isolation from the other tenses, simply are what they are; whatever is here is what is here. To get to the idea that something is *missing* I have to see what is presently here in light of a futural goal that I cannot accomplish without the hammer which I can *now* see is absent. In Sartre's formulation, its absence is present to me.[3] It is only if I project myself onto a towards-which – say, building a birdhouse – that I find the hammer broken because it cannot enable me to accomplish my goal (406–7/354–5). Without this futural teleological openness I would just see disconnected bits of wood and metal, not a broken hammer. This is a little like Kant's argument that time and memory underlie arithmetic. If I were to keep forgetting what I have counted up to now, I would not be able to count; I'd be stuck repeating "1 . . . 1 . . . 1 . . ." forever. I need to retain the fact that I have already counted one in order to move on to two. Where Kant focuses on the past memory of what I have already done, Heidegger emphasizes the future anticipation of my goal, though his temporal holism certainly includes the past as well: I *find myself* inclined towards building the birdhouse, as already on the way towards making it, to let me see the context in terms of its suitability to complete the task.

¶69(a) brought back Division 1's discussion of equipment to show how its mode of being – readiness-to-hand – is based on a form of temporality. ¶69(b) continues the Hermeneutic Spiral by explaining how the topic that followed equipment in 1.III.¶16 – the way concernful dealing with equipment can turn into the theoretical analysis of present-at-hand objects – also presupposes a form of temporality. Since theoretical observation is the stance of science, this discussion also yields "an *existential conception of science*," that is to say, an explanation of how science is possible for a being who has existence as its way of being (408/357). Heidegger's not interested in the ontic events that lead to the rise of science like Newton's getting struck by an apple falling. He is looking for what it is in our ontological constitution that allows us to approach the world in this distinctive way.

Heidegger first dismisses a facile distinction between the practically involved mode of being-in-the-world that characterizes our everyday doings and a scientific attitude that withdraws from all interactions or manipulations of the environment. This way of accounting for science won't do since engaging in science is itself a doing which uses equipment of its own—microscopes, test tubes, at least pen and paper. So the idea of withdrawing entirely from the world of use to merely observe in a purely intellectual fashion turns out to be a caricature that simply isn't available for creatures like us.

He then briefly reminds us of the relevant features of circumspective concern. This way of acting sees things in light of future goals and already present environmental totalities of equipment. It operates according to an "if-then-so" schema: if I want to build this birdcage, then I need wood and a hammer in-order-to do it, so let's rummage around to find them. This lets us experience the hammer *as* something, namely an instrument for driving in nails, although this interpretive perception takes place at the pre-predicative level. In other words, I don't need to express the hammer's purpose in words or consciously think about it, but just enact it, as explained in 1.V.¶32. And, as we just saw in 2.IV.¶69(a), this scheme is based on ecstatic temporality where the three tenses intertwine. The pre-predicative use of the hammer encounters it as "too heavy" or "just right" only in the context of the futural goal I am using it for and the surrounding tools it is used with, such as wood and nails.

But this can fundamentally change, which gets reflected in how I talk about it. If I stop seeing the hammer in light of the goals I want to use it for and simply look at it for its own sake, its involvement in the environment, equipmental context, and towards-whichs all dry up, leaving behind a static, self-sufficient object. Since it has no intrinsic relationship to a goal, it can't be "just right" or "too heavy;" these qualifications only make sense in relation to an activity to which it is well or poorly suited. Stripped of this instrumental context, the hammer now "has the 'property' of heaviness. . . . We have now sighted something that is suitable for the hammer, not as a tool, but as a corporeal Thing subject to the law of gravity" (412/361). Instead of being "too heavy" it now has a mass which can be measured and remains the same for all observers. This is a fundamentally different kind of property than "too heavy," which is related to particular users and tasks and varies with them.

What accounts for this modification in the way we see and talk about the hammer is that we have changed our stance towards it. Remember, one of the over-riding points of the book (indeed, of all of Heidegger's thought) is that how we experience something and what kinds of things we find appropriate to do with or say about it follow from how we understand its way of being. This is why the question of being has an unsurpassable priority over all other questions. Here, we have switched the hammer's way of being from ready-to-hand to present-at-hand by turning from using it to staring at it. "We are looking at the ready-to-hand thing which we encounter, and looking *at* it 'in a new way' as something present-at-hand. The *understanding of Being* by which our concernful dealings with entities within-the-world have been guided *has changed over*" (412/361). The change-over in our way of understanding its being due to our having stopped using it to just stare at it causes it to change the way it appears to us. Since how things appear is how they are according to phenomenological ontology, it now is in a different way. Although we can take ready-to-hand entities as the object of sciences such as anthropology or economics, doing so inevitably treats it as in some sense present-at-hand, albeit a strange hybrid of the two modes of being, perhaps like the transitional state of a broken tool we're trying to repair (103/73).

When we do science, we strip away the features of environmental significance that define ready-to-hand equipment. For one thing, this change-over repeats what we saw happen in Descartes' mathematical space in 1.III.¶21. A tool's "place becomes a spatio-temporal position, a 'world-point', which is in no way distinguished from any other" (413/362). Whereas the lived-space of the world is meaningfully arranged into regions organized around particular activities, science sets up Newton's absolute space as an inert homogeneous container that has nothing to do with its contents. We will see the same thing happen to time in 2.VI.¶81.

There is an interesting hermeneutic point lurking here. We like to think of objectivity as giving us the world the way it is in-itself without any modification, interference, or interpretation on our part. We must be the soft passive wax which receives the imprint of experience, the white paper on which sensory data writes, the pure untroubled mirror of the world if we are to show things accurately. But Heidegger is arguing that the scientific characterization of the world is itself simply another interpretation that is based on our projection of a particular understanding of being. It doesn't give us the world as it is independent of all Dasein – that's not something that we, as Dasein, can get at, as he argued in 1.VI.¶¶43–4. Instead, it gives us the way the world looks when we look at it in a particular way. "Only 'in the light' of a Nature which has been projected in this fashion can anything like a 'fact' be found. . . . In principle there are no 'bare facts'" (414/362, compare with 190/149). This last phrase could be the fundamental motto of hermeneutics, similar in function to phenomenology's "to the things themselves." However, its meaning is in some tension with that very slogan since the hermeneutic claim is that there is no such thing as things *themselves*, but only things as seen in this or that horizon or projection or understanding of being. There simply is no such thing as a direct, non-interpreting, passive intuition of the world, which Husserl seems to have believed phenomenology offered us (191–2/150). "Thus the paradigmatic character of mathematical natural science . . . consists rather in the fact that the entities which it takes as its theme are discovered in it in the only way in which entities can be discovered – by the prior projection of their state of Being" (414/362).

Heidegger calls science's specific form of projecting "thematizing," and it turns equipment into objects. Thematizing frees entities from their involvement in the web of in-order-tos that make up the worldhood of the world, and lets us look at them just to see them. As present-at-hand, these objects appear to be what was really there before and wholly independent of our encountering them as we discussed above, but Heidegger follows Kant and Husserl in arguing that it is our stance or attitude that constitutes them as objects: "thematizing Objectifies" (414/363). This approach allows us to explicitly grasp the way of being of a type of entities that we pre-ontologically understand in use such as money or minds or matter, as mentioned in the Introduction ¶3.

The point of this section is that the scientific thematizing attitude takes place on the basis of a specific form of temporality (although to fully appreciate how this happens one needs to also see the discussion of what he calls the ordinary conception of time in 2.VI.¶81). The temporality of circumspective, concernful being-in-the-world is ecstatic: I am open to the future goals which refer me back to the already present context of equipment available to me from which I can take up a tool to do the work. All three tenses are necessary and the future is in a sense the origin of the process because I have to start from my goal. Thematizing, on the other hand, cuts the entity off from its context, isolating it from its connections to the world. Just as it presents the object in a meaningless space-point, it also places it in an inert, isolated now with no intrinsic relationship to the future or past. The object simply is what it is without being stretched out towards anything else.

2.IV is then rounded out by a number of discussions I find incomplete, misplaced, or otherwise underdeveloped. ¶69(c) takes up the notion of transcendence and horizons, which does not get explained well here and seems mainly of interest to those who want to compare Heidegger's views with Husserl's.[5] ¶70 tries to show that spatiality is based on temporality, though it doesn't do a great job of it. The main point is that spatiality is based on care – we make room and organize regions in order to pursue our business – and this pursuit is temporal, as we have seen. This makes sense and is interesting, but he really doesn't develop the topic in the detail it needs.[6] Finally he points out that even the term "everydayness" is a temporal qualification, a point he often makes about "a priori." But once again, little is made of it. Were these sections written in preparation for a more developed analysis in Division 3? Did he not get a chance to address them at sufficient length because of publication pressures? I don't know. All I can say is that this part of the book strikes me as unsatisfying.

Being and Time 2.V Historicality

Chapter V opens with a very clear restatement of the overall strategy of the book. We are looking for the meaning of being which we will find in the being that already possesses this meaning because it understands being by its very nature – Dasein. Although it sounds a bit like Dr Seuss Does Ontology, we will understand being by understanding the being who understands being. This is why the existential analytic – the analysis of Dasein's way of being, existence – is fundamental ontology – the basis on which we will conduct ontology or the inquiry into being (424/372). This is another reason, in addition to the primacy of the future, why understanding enjoys a certain privilege, as we just saw in 2.IV.

Obviously this strategy requires us to understand all of Dasein, to make sure that we aren't leaving anything out) which could prove to be an essential component of her understanding of being, a worry that troubles Heidegger at several points in the book. We made significant strides towards capturing existence as a whole by explaining the various components of being-in-the-world in 1.I–V and then showing their unity and deeper meaning in care in 1.VI. Division 2.I–III extended this analysis by adding Dasein's authentic mode of existence to Division 1's account of inauthenticity. It also continued the Hermeneutic Spiral of deepening our understanding of these components by showing how authentic care is based on temporality (in 2.III.¶65, how understanding or disclosedness is based on temporality in 2.IV.¶68, and how temporality makes possible two of Dasein's basic stances: everyday concernful being-in-the-world in 2.IV.¶69(a) and theoretical observation of objects in 2.IV.¶69(b).

Now, in Chapter V, Heidegger returns to the concern that opened Division 2: have we truly gotten Dasein as a whole in our sights? Death represents her ownmost potentiality which, because it cannot be outstripped, seemed to give us a way to capture all of Dasein: our lives necessarily take place before our death, making it a kind of outermost boundary of all of our possibilities. Examining existence in light of its ultimate possibility seemed to guarantee that we had all of it (309/264).

But now Heidegger questions this achievement. After all, death "is just *one* of the ends by which Dasein's totality is closed round. The other 'end', however, is the 'beginning', the 'birth'" (425/373). If we want to grasp Dasein as a whole we need to get Dasein as she is between *both* ends, not just on this side of one. As always, given the ecstatic open nature of time these "ends" are not deposited in a distant separated future or past but are lived at every moment. Our temporality does not consist in the coming up and passing away of a series of disconnected now-moments, as we will discuss in 2.VI, but in the inextricable mixture of all the tenses all the time. The present is not an isolatable self-sufficient shard of time; it is the meeting place of the future and the past. It is not their source but the outcome of their interactions. Dasein continuously incorporates both ends into her life by stretching herself out between them, which is why time is ecstatic (or perhaps Dasein stretches itself because time is ecstatic – I prefer the former, but I think Heidegger means the latter, at least here). Heidegger says here that this stretching is historizing (427/375) which strikes me as odd. Historizing seems to me as if it should be one element of this stretching, the one oriented towards the past, rather than the whole of it.

¶73 begins with the way we normally talk about history, for example about historical objects displayed in a museum. What does it mean to call a 400-year-old hairbrush historical? The entity is here in the present, so how exactly is it past? Heidegger's answer is that although the tool is still here, the particular world within which it found its environment and equipmental context isn't (432/380). The brush itself, considered as a present-at-hand object, just is what it is; nothing of the past clings to it physically. But because it had been taken into a world which has now passed away, it can vicariously partake in Dasein's openness to the having-been. The ghost of a world still hovers over the tool like smoke over ashes because of *our* ability to perceive the world that was but is no more. When we see it in a museum, we imaginatively conjure up a quasi-world around it, the way paleontologists reconstruct an entire skeleton from a dinosaur's toe bone. Non-Dasein entities can be historical by their inclusion in worlds, and worlds are historical because they are a component of Dasein who is historical in her being, an idea Heidegger repeats later in "The Origin of the Work of Art" (BW 166). Thus, "what is *primarily* historical is Dasein. That which is *secondarily* historical, however, is what we encounter within-the-world. . . . Entities other than Dasein which are historical by reason of belonging to the world, are what we call 'world-historical'" (433/381).

¶74 is the heart of 2.V, fleshing out the past side of authenticity to accompany his earlier discussion of futural death. Authentic temporality involves the anticipation of death: I have to realize deep in my bones that I will die. This marks the breakdown not of a particular tool or environment but of my being-in-the-world as a whole, thereby lighting up my existence. It throws me back into the situation in a moment of vision where I see my possibilities anew in light of their eventual *im*possibility. Death helps me stop chasing after pipe dreams and realistically assess what options are actually open to me, given the stage in life I find myself in and the abilities and limitations I find in myself. It brushes aside the particular roles and projects I happen to find myself in or that I maintain simply through the inertia or conformity to doing what "one" does, so that I can explicitly choose what I genuinely want to do and the kind of person I really want to be.

However, this realization is a formal one: I realize that I have a limited time on this planet and that I need to stop coasting through life letting the they live for me. I need to take the reins and actively live my life, choosing to choose (312–13/268). But what can I choose? I must be resolute, but where do I get the options I can resolve upon? Unlike most previous philosophers, Heidegger argues a number of times that there is no special task written into our souls or the universe: conscience does not give us "any concrete single possibility of existence" (325/280); there is no "potentiality-for-Being which belongs to existence" (393/343); "death, as possibility, gives Dasein nothing to be 'actualized', nothing which Dasein, as actual, could itself *be*" (307/262); "those possibilities of existence which have been factically disclosed are not to be gathered from death" (434/383). This is why he does not preach a particular vocation or activity – no existentiell project enjoys an existential privilege.

Philosophers have traditionally sought some external transcendent perspective from which to judge imperfect temporal society, adopting what Hilary Putnam calls a "God's Eye point of view" on the universe through philosophy or religion or science.[7] Although this is a common aspiration, it reaches a particularly clear expression in Husserl's notion of phenomenological bracketing which was supposed to strip away all of our presuppositions to let us see the things themselves.[8] Because Dasein is essentially and inescapably being-in-the-world, however, Heidegger does not think that such a perspective is available to us. We are always already immersed in the ideas taken for granted in our society so we cannot achieve an innocent eye that could look upon the world free of all prejudice, as he argues in the hermeneutic portions of 1.V.¶32 (especially 191–2/150). Even rebelling against your culture's understanding of how people should act must begin from those views both because you have to start with *some* sense of how to behave in order to get the skills necessary to later come up with your own ideas and because rebelling against something still takes place in relation to it and so is shaped by what it is rejecting (435/383). Heidegger uses this latter argument in his later work against philosophers like Nietzsche who take themselves to be rejecting metaphysics, as we will see.

Anticipating death allows you to enter the situation in a moment of vision, the authentic version of the present. This means that you see what possibilities are truly open to you and what pursuing them will require. The possibilities that we find in the situation are those we are thrown into, and resolutely accepting our guilt means accepting that we did not create and do not control what is open to us. Heidegger is now adding that the possibilities in our particular situation represent our "heritage." Whereas his earlier discussion of guilt presented this in largely negative terms – we have to accept guilt and nullity by reconciling ourselves to the limitations of what we find – he now presents the idea with a positive spin. These roles and projects we find open to us are our inheritance. We need to have some possibilities to be able to be-in-a-world at all, just to be Dasein, so we should celebrate our finding ourselves so generously endowed. Thus, while our desire for autonomy and control may chafe at the givenness of our world, we should also be profoundly grateful for being thrown into one. The givenness of the world represents a gift, as he will emphasize in his later work where history becomes far more prominent. In fact, one could almost say that whereas *Being and Time* makes the future primary, the later work shifts this privilege to the past, and we can see the outlines of this move here in ¶74.

We cannot step outside of our particular world to find some kind of metaphysically special role or task; our possibilities are essentially worldly since they are for-the-sake-of-whichs which are themselves made up of instrumental chains of tasks, equipment, and contexts. We find these for-the-sake-of-whichs handed down to us by our society. Negatively, we did not create them, which fundamentally compromises our autonomy as discussed in 2.II.¶58. Positively, these pools of possibilities have been given to us, enabling us to project some of them and thus open up a world we can live out a life in. Without this gift, we could not be Dasein; in an important sense, it is this inheritance that gives birth to us as Dasein.

While this givenness prevents absolute autonomy, it is what enables choice and action to take place at all. I can only become something that my society allows for; were there no institutes of higher learning in twenty-first-century America, I could not be a student no matter how many student-type activities I engaged in. Of course I still have the option to drop out or not go to college in the first place. The range of possibilities is made for me, while the specific choice among them is made by me. Although inauthentic Dasein is lived by the they, this is ultimately a fleeing from an inescapable fact: we must take up and live out our lives for ourselves, up to and including dying our own deaths. This inheritance only limits, it cannot eliminate free choice. Indeed, it is the necessary condition for decisions since we must have something to decide upon.

Thus one does not merely passively receive this heritage; "there is hidden a *handing down* to oneself of the possibilities that have come down to one" (435/383). We are given these roles and projects but, while we often try to avoid it, the decision still comes down to us which we will take up and how we will do so. Will I be studious or a slacker? Will being a student define me or only be my day job? Dasein's being remains unsettled so I can never surrender all thought and choice to simply become a student, letting its tasks take over my life while I go on autopilot. This is what I attempt to do in inauthenticity, but it happens as a denial of what I know deep down to be true. Heidegger calls the authentic resoluteness towards one's heritage "fate" (435/384) although, in light of what was just said, we must ignore the deterministic connotations of the word.

This is how Heidegger salvages a form of autonomy, one that is compromised but still real. He finds it in a paradox: "Dasein *hands* itself *down* to itself, free for death, in a possibility which it has inherited yet has chosen" (435/384). On the one hand, all possibilities are inherited; even changes one makes to them depend on them. On the other hand, choosing from among them does make them one's own, and one makes one's self out of them. This solution resembles Nietzsche's *amor fati* or love of fate where one looks back at one's life and "wills" it in the sense of accepting and approving one's past since it is what has led up to the present and made one what one is. Accepting the eternal recurrence of all that has happened "recreate[s] all 'it was' into a 'thus I willed it.'"

Heidegger is trying to walk a tightrope between giving Dasein too much power over herself and too little. We are never completely free or undetermined; we're always thrown into a particular world, set of possibilities, personal traits and preferences, and so on. Without these we couldn't make any choices at all. Yet neither are we entirely determined by our context or past. It is always up to us to decide which possibilities to take up and how to do so. The paragraph on p. 436/384–5 does seem to tip the balance a bit towards the freedom/power/control side, though. He seems to be saying that the anticipation of death can in some sense take away the "powerlessness" of thrownness rather than just interact with it. Completely taking over the nullity of our thrownness almost neutralizes its nullity, the way Nietzsche's eternal recurrence allows us to will retroactively. Heidegger's idea sounds a bit like Kant's notion of the sublime, which is an experience that overloads our comprehension – something of enormous scale or power. Rather than feeling diminished in its presence, however, Kant believes that the experience reinforces our ego and self-assurance since we realize that even such an overpowering phenomenon could not force us to act against our will.

If being-with is an essential component of existence, then our fate is also caught up with others. The collective fate of a people is what Heidegger calls "destiny" (436/384). Members of the same generation who were socialized into the same culture share a common pool of possibilities giving them an ontological sympathy that foreigners can never achieve no matter how complete their assimilation. We can see here the roots of Heidegger's later views about the importance of the Fatherland which predisposed him to the Nazis' emphasis on soil and blood, although the emphasis is on soil to the exclusion of blood.

Like the passage at 401/350, Heidegger summarizes his discussion of authentic temporality and emphasizes the holistic interconnection of the ecstases on 437/385. Projecting ourselves into the future onto our death repels us back to the past so that we can hand down our inherited possibilities to ourselves and act on them in the present moment of vision. Even in dealing with history, the future is still primary because it is our interests and projects that select what we look for in the past and how we understand it (447/395). Our temporality is what makes the experience and the discipline of history possible, and authentic temporality is what allows us to claim our fate.

The resolute taking up of what we were thrown into is called "repetition," likely derived from the title of a book by Kierkegaard. Heidegger also calls this "choosing your hero" in the sense of picking an inspiring figure from history who embodies qualities you want to emulate. It is important to note that past possibilities can never be simply repeated but must always be applied to the specifics of one's situation, making repetition into "a *reciprocative rejoinder*" (438/386). Like Aristotle's *phronēsis*, we must always adapt these former possibilities or role models to present circumstances. This is the authentic way to bring your birth into existence, the way anticipation brings death into the choices you make (442–3/391).

Heidegger closes the chapter with some brief comments on the discipline of history – called "historiology" – which follows the ideas about science laid out in ¶3 of the Introduction (29–31/9–11).

Science takes up what Husserl called an ontological region – a particular kind of being such as language or money – that we have a pre-ontological familiarity with and studies it explicitly (445/393). This means that Dasein must have a pre-scientific sense of history in order to study it as a discipline or, in Heidegger's terms, historiology presupposes Dasein's historicality. We have to be historical in our being in order to be capable of thematically studying history as a subject. He also matches up his conception of history with Nietzsche's three ways of doing history in his essay "The Uses and Abuses of History" (448–9/396–7) and then devotes ¶77 to a comparison of his own views with those of Wilhelm Dilthey and Count Yorck as expressed in letters between the two.[10]

Being and Time 2.VI Dealing with everyday time

2.V discusses, among other topics, the way Dasein studies history as a discipline or "historiology." But, as 2.V.¶76 shows, Dasein can only study history if she is already open to the past, a more basic state Heidegger calls "historicality." We have to have a prescientific sense of what history is if we are to thematically examine items and events in a historical manner. And since historicality is a form of temporality we must encounter time in our pre-scientific being-in-the-world as well; this applies to all scientific studies that involve time. "Before Dasein does any thematic research, it 'reckons with time' and regulates itself *according to it* . . . a way of reckoning which precedes any use of measuring equipment" (456/404). The final chapter of the book takes up the way we encounter time in our average everyday lives, thus continuing the examination begun in 2.IV.¶69(a) The Temporality of Circumspective Concern.

Heidegger wants to describe our average everyday experience of time, what some phenomenologists call "lived-time" – time as we experience it rather than time as we think about it, which would be theoretical or philosophy time. He argues that the latter "levels" or "shears off" features of time as we usually experience it. In many ways, this revisits the distinction between readiness-to-hand and presence-at-hand but now in terms of their temporal bases, thus carrying on the book's Hermeneutic Spiral by re-examining earlier topics in light of deeper discoveries. The bottom level we reach is the temporal foundation of all that Dasein is and does, as announced in 2.III.¶65: "all Dasein's behaviour is to be Interpreted in terms of its Being – that is, in terms of temporality. We must show how

Dasein *as* temporality temporalizes a kind of behaviour which relates itself to time by taking it into its reckoning" (456–7/404–5). This is what it means to say that time is the meaning of Dasein's being.

The very first thing Heidegger told us about Dasein is that our being is an issue for us (32/12). We try to settle this issue by taking up for-the-sake-of-whichs that can only be enacted in-the-world: to be a student means to be-in the environment (*Umwelt*) of a college by dealing (*Umgang*) appropriately and intelligently (*Umsicht*) with student-gear and performing appropriate student-actions. We are proximally and for the most part caught up in our lives by concernfully dealing with equipment and tasks, and this is where we encounter average everyday temporality. In taking care of tasks, we are always also dealing with time. We have to meet deadlines, plan out when to do various activities, decide whether we have enough time to do this or that, and so on. Even if we don't notice it, interacting with our environment continuously involves reckoning with time as well.

Dasein is essentially in-the-world, as Division 1 showed, and Dasein is essentially temporal, as Division 2 has demonstrated. ¶79 now brings these two layers together to show that our common experience of time takes on the properties of worldhood, making it "world-time" (467/414). Heidegger defines world-time in terms of three attributes: datability, span, and publicness.

First, world-time is datable, which means that it's always related to activities and events (459/407). Time isn't a neutral container but is intrinsically involved with its "contents." We experience time through the things that happen at and for particular times. "Now" is "now while I'm reading this book;" "a few moments ago" is "earlier, when I was ransacking the fridge for a snack;" "in a little while" is "soon when I will have dinner with my friends." These moments are not inert, empty place-holders but caught up with what fills them, the way, say, December 25th isn't simply another day but is Christmas which has its own rituals and even a distinct feel for many people. Because our living in-the-world is made up of performing actions, everyday temporality is always the time of doing things. In other words, temporality has the property of intentionality, one of the founding ideas of phenomenology. Consciousness, Husserl said (borrowing from his teacher Brentano), is always consciousness *of* something. You can't just think about nothing; to think or feel is essentially to think or feel *about* a particular topic (Heidegger later challenges this idea in "What Is Metaphysics?").

Heidegger is saying the same thing about world-time: it's always the time *of* or *for* something since we are-in-the-world by dealing with equipment and doing jobs. Thus, world-time's datability "*reflects the ecstatical* constitution of temporality" (461/408). World-time is outside-of-itself by being *in* activities and events.

As the time of our worldly actions, everyday time takes on their contours. World-time has a span or a breadth which depends on what we're engaged in (462/409). Now can be as brief as the blink of the eye, or it can stretch out to varying dimensions: "now while I'm eating breakfast," "now while I'm in college," "now while I'm in the prime of my life," or even "now while I'm still alive." This refutes St. Augustine's argument of the vanishing now point. He said that if I closely examine a now – for instance, now while I'm reading this book – I will realize that a portion of this activity has already passed and some is yet to come, so I should really narrow what is actually now to, say, reading this page. But then, some of this page has already been read while some is still outstanding, so the now should really be this sentence. But even while reading this sentence, I have finished some of the words and have yet to read others, and so on. No matter how thinly I slice the now, it seems like it can always be further divided until the now shrinks to an instant without duration, like Euclid's point that takes up no space. Time then would be built from instants that contain no time themselves.[11]

Heidegger avoids this paradox by arguing that lived-time, like ready-to-hand equipment, behaves differently when being experienced than observed. "When Dasein is 'living along' in an everyday concernful manner, it just never understands itself as running along in a continuously enduring sequence of pure 'nows'" (462/409). Empty theoretical nows may fall to Augustine's Paradox but the worldly now does not – it has a span or temporal breadth. Like datability, span is also due to temporality's ecstatic nature, now understood as stretched out to encompass the activity or event that occurs in it (462/409). Once again, the attributes of world-time take on versions of temporality's defining features.

One of the defining features of inauthenticity is that we lose ourselves in our activities. This means, as discussed phenomenologically in Division 1, that we don't pay much attention to what we're doing while busily attending to business. In the existential analysis of Division 2, this becomes the fact that we inauthentically forget ourselves, relinquishing control of our lives to the they and understanding ourselves entirely in terms of our job. You can see the two versions coming together in passages like this: ("the Self must forget itself if, lost in the world of equipment, it is to be able 'actually' to go to work and manipulate itself") (405/354). This expresses both the neutral claim, expanded by scholars like Hubert Dreyfus, that we must not think about ourselves if we are to engage successfully in the flow of actions, and the negative judgment that this amounts to being "lost."

As inauthentic Dasein understands itself in terms of the they's possibilities, so world-time is public time. Like the shared meanings of equipment, time is communally agreed upon so that we can meet for dinner at the same time or show up for work on time. This means that time is not my own and that it can be taken from me, used by others such as employers, and that I can surrender it so completely to business that I have no time and live in continual busyness. This is in contrast with the authentic present of the moment of vision which places me in the situation where I see what is truly important and can arrange my priorities correspondingly. I always have time for what really matters because I can make time for it if the situation demands it (463/410).

Because Dasein is essentially falling into the world, she encounters time for the most part by reckoning with it in pursuing tasks. This opens up world-time and the entities we encounter in the world are called "within-time." Whereas temporality is existential or Dasein's time, within-time is the category that applies to non-Dasein beings. Since fallen inauthentic Dasein "understands itself in terms of its daily work" (465/412), it views the time of ready-to-hand and present-at-hand entities in terms of its work schedule, dating time-spans to activities. Just as space gets divided up into regions like the workshop organized around particular tasks (136/103), so time also has a meaningful shape. It gets portioned into what we might call periods (though Heidegger doesn't use this term) that possess significance in relation to tasks. For example, before effective and cheap artificial light was widely available, "while the sun is up" was an important period because it was only then that most work could be done. Obviously, periods are not neutral tickings of the clock but possess significance; they are appropriate or inappropriate for activities (467/414). Similar to the way an environment has a towards-which, periods are times-for doing various things: daylight is time to work in the fields; the night is when we socialize and sleep. Regularly occurring periods like morning, mid-day, and night give a shape to our daily (itself a temporal term) routine, and the same goes for what the seasons do for the year, supplying time with what the Greeks called a *cosmos logos*, an intelligible pattern to the universe (466/413).

This changes with the invention of the clock which strips the significance from time, rendering it an inert, continuous sequence of identical now-points. Just as Descartes' insistence on mathematical measurements turned lived-space into a homogeneous, featureless container,[12] so clocks change time. Lived world-time can speed up and slow down; "daylight" – an essential unit of world-time – shrinks and expands with the changing of the seasons, while "the time it takes to get ready in the morning" has a span that varies dramatically among people. Clocktime, on the other hand, gives us exact lengths which correspond to the change-over from readiness-to-hand to presence-at-hand: "the idea of a standard implies unchangingness; this means that for everyone at any time the standard, in its stability, must be present-at-hand" (470/417, compare with space at 128–9/95–6). Heidegger hints at the idea that this marks a case in which an ontic fact – the invention of the clock – has an effect on an ontological feature of Dasein – the way we think about and, when disengaged, observe world-time (471/418). This could undermine the division between historical, contingent ontic facts and what appear to be ahistorical, essential ontological facts about Dasein's way of being, though he doesn't explore this possibility.[13]

Heidegger concludes ¶80 with one of his nesting charts of the ontological layers that make more superficial phenomena possible: "temporality, as ecstatico-horizonal, temporalizes something like *world*-time, which constitutes a within-time-ness of the ready-to-hand and the present-at-hand" (472/420). Temporality is the bottom layer reached in the book, the meaning of Dasein and all of her experience. Here we see how this lays the ground for world-time as the time we reckon with in our average everyday lives and it is within this time that we discover ready-to-hand equipment and present-at-hand objects. We have largely covered how readiness-to-hand is based on a particular form of temporality, both here in ¶¶79–80 and in 2.IV.¶69(a). Now, in ¶81, Heidegger turns to explain the temporality of presence-at-hand, thus continuing the discussion of 2.IV.¶69(b).

He calls this the "ordinary conception of time," though the emphasis is on "conception" rather than "ordinary." This is not our usual *experience* of time, which is world-time, but rather the way we tend to think about it once we have disengaged from activity and switched over to observation. The changes that follow from this switch of stance are one of the recurring themes of the book.

Although it took some time before consistently performing artificial clocks were invented, the idea that time has to do with numerical sequences or the counting of moments started with Aristotle and, in keeping with his view of the history of philosophy at this point in his career as primarily continuous, Heidegger thinks that everyone since has more or less "clung *in principle* to the Aristotelian definition" (473/421). Since each moment counted represents another identical unit (if they differed qualitatively, you couldn't just count them out one-by-one), time is understood as a stream of interchangeable nows that are constantly coming along and passing away at a perfectly steady rate, only differentiated by their order. Heidegger calls this conception "now-time" (474/421).

Mirroring his description of the switch from ready-to-hand to present-at-hand, he says that "world-time gets leveled off and covered up by the way time is ordinarily understood" (474/422). The features we assigned to world-time are stripped away in now-time: these points have no significance; they don't change regardless of what fills them, and they don't stretch. They are Newton's absolute time – an inert container that doesn't interact with its contents and never changes. Each now-point is sealed off from the future and past, making time a row of self-sufficient moments like a string of pearls. Like substances, nows are not open to other tenses but just are. Furthermore, this sequence is infinite: no matter what happens to the universe, time keeps on ticking.

Although this sounds innocent enough, Heidegger sees an inauthentic fleeing concealed in this ordinary conception of time. Seeing it as a sequence of nows that are closed off from each other places death as an actual event safely in the future. Since the future strictly speaking doesn't exist yet and since the present now exists entirely on its own, I don't have to worry about my death. That's a thought for another day, for when it becomes actual. As long as it is a mere future possibility it has nothing to do with me now, so I can and even should ignore it and live in the moment. It is only on the basis of authentic ecstatic time, where my now is formed and informed by the future, that I can live my death as a possibility which is always relevant. Thus, the inauthentic suppression of morbid thoughts is enabled by the ordinary conception of time whereas the authentic anticipation of death and living as a mortal takes place on the more primordial form of ecstatic time.

Note, however, that Heidegger does not dismiss the ordinary conception of time as incorrect. We do encounter this kind of time, especially when disengaged and observing or running experiments and, according to phenomenological ontology, whatever manifests itself is real. The problem is that this ordinary conception, much like present-at-hand ontology, tries to insist that it is the only true form of time while the world-time we usually live in gets demoted to the merely subjective (478/426). Not only are there other modes of time – world-time and Dasein's ecstatic temporality – but arguments can be made that these are actually more primordial than the ordinary conception. World-time is far more prevalent in our lives, again like ready-to-hand equipment, while ecstatic temporality is the necessary condition for now-time, making it more primordial in Heidegger's sense (479/426).

¶82 closes this discussion by comparing Heidegger's views with Hegel, another philosopher who thought a great deal about time, as well as history. His main point here is that while Hegel took time more seriously than most philosophers in the canon, who write it off as a merely accidental feature of the empirical world that signals its unreality, Hegel still ends up making temporality a condition that happens to spirit. Spirit first exists, and then it falls into time. For Heidegger, on the other hand, there simply can be no Dasein except as temporal (486/435–6).

Further readings

The classic work on Heidegger, time, and idealism is Bill Blattner's *Heidegger's Temporal Idealism*. Other books on the connection between Heidegger and Kant are Taylor Carman's *Heidegger's Analytic: Interpretation, Discourse and Authenticity in Being and Time*; Frank Schalow's *The Renewal of the Heidegger–Kant Dialogue*; and Charles Sherover's *Heidegger, Kant, and Time*, as well as a number of essays in Steven Crowell and Jeff Malpas' *Transcendental Heidegger*. Many authors have taken up the relationship between Heidegger and Husserl, including Steven Crowell in *Husserl, Heidegger, and the Space of Meaning: Paths Towards Transcendental Phenomenology* and Timothy Stapleton in *Husserl and Heidegger: The Question of a Phenomenological Beginning*. For discussions of Heidegger's analysis of history, you might look at Werner Marx's *Heidegger and the Tradition* or Jeffrey Andrew Barash's *Martin Heidegger and the Problem of Historical Meaning*.

6

Being and Time: *Conclusion*

It is a tantalizing question that keeps continental philosophers up at night, a party game for Heidegger scholars: what would Division 3 of *Being and Time* have been like? We know a good bit about what Part II of the book would have said. It was going to trace the history of philosophical conceptions of time and being, focusing on Kant, Descartes, and Aristotle in that order, as sketched out in ¶6 of the Introduction. We can to some degree reconstruct this part since Heidegger drops a number of hints about his views on Kant (2.III.¶64.pp. 366–8), Descartes (1.III.¶21), and Aristotle (2.VI.¶81.pp. 473–4) along the way, and several contemporaneous lecture series take up these figures in some detail.

But Division 3 was to be the conclusion of the book, the moral of the story, the ontology that the existential analytic, covered in so much detail in the first two divisions, was providing the foundation for. Let's summarize the book's structure to see where we have gotten to and then we'll see if that provides any clue as to where it might have gone.

Being and Time is about the meaning of being. Even though we use the word all the time and are continuously interacting with beings, both of which imply that we have some grasp of what it means to be, we are unable to define it. Nor do we feel the astonishment about this inability invoked in the book's opening quotation. So Heidegger will reawaken this question and try to give us an answer: time; hence the title. In fact, he gives us the answer in the very first proper paragraph of the book: "our provisional aim is the Interpretation of *time* as the possible horizon for any understanding whatsoever of Being" (19/1). It almost sounds as if he were changing the subject here, from the meaning of being to the horizon for understanding being, but this is his point. Meanings only exist in relation to entities that can understand them. They are not part of the physical furniture of the universe that can just be there independently of anyone grasping them. By the Law of Transcendental Transitivity, whatever determines the ways we understand being at the same time determines the meaning of being, similar to the way facts about the way we see determines facts about everything that can be seen.

This is why fundamental ontology – that which must provide a foundation for all interpretations of what being means – is to be found in the existential analytic – the analysis of how we are: we are the being that understands. This is also why the factors organized around the clearing, understanding, and future enjoy a priority in Heidegger's various three-part layers. Although we could not exist without the other two factors, what is most essential about us is that we are the clearing, an emphasis that becomes more prominent in the later work.

So the meaning of being is time *because* the meaning of Dasein's existence is temporality.

> Whenever Dasein tacitly understands and interprets something like Being, it does so with *time* as its standpoint. Time must be brought to light – and genuinely conceived – as the horizon for all understanding of Being and for any way of interpreting it. In order for us to discern this, *time* needs to be *explicated primordially as the horizon for the understanding of Being, and in terms of temporality as the Being of Dasein which understands Being.* (39/17)

We can only be an understander if we are temporal: we must be stretched out in order to open up a clearing to let the light in. It is only by being-in-a-world by being open to future goals, already available contexts and choices, and present tools that we can allow being to manifest itself. Since the clearer is temporal, the clearing is temporal, and all that is cleared is as well. Even apparently nontemporal beings like present-at-hand substances just have a different mode of temporality, one based in the unchanging now. Even differentiating realms of beings according to whether they are temporal or atemporal bases ontology on time, thus unwittingly conceding its importance while denigrating it. Even ideas that seem to have nothing to do with time are still couched in temporal terms, like "a priori" or "everyday."

Since we are at bottom temporal (*"Dasein itself . . . is time,"* as he puts it in his 1925 lectures (HCT 197)) understanding is temporal, so we understand being in temporal terms and thus being is temporal. This is sometimes called Heidegger's temporal idealism since it follows the contours of Kant's main argument in the *Critique of Pure Reason*. Kant says that the laws that rule our mind in processing experience are, at the same time and for that reason, the laws that govern everything we experience, that is, phenomena. When we do math and science we are unwittingly (and only partially – the world plays an important role, too) doing transcendental psychology since we're actually studying our mind's effects on experience.

Heidegger is making a similar move with three important differences. First, Heidegger expands experience to include more than just what we discover scientifically. In fact, the theoretical observation of present-at-hand objects is a relatively minor, albeit legitimate, way to experience the world. Far more prevalent and important to our lives is our average everyday experience, as well as those moments of existential crisis that form the focus of the first half of Division 2. Second, and related to the first point, there is more than one way that the mind can organize experience. Kant thought that the mind only had one set of structuring principles which never change. Heidegger allows for three different understandings of being – existence, readiness-to-hand, and presence-to-hand – which present very differently behaving beings. Third, Heidegger rejects Kant's notion of noumena, that is, the world as it is in-itself independently of us. For Heidegger, phenomena are what are because being means appearing to Dasein. This is what allows him to move directly from claims about the way being is experienced by us to claims about being itself: there is nothing to being besides its manifestations and the fact of its manifesting. "If Being is to be conceived in terms of time, and if, indeed, its various modes and derivatives are to become intelligible in their respective modifications and derivations by taking time into consideration, then Being itself (and not merely entities, let us say, as entities 'in time') is thus made visible in its 'temporal' character" (40/18). This is why phenomenology is ontology.

Heidegger also solves a problem with Kant's system. As many German Idealists pointed out, the particular forms of the mind's faculties, especially the twelve concepts of the understanding, seem rather arbitrarily adopted, many plucked from the math, science, and logic textbooks of the day. Kant isn't able to justify his choice of these specific concepts or the particular forms of the intuition; they seem transcendentally arbitrary. One of the principal projects of German Idealism was to find a way to unify all the mind's categories as issuing from a single idea or fact which was itself necessary.

Heidegger has given just this kind of solution with temporality. Division 1 lays out the diverse ways Dasein understands the world and the various aspects of her own existence, then a turn of the Hermeneutic Spiral shows that these are all forms of temporality. That is what it means to say that temporality is the meaning of existence: it is what explains and unifies the various features of existence by showing them all to be facets of a single phenomenon. At bottom, Dasein is temporal and all the particular features of our existence emerge out of that. It is only as temporal that we can care, and so be-in-the-world, and so have an unsettled being, moving backwards through the layered definitions of Dasein.

So it appears that we have not just reawakened the question but have actually answered it. Since "Being cannot be grasped except by taking time into consideration" (40/19), being as grasped – that is, being as meaningful – is temporal. But we must be careful here. Heidegger warns us in the Introduction that when it comes to questions of this magnitude, "one is constantly compelled to face the possibility of disclosing an even more primordial and more universal horizon from which we may draw the answer to the question, 'What is "Being"?'" (49/26). In other words, although we may feel that we have reached bedrock with temporality, we must be sensitive to the possibility that further layers could be uncovered. Indeed, the final sentence of the book seems to throw its own answer back into question: "does *time* itself manifest itself as the horizon of *Being*?" (488/437). He even seems to doubt the book's strategy of fundamental ontology, saying in ¶83, the last paragraph of the book, that "our way of exhibiting the constitution of Dasein's Being remains only *one way* which we may take" to get at the meaning of being (487/436).

One problem is that in order to do fundamental ontology as the existential analytic, we need to distinguish Dasein as the existing entity from those beings with different modes of being, ready-to-hand tools and present-at-hand objects. But, Heidegger argues, we can only differentiate specific ways of being if we already have an understanding of being in general. Without a proper grasp of being in general we can't give a fully thought-out explication of the various modes of being, even though it seemed like the two divisions did a pretty good job of this. Thus he calls for another spin of the Hermeneutic Spiral to re-examine the ideas already addressed, especially Dasein's existence, in light of a proper understanding of being itself (382/333, 487/436). This must have been what was planned for Division 3.

However, he gave a good explanation of being in his discussion of phenomenology in ¶7 of the Introduction, and his discussions of reality and truth at the end of Division 1 (1.VI.¶¶43–4). There being is defined as manifesting or appearing to Dasein. This is why phenomenology as the study of how things appear to us is equivalent to ontology or the study of being itself (60/35). It's why it makes no sense to try to prove that the world exists – if we experience it, then that's real being (249–50/205) – and why Reality as wholly independent of Dasein is itself a form of experienced being (and thus still dependent on Dasein) (255–6/212, 414/362). And this meaning of being also explains why truth means becoming unconcealed or showing itself to Dasein (269/226). As I indicated above, the discussions of ¶43 and ¶44 strike me as appropriate for Division 3, which is further supported by the fact that they are so out of place in the book's architectonic.

Once Heidegger lays out being as appearing to Dasein, he can go through and re-examine all the ways that the aspects of existence contribute to setting up the clearing. These ideas were already there – just think, for example, of his description of moods as disclosive (175/136) – but Division 3 might have made this explicit as another turn of the Hermeneutic Spiral. In this way, it would have done for Divisions 1 and 2 as a whole what the latter half of Division 2 did for Division 1 when it showed the temporality of being-in-the-world, which had been suggested by terms like "ahead-of" and "already-in" but had not been explicitly stated. Division 3 might have explained being as manifesting and Dasein as the being that is manifested to, which all the particular features of existence serve. Without introducing anything completely new, it would have spelled out the consequences of the ideas already discussed to show existence in a new light. And in fact, as we will see in the second half of this book, this is precisely the direction Heidegger turns after *Being and Time*.

Further readings

There are many excellent resources for readers trying to come to terms with *Being and Time* as a whole. Richard Polt's *Heidegger's*

Being and Time: *Critical Essays* and Mark Wrathall's *The Cambridge Companion to Heidegger's Being and Time* collect a number of superb papers on various aspects of the book. Dreyfus' *Being-in-the-World: A Commentary on Heidegger's Being and Time, Division I* is a seminal work on the subject, although it has a strong interpretive bent with an overwhelming focus on Division 1. Bill Blattner's *Heidegger's Being and Time: A Reader's Guide* is a reliable and helpful guide to the book. The last two thirds of Heidegger's own 1925 lecture course *History of the Concept of Time* contains early and often much clearer versions of many of the ideas that get worked out in more detail in *Being and Time*. I will soon be coming out with a collection of essays by Heidegger scholars speculating on what the missing part of the book might have said, titled *Division III of Being and Time: Heidegger's Unanswered Question of Being*.

Part II

Later Heidegger

7

Introduction to the Later Heidegger

Heidegger changed his mind; that's why we talk about an early and a later Heidegger. Now, a simple bifurcation like that is too stark. For one thing, over his many years of thinking and writing Heidegger changed his mind a lot, not just once. Almost every decade of his career a new topic surfaces as the one central idea which then gets retrospectively read into not just his own previous work, but the history of Western civilization as a whole. However, the change that took place around 1930 does strike me as sharper and deeper than the later transitions among focusing on, for example, truth, *Ereignis*, the fourfold, etc.

Nor need we exaggerate this change – often called the "turn" or "turning" (*"die Kehre"*) – into anything like a complete break in which he came to repudiate his early work. Of course there are continuities of topics, views, approach, and so on. Later and early Heidegger are both recognizably – indeed unmistakably – Heidegger. But these continuities are incomplete. *Being and Time* certainly contains an important discussion of truth, for example, which already makes the crucial move of defining it as unconcealment (1.VI.¶44). But the twenty-odd pages there are a far cry from his extensive, complex, multi-faceted discussions of the topic in the 1930s and throughout the rest of his career. The early discussion is like a musical theme that appears in a composer's youthful sonata, only becoming fully developed into a symphony later on.

Of course, the primary continuity – the primary fact about Heidegger's thought in general – is the question of being. He never strays far from this home key, even when he modulates it or even crosses it out in favor of other terms. But that's one of the funny things about *Being and Time* – there's more time in it than being. He tells us from the outset that he wants more to reawaken the *question* rather than provide an answer, to revive a long-dormant puzzlement rather than settle it, and in this aim he has surely succeeded. The part of the book that was to have dealt directly with being – Division 3 of Part I – was never published, making it impossible to construct a substantive continuity between his early and late work on the basis of his views about being. What we get in *Being and Time* is a thorough discussion of three ways of being, and some brief discussions of being itself as appearing or manifesting to Dasein.

While the continuities are vague and sketchy, we find ideas in the later work that conflict rather directly with his early thoughts. Heidegger himself wrote of a Heidegger I and a Heidegger II in a famous letter (HR 304), although he also insisted that each could only be understood via the other. Following this suggestion, I will use his early work to help us gain a foothold in this vast, forbidding later thought.

Heidegger is not a systematic philosopher; he read too much Kierkegaard and Nietzsche for that. Besides, phenomenology refuses to put anything above fidelity to experience and experience is messy. However, he is a holistic thinker in that his thoughts about the wide variety of topics he deals with all interconnect, all being facets of a single insight. "Every thinker," he writes in words that apply especially well to himself, "thinks only one thought" (WCT 50). We should take Heidegger at his word when he says that being is the skeleton key to all philosophy, particularly his own. Unlike *Being and Time*, which the reader can get quite a bit out of without paying much attention to being, it's hard to advance a single step in almost any of the later volumes without a solid grasp of what it means.[1] With a grasp – well, it's still tough going, but one can make progress, so let's turn to being.

Being and Time teaches us the ontological distinction between beings and being. Whereas beings are just the various entities that populate our lives, their being means the kind of entities that they are. It's quite close to the traditional notion of essence, though Heidegger's ontology is more dynamic: things actively *are* or, in a sense, behave in certain ways that determine what is appropriate to do with them. Perhaps the main point of the book as we have it is that we tend to interpret the two kinds of being most common to our experience – tools' readiness-to-hand and Dasein's existence – inappropriately (*uneigentlich*) in the manner of present-at-hand objects, so he spends much of the book laying out these neglected modes.

Now Heidegger still holds to this idea in his later work, although he adds more kinds of beings: artworks, technology, and what he calls "things," for instance. But he also adds a third layer to the ontological difference that barely appears in *Being and Time*, which he sometimes calls being itself or the truth of being (or *Seyn* or appearing in the clearing or the "there is"). This means the manifestation of beings to us, the fact that we can become aware at all. Thus the whole set-up gives us: entities that get unconcealed (beings), the kind of being these entities have (the being of beings or beingness), and the fact of unconcealment (being itself). None of these layers can exist on its own – being is always the being of a being (29/9) – but we can distinguish them.

This third level, being itself, turns out to be the most inconspicuous phenomenon of all. In fact, each level conceals or covers over the next: we experience (1) particular entities in terms of (2) the kind of being that they are (using tools or talking with people), but we're so absorbed in interacting with them that we rarely think about their mode of being. I never contemplate shoeness or, more generally, equipmentality when putting on my shoes, for example, and certainly not while taking a walk. Explicitly examining these (2) modes of being, as metaphysicians do, occludes the far more basic fact that (3) something is manifest to us at all. While *Being and Time* basically moved us from no. 1 to no. 2, laying out the traditionally neglected modes of ready-to-hand and existence in great detail, Heidegger's goal now is to highlight no. 3, this ever-present but ever-hidden fact of awareness, to awaken us that we may become awestruck by it. All philosophy is born of wonder and what is more wondrous than that we can be struck by wonder at all, that there is something to wonder at? This amounts to the logical culmination of phenomenology, the awareness of awareness itself – phenomenology squared if you will, whereby "the clearing belonging to the essence of Being suddenly clears itself and lights up. . . . It brings itself into its own brightness. . . . The essence, the coming to presence, of Being enters into its own emitting of light" (QT 44–5).

If we pass by a tool's way of being in using it, falling into autopilot as we act, we think about the simple fact that we can think or experience anything at all even less, even though this pervades every waking moment of our lives. Indeed, the logic of inconspicuousness suggests that this ubiquity is one of the reasons *why* we ignore it: "on account of its obviousness, Being is something forgotten" (BQ 159). Heidegger often says that in revealing beings, being conceals itself, but this is not because being is an esoteric or transcendent entity – that would be treating being as *a* being, confusing the ontological difference in a mistake he calls onto-theology. Rather, being withdraws by its very nature as the revealing of beings. "Being is not merely hidden; it withdraws and conceals itself. . . . It shows itself and withdraws at the same time" (BQ 178). It is their visibility, so to speak, which isn't the kind of thing we can see, even though seeing presupposes it. Heidegger sometimes compares it to light, echoing Plato. We see things by means of light, but if light itself were visible then it would block our sight of the scene; we would be encased in an opaque block of luminous amber. We have to *not* see the light if we are to see that which is lighted. "In order to bring into view what resides in a visual field, the visual field itself must precisely light up first, so that it might illuminate what resides within it; however, it cannot and may not be seen explicitly. The field of view, ἀλήθεια [*alētheia* or truth], *must* in a certain sense be over-looked" (BQ 127–8). Necessarily, every unconcealment is at the same time and in itself a concealment, a concealment of that very unconcealment by unconcealing beings (to revert once more into Dr. Seuss ontology).

When he discusses philosophers, Heidegger sometimes criticizes them for "forgetting" being in that their ideas make it harder to grasp this one essential thought. Plato is often blamed for instigating this process that wends its way through the history of philosophy. The "fault," however, lies not in ourselves but in being itself, that we are forgetful. "What, in an exceptional and unique sense, conceals itself in the domain of open beings is Being. We experience this in the most prosaic and yet most enigmatic event, namely that beings most immediately press upon us and impose themselves and that only beings seem to be" (BQ 183, compare with 59/35). This is how he reads Heraclitus' saying that nature or, on Heidegger's reading, being loves to hide (PM 229–30).

Being aware of the world was the defining feature of Dasein in the early work, but there he explained our awareness by appealing to our nature the way idealists like Kant and Husserl do. It is because we are the kinds of creatures that we are and because we do the kinds of things that we do that beings show up for us at all and in the specific ways that they do. The later work turns this formulation around: it is because beings show up for us and in the specific ways that they do that we are the kinds of creatures we are and do the kinds of things we do, Being is something that happens to us rather than something we enact, even autonomically. This, along with its dynamic sense, is why he comes to use the term *Ereignis*: being manifesting itself is an event in which we are caught up rather than an act we perform.

This changes everything. *Being and Time* sets out the project of "fundamental ontology" which founds the study of being on a grasp of ourselves since being, in a Kantian way, reveals itself in our projection. The later work reverses "fundamental ontology" into an ontological foundation: everything must be understood in light of the fact and way that being appears to us. This is for Heidegger the inexhaustible source and provocation of all thought and wonder and, thin as it may seem, he derives an astonishingly rich and diverse array of insights from it. I don't think it's much of an exaggeration to say that the later work as a whole can be described as working out the consequences of this one insight. "'For there is Being.' The primal mystery for all thinking is concealed in this phrase" (BW 238). Heidegger patiently, doggedly, takes up one topic after another and works out new understandings of them in light of this idea. And so shall we.

Heidegger's later work is massive and sprawling, without a single summative work like *Being and Time* for his early thought. I've focused on topics that I consider essential to his thought and that are important philosophically, but there is no way to do this without leaving out many interesting and important topics, which I have done. Others would and have made somewhat different choices. At the end of each chapter, I will indicate the primary and secondary texts I find most helpful for that topic.

Further readings

Of Heidegger's own writings, I find *Basic Questions*, especially the Appendices, his clearest explanations of being. Thomas Sheehan has a wonderful essay on this, called "A Paradigm Shift in Heidegger Research." On the turn, you might look at the essays in James Risser's *Heidegger Towards the Turn: Essays on the Work of the 1930s*.

8

History, Nazism, the History of Being and of its Forgetting

No major philosopher, except perhaps Hegel, takes history more seriously than Heidegger. At the end of his long career he said that his "entire work in lectures and exercises in the past thirty years was mainly just an interpretation of Western philosophy" (HR 328). While this is a bit of an exaggeration, there's no question that history dominates his later thought. Where his early work entwines ontology with phenomenology, his later work makes the study of history internal to the study of being rather than just an addition to it.

Being and history

Phenomenology is the study of reality as we experience it. Since we can only study what we have access to, the study of being – ontology – can only be the study of the way being appears to us – phenomenology (BT 60/35). *Being and Time* joins a Kantian project to this approach. To understand reality we must study experience, and we understand experience by discerning Dasein's ways of experiencing, much the way Kant explained the scientific and mathematical features of experience by our transcendental faculties. By the Law of Transcendental Transitivity, what is true of the experiencer's ways of experiencing gets transferred to the experience, the way an artifact of a lens gets reflected in the light that passes through it. The conclusion was that because of the kinds of beings that we are, we experience the world in certain ways – specifically, in terms of care and ultimately as temporal.

One of the ideas that appears late in *Being and Time* is that we are historical creatures, which means that experience is historical through and through. Dasein is essentially in-a-world, but worlds differ among communities and time periods; worlds can be born and can die, which is what makes artifacts historical. The content of our lives, the specific vocations and projects we take up are supplied by our society so that a person brought up in one culture will have a different range of for-the-sake-of-whichs open to her than people brought up in others. I, a twenty-first-century American, can be a philosophy professor or a race-car driver, but not a samurai or knight-errant.

As far as I can tell, however, history doesn't go all the way down in Heidegger's early account. The *material* of our lives comes from historically varying contexts, but the *way* we assimilate it, the formal structure of Dasein's being – the set of *existentialia* – appears to remain the same for everyone at all times and places. By transcendental transference, this means that the modes of being remain constant as well. A samurai's shoes will withdraw from his notice in the heat of the battle the same way mine do in the heat of a lecture because both pairs of shoes have the same mode of being, readiness-to-hand. He is defined by care just as I am, even though the particular things he cares about – saving face, honorable service to his lord – differ from my concerns – teaching my students well, getting rich from my books.

Now one of the main goals of Heidegger's early work is to overcome philosophy's metaphysical allergic reaction to change. Ever since Parmenides, time and change have been associated with unreality, whereas true being must be impervious to alteration. The meaning of the book's title is to turn the traditional mutually exclusive dichotomy of being *or* time into a synthesis of being *and* time, reintegrating time and change back into reality instead of treating them as symptoms of ontological inferiority. "But why should what comes into existence and passes away count as non-being? Only when beingness is already established as constancy and presence" (CP 137/¶100). But we can see that Heidegger didn't free himself entirely from this prejudice. He preserves the essential formal structure of Dasein as an unchanging nature, just as Kant assumes that all humans have the same transcendental faculties.

Heidegger's later work fulfills phenomenology's commitment to experience as it presents itself by taking history seriously. Being is what it manifests itself to us as, and he now realizes much more fully than before just how differently it has manifested at different times. We don't discover this through phenomenology's standard method of describing first-person experience since we naturally live in only one period, or at most two. Rather, we discover this diversity by examining the records from earlier periods. Heidegger sees the canonical works of metaphysics as the best accounts of an epoch's general way of thinking. This is why he spends so much time in his later works slowly, meticulously reading these texts: he is trying to painstakingly piece together a being-in-the-world that is gone, like a paleontologist rebuilding the skeleton of an extinct animal from a handful of bone fragments.

This kind of historical phenomenological excavation is trickier than describing one's own experience. Hermeneutics, which appeared in the early work, plays a larger role in our attempts to indirectly reconstruct someone else's experience via written records, a point he was planning on addressing in Part II of *Being and Time* (BT 43/21). Further complicating the task, each epoch's understanding of being pervades a culture completely like Hegel's *Zeitgeist*, making it so self-evident that it becomes inconspicuous to those living in it. It becomes so taken for granted that few explicitly articulate it, leaving us with little direct discussion of it. Luckily, there have been a small number of special people sprinkled throughout history who have stood back from their daily actions to ask general questions about the nature of reality: philosophers. At one point, Heidegger imagines the primal scene of the awakening of metaphysics: "the ek-sistence of historical man begins at that moment when the first thinker takes a questioning stand with regard to the unconcealment of beings by asking: what are beings?" (BW 126, see also BQ 175). Philosophy was born in ancient Greece when someone looked up from plowing the field or tying their sandals to ask not, what is this particular thing or that, but what is being in general? What does it mean to be? In terms of the ontological difference, these individuals move from dealing with beings to inquiring into the being of these beings, that is, their mode of being or the way they are.

We find the answers to these questions in the great works of metaphysics; these works are for Heidegger attempts to define "beingness," that is, the qualities whose possession makes something count as existing. Metaphysicians describe their epoch's understanding of being by capturing "the totality of beings as such with an eye to their most universal traits" (PM 287); they attempt "to find words for what a being *is* in the history of its Being" (N IV: 7). Whereas the three modes of being in *Being and Time* appeared to hold constant for all Dasein, now Heidegger sees the form of being as remaining constant throughout all the activities and institutions of an era but then changing when a new epoch descends. For the ancient Greeks being was constant presence, as exemplified for Plato by the Forms. Plato divided beings into the empirical, changing things around us which are less than fully real because they do not embody the contemporary notion of beingness, and the timeless, unchanging Forms that are because they do. Medievals then transferred these Forms into the mind of God, so that what it meant to be at that time was to be God or, at a lesser level, a creation of God. The early moderns created an anthropocentric metaphysics with the self as the unquestioned center and all else being real to the extent that we can represent it. The ideas that matter became those within our heads rather than God's, specifically those that don't change across time and observers, like quantifiable measurements. Our own age extends the early modern conception to the point that beings appear exclusively as resources for us to use to get what we want, reaching its epitome in technology.

As *Being and Time* showed us, the way one understands an entity's being determines what kinds of actions will seem natural and appropriate to take with it. Heidegger's later work breaks the history of thought into epochs organized around specific "understandings of being," that is, basic understandings of what it means to be, which shape a culture's entire way of acting and thinking. "Metaphysics grounds an age in that, through a particular interpretation of beings and through a particular comprehension of truth, it provides that age with the ground of its essential shape. This ground comprehensively governs all decisions distinctive of the age."[1] Ontology is still the foundation for all else, but with a significant difference. Whereas Dasein could switch between different stances (engaged use and disengaged study) and thereby induce a "change-over" in the beings dealt with (ready-to-hand tools and present-at-hand objects), now an era's beingness governs *all* interactions during that period, with little if any room for alternate ways of understanding and acting.

The change-overs now happen across time rather than between Dasein's comportments.

We call "natural" what is understood without further ado and is "self-evident" in the realm of everyday understanding. . . . In the Middle Ages everything was "natural" which obtained its essence, its natura, from God. . . . Therefore, it follows: what is "natural" is not "natural" at all, here meaning self-evident for any given ever-existing man. The "natural" is always historical. . . . There must have been a time when the essence of the thing was not defined in this way. . . . The formation of this essential definition of the thing did not, then, at some time just fall absolute from heaven, but would have itself been based upon very definite presuppositions. (WT 39–40, see also IM 56)

The actions that appear self-evident do so in light of a very basic sense of what things are like. It is this which determines what is common sense and what nonsense. We can see that Heidegger is still employing something like Kant's transcendental idealism where we find the world to be spatial, temporal, causal, substantial, etc. because of a "conceptual scheme" that structures our experience. But Heidegger now disagrees with Kant's removal of this scheme from history. Instead, there have been several different schemes – even within science, as Thomas Kuhn later argues – each unified around a particular understanding of being, and when these change the world appears differently. Heidegger also severs the scheme from consciousness: it does not emanate from us but descends upon us and the world alike.[2]

Let's look at one era in a little more detail to get a better sense of Heidegger's idea. For the medievals, to be was to be the creation of God. Having been created by God is not just a contingent fact about things but what defines them as the particular things they are and simply as being anything at all. This ontology implies a cosmology – the world exists because God made it; an ethics – being a good person means living up to God's Idea of us; an aesthetics, and ultimately an entire worldview. If the world is as it is because God made it that way, then trying to change it can only be hubristic rebellion. If your king is rotten, it is your duty to put up with him as an assuredly just divine punishment. Thus an epoch guided by this understanding of being will not give rise to the kinds of widespread revolutions or democracies which become natural under the later understanding which emphasizes taking control of the now inert or "disenchanted" world to improve our condition. Suffering from disease is a humbling of the flesh we should embrace, not a problem to be fixed, so medicine and science more generally will not take root in this soil. As in the early work, what may initially appear to be an esoteric, abstract metaphysical doctrine has enormous concrete effects. Heidegger constantly, tirelessly, occasionally tiresomely, insists on the question of being because all else is superstructure to it, taking on the form of this foundation.

This kind of ontological perspective can be a very powerful interpretive tool, illuminating vast swaths of a period's actions and works with a single idea, although for the same reason it risks simplification, reducing all else to mere metaphysical epiphenomena. Michel Foucault, one of the most influential figures of the twentieth century, takes up this idea though he emphasizes pedestrian, marginal texts like prison timetables or store inventories as the best evidence for an era's way of thinking. Like Heidegger, he wants to know how humanity got the form of subjectivity that it now has; indeed, Foucault starts from the position that history goes all the way down, the position that Heidegger only achieves in his later work. But Foucault looks for the answers among the mundane details of everyday life – the way handwriting was taught, or the structure of botanical taxonomies, or the kind of prescriptions against childhood masturbation that physicians issued.[3] As mentioned above, this blurs the line between the ontological and the ontic, layers Heidegger kept separate. Heidegger's lofty approach also makes him insensitive to basic human concerns, as I will discuss below.

Whereas in his early work history supplies the content to be fitted into Dasein's ahistorical formal structure, the later work makes being historical all the way down. In particular, he makes man (his preferred term now instead of Dasein) historical. Dasein had been the anchor, the foundation of ontology in *Being and Time*: our structure, the ways we act and experience set the modes of the beings we interact with and experience. Since we deal with beings, they have the mode of ready-to-hand; we also stand back and observe so beings can be present-at-hand. Now the mode of beings depends not on our behavior but on the understanding of being that being "sends" to us at a particular historical period. And our way of being changes with them so that a Greek citizen, a medieval monk, an early modern gentleman-scientist, and a modern iPhone user are different kinds of subjects. Man still retains the essence of being open to being, that is, being able to become aware of things, but the things we can be aware of and the way we are aware of them alter fundamentally across time.

"The greatest stupidity of my life:" Heidegger's involvement with the Nazis

The ugliest stain on Heidegger's life, the act that can never be forgotten nor completely forgiven, is his membership of the National

Socialist or Nazi Party from 1933 until 1945. The facts have been partially obscured by so much discussion, and by some intentional obfuscation by Heidegger, but it is undeniable that he was at least initially an enthusiastic member of the party and, when he became rector of Freiburg University in April 1933, he carried out many of the party's policies.[4] His inaugural address, "The Self-Assertion of the German University," proposed to remake the university in unmistakably Nazi phrases. He resigned the rectorship in April 1934 and withdrew from active political life, although he never officially renounced membership of the party.

These facts may be uncontested, but their significance has been the subject of considerable debate, ranging from the opinion that Heidegger did the best he could to restrain Nazi policies from within (Heidegger's own account of his behavior after the war (HR 313–18)) to the view that he vigorously and enthusiastically implemented them. Also in dispute is the meaning of these actions for his work; views here extend from the idea that Heidegger's personal decisions have nothing whatsoever to do with his thought and are therefore irrelevant to philosophy, to the belief that his actions demonstrate that his work is at best worthless, at worst deeply pernicious. I will try to give a balanced account of the topic.

We have to qualify the simple assertion that Heidegger was a Nazi, since he was an enthusiastic member for less than one year, from May 1933 to early 1934. This is important for two reasons. First, when we hear the word "Nazi" we think of them as what they became by the end: the paragon of evil who butchered millions horrifically. The Nazis in 1933 were brutal, anti-Semitic thugs who used force and violence to get their way, no doubt, but they were not the absolute monsters they later became. I want to emphasize that they were awful even then, but being enthusiastic about them in 1933 is a very different thing from being so in, say, 1943, when the concentration camps were running.

Second, Heidegger quickly became disenchanted with the party. It's possible – though I am speculating here – that he had been less aware of their true nature before he dealt with them and that, as he got to know them, he recoiled from what he found. He does occasionally differentiate between what he sees as the party's essential nature and the unfortunate state it existed in, and he apparently interceded on behalf of some Jewish professors and helped others escape. The Nazis, moreover, became equally disenchanted with him, refusing to exempt him from potential active duty despite his great fame and poor health.[5] On the other hand, he did apply Nazi racial policies to the university and he continued to make positive references to the party even after his resignation in 1934.[6] Furthermore, many have speculated that his disenchantment was due less to his dawning realization of their evil than to the fact that they did not sufficiently stroke his ego by seeking his intellectual counsel and countenance; apparently, many Nazis found his talk of being incomprehensible and irrelevant to the running of a country or a war. Thus, he might have withdrawn more because of wounded pride than moral repugnance.

Others have argued that worse than his membership during the war is his behavior afterwards. Although he called his involvement "the greatest stupidity of his life" (Petzet 1993, 37), he never gave anything like a real apology or acknowledgment of wrong-doing, nor did he ever give the Holocaust sustained discussion of any kind, a gap that has become known as "Heidegger's silence."[7] His few direct discussions tend to be self-serving or appallingly insensitive, equating the concentration camps with the massive displacement of Germans after the war or modern industrialized agriculture, for example.[8] Perhaps his pride prevented him from feeling the appropriate shame.

He later defended his actions during the war, insisting at one point that his 1936–1940 lectures on Nietzsche were a kind of intellectual guerilla warfare against the Nazis, an exceedingly peculiar idea.[9] While troops were fighting and Jews were being rounded up and killed, his political resistance consisted in talking about a nineteenth-century philosopher, albeit one who was important to the Nazis and in a way that conflicted with the party line on him. This may be another indication of Heidegger's detachment from the concrete details of life (ironic for someone whose existential phenomenology was unprecedentedly attuned to the concrete and everyday) and his deep belief in the importance and influence of philosophy. Elsewhere, for example, he dismisses the atom bomb as a mere consequence of the far more profound destruction wrought by an inappropriate ontology.[10] Throughout his career Heidegger shows indifference to "ontic" concerns in favor of philosophical, ontological issues. Pollution isn't the problem with technology; our distorted relation to being is what we should be concerned about. People living on the streets is of less concern than the fact that we don't know how to dwell. He once claimed that "compared to [our encounter with Nietzsche], world wars remain superficial!"[11]

Such statements seem prime examples of a philosopher with his head in the clouds, ignorant of and unmoved by petty concerns like human suffering. There is a more charitable reading, however, which appeals to his understanding of history. Recall that Heidegger believes that the way an era understands what it means to be sets the parameters of acceptable and reasonable behavior for that period. This makes philosophy necessarily, essentially more important than any actions taken or events that happen, because these are merely the effects allowed or encouraged by that epoch's understanding. Thus, if we are to understand why the twentieth century had mass killings or total warfare, we must look beneath these events to the understanding of being that gave rise to them, which is best captured in philosophy. An age's metaphysics "comprehensively governs all decisions distinctive of the age. Conversely, in order for there to be adequate reflection of these phenomena, their metaphysical ground must allow itself to be recognized in them" (OBT 57). This explains his notorious statement that "farming is now a motorized nutrition-industry, in essence the same as the fabrication of corpses in gas chambers" (HR 270). This is, on the face of it, simply hideous. But if we understand what Heidegger means by "essence" and how he understands the essence of technology, which we will turn to in Chapter 11, what he is saying is that the same understanding of being underlies both. I leave it to the reader to decide whether this demonstrates a profoundly illuminating explanation or a repulsive lack of human decency or, as I see it, some of both.

Some, such as Richard Rorty, see no connection whatsoever between Heidegger's thought and his deeds; after all, Frege was a rabid anti-Semite and no one thinks that this affected his work on logic.[12] Others argue that Heidegger's ideas lead to Nazism, or something similar.[13] I want to draw a middle path between these two extremes. There are certainly elements in his early work that seem incompatible with Nazism. Could anything be further from Dasein's individualistic, resolute mineness than the uniform masses marching in lockstep at the Nuremburg rallies? But one feature is in harmony with it, as Heidegger pointed out to Karl Löwith, a former student, in 1936: "I was of the opinion that his partisanship for National Socialism lay in the essence of his philosophy. Heidegger agreed with me without reservation, and added that his concept of 'historicity' formed the basis of his political 'engagement.'"[14] Being and Time portrays Dasein as a deeply (although not entirely) historical being. We cannot be-in-the-world without pursuing some kind of project, since part of what it means to care about ourselves is to try to construct a self to care about. We derive these projects from our particular culture which makes historicity a kind of content that gets taken into the ahistorical structure of *existentialia*, as explained above.

In the later work history reaches all the way down, so that not just our vocations but our very nature changes with history and culture. Now if this is true, then we do not all possess the same timeless nature but are determined from the ground up by the society we grew up in. *Being and Time*'s Kierkegaardian individualism gives way to a Hegelian communitarianism (bits of which were there too), where we derive our very selves from our community.[15] This means that people who are socialized into the same culture are fundamentally, even *ontologically* closer than those from elsewhere. This harmonizes strongly with the Nazis' quasi-mystical emphasis on the special bond Germans share as offspring of the Fatherland. What was jingoistic for them is metaphysical for Heidegger.

One interesting consequence of this interpretation is that Heidegger's views not only don't lead to anti-Semitism, they actually argue against it. A German Aryan is fundamentally similar and related to a German Jew in a way that she can never be to, say, a blue-eyed, blond-haired Californian surfer. Socialization replaces biology on this reading; soil trumps blood.

The history of being

Heidegger defines the discipline of metaphysics as it has taken shape in the history of philosophy as the attempt to determine the nature of reality, distinguishing the genuinely real from what is not fully real: "metaphysical thinking rests on the distinction between what truly is and what, measured against this, constitutes all that is not truly in being" (N II: 230). The story of philosophy is the story of the series of candidates for these roles based on the changing sense of what it means to be. Since, according to Heidegger's later ontology, being manifests itself in epochal forms, the various periods of metaphysics are our only access to reality, which is why he spends so much time poring over and boring into the tradition's metaphysical texts. One of his greatest achievements is to offer an innovative history of philosophy that shows how the various phases come together into an intelligible, overarching narrative. He gives penetrating analyses of individual books, thinkers, and epochs, showing the deeply held assumptions that hold together a figure's various ideas, the members of a school, or even the competing schools of an age. He also offers a comprehensive history of how these thinkers and epochs fit into a sweeping narrative of being's adventures as a whole, the story of being.

I find Heidegger to be of two minds about this overarching history. On the one hand, he often seems to hold a view similar to philosopher of science Thomas Kuhn that the epochs are incommensurable. This means that their dissimilarity goes so deep that they cannot be directly compared or connected. Ancient and medieval understandings, for example, are apples and oranges which cannot be put into a story with logical transitions or judgments of overall progress or regress. Each epoch's understanding of being includes its own criteria by which to judge the success of an era, so comparing two of them would require picking one set of criteria or the other, and how do you choose? Importing a set of meta-criteria wouldn't solve anything, since these would simply form a third party to the dispute whose authority would also need justification, as the ancient skeptic Sextus Empiricus argues. Heidegger sometimes seems to hold this view, which undermines the telling of the history of being as a story where the order of the phases makes sense, where each leads rationally into the next. He was recorded in a late lecture contrasting his take with Hegel who does give a story of intelligible transitions among periods with overall progress: "for Hegel, there rules in history necessity. . . . For Heidegger, on the other hand, one cannot speak of a 'why.' Only the 'that' – that the history of Being is in such a way – can be said."[16] The understandings we receive are fundamentally mysterious; we cannot make any sense of why they are the way they are or why they are in the order they are, any more than we can of the fact that they are at all.

In a number of writings, however, Heidegger *does* give us just this kind of explanatory narrative. If it never quite comes up to the level of necessity, we can understand why and how one phase turned into the next. And the order as a whole does describe a specific development, namely, the increasing forgetfulness of being. Western civilization started off, according to this account, with a robust awareness of and wonder at being, but ever since has been paying less and less attention. I will briefly sketch out this story, gathering it together from the various places he scattered it throughout his later works.

The pre-Socratics

Heidegger's history, which has biblical undertones to it, begins in the philosophical garden of Eden with the pre-Socratics. They understood being as *physis*: beings naturally, almost organically rise up into reality, a bit like a plant breaking through the shell of its seed and pushing through the soil to emerge in the light of day. Truth, always an important part of an epoch's understanding of being, is for the pre-Socratics *alētheia*, which becomes Heidegger's own favorite word for truth. He stresses the privative prefix ("a-") which means the absence or withdrawal of something, while "*lētheia*" means hiddenness or concealment (think of the river Lēthē in Greek mythology which relieves those entering the underworld of memories of their former lives). Putting them together, truth means unconcealment, the drawing of something out of hiddenness into the open. Notice how well this works with the view of being as entities emerging out of the nothingness in which they lie concealed into reality where they are revealed. Heidegger sees all aspects of an era as harmonized into a coherent whole, especially its notions of truth and being.

Heidegger feels a great affinity for the pre-Socratics, the era whose views he finds closest to his own. He likes the way they make being and truth dynamic: each is understood as an event ("*Ereignis*"), a term Heidegger uses a lot in his late work. Truth isn't a static relationship like resemblance or correspondence, but something that happens. This fits with our experience of beings as dynamically be-ing and truth as a process of discovery and encountering, as captured in his phenomenological description of checking to see if the painting on the wall is straight in *Being and Time* (BT 260–1/217–18). Heidegger also likes the fact that on the pre-Socratic account, these processes are not centered on us. They are events in which beings and language and perception and thought are all caught up and commingled rather than being under our control (OBT 79–80). This is not anthropocentric but onto-centric: things appear. There is no place here for representations lodged in the innards of the mind. Everything takes place out in the open since being takes place as the place of opening.

Plato

After Eden comes the fall, and the apple in Heidegger's story is Plato's Forms. Metaphysically, Plato divides reality into two planes:

the empirical, changing realm we spend our time in and the eternal realm of the Forms, where true reality and real truth lie (Heidegger agrees with Nietzsche that this distinction begins philosophy's long degradation of the changeable and mundane in favor of the static and transcendent). If true reality dwells elsewhere, we ought to shun this half-real plane of shifting shadows and turn our eyes upwards (but one of the major goals of his early work is to rehabilitate time, change, and the average everyday). He invokes a story about Heraclitus: upon disappointing some tourists who, looking for an ostentatiously wise man, found him merely warming himself by the stove, he tells them that even in this humble place and action gods dwell.

For Heidegger the separation of the knowable from the actual thing is even more significant. Plato peels the truth of things off them like a film; when I know this dog, I'm actually dealing with the Form dogness which is severed from it and resides in the changeless plane (Forms do not emerge out of non-being like *physis*; they are always there, purified of all hiddenness) (although Heidegger spies vestiges of the older view in Plato's doctrine of recollection). Truth stops being an event and becomes a relationship I enter into with a permanently static thing. Although the Forms are not human creations, the grasping of them is an action I perform rather than an event I merely participate in, and it becomes something that is far more digestible by the mind than the event of a being manifesting itself. Thus begins the long road to modern anthropocentrism (OBT 69).

Medieval

All now centers on God. The Forms have become ideas in His head. He is the seat of truth and reality on which we all depend and which all imitates and longs for. This is more anthropocentric in that God created the universe for us. On the other hand, we are considerably far down the great chain of being, above rocks, plants, and animals, but below angels and God. Christianity preserves the Platonic notion of the world we live in as fundamentally inferior – ontologically, epistemologically, ethically, and so on – now cast as sinful and fallen.

What is new is that we now have a conscious agent at the base of reality who creates and knows the world. God thinks and acts like us, just more so. His mind contains the Ideas that are the models for the things in the world, and He makes the world for our benefit. Furthermore, He created Himself and so enjoys absolute autonomy. Thus the Forms become mental entities and truth becomes a relationship between the things in the world and the Ideas in His head, although the direction of resemblance must flow from things to Ideas rather than the other way around.

Modernity

At the beginning of modernity, a number of pieces set out by previous eras are now put into a new arrangement that drastically alters their significance. In particular, several of the features given to God are now transferred to humanity. For one thing, autonomy – which God enjoys due to His self-creation – comes to the fore as a central goal for us in the Scientific Revolution and the Enlightenment, both epistemologically and ethically. Instead of following what traditions have told us or even what God tells us, we must discover how the universe works for ourselves and make up our own minds about what is good and evil. Descartes rejects all that he had been brought up to believe because, if he didn't consciously and deliberately decide whether he actually believed these ideas, then he didn't really believe them; they were just there, installed in his mind when he was too young to do anything about it. And since the self is largely made up of what one believes, that means that he didn't really have a self; he needs to make one in order to have one. Kant cements this epistemological creativity in his transcendental idealism: all that we know are facts that we have, unbeknown to ourselves, made. He also installs the ideal of autonomy in the realm of ethics. We have an empirical self that, like Descartes' weak and dependent youth, is buffeted by the vicissitudes of the world. It gets banged and battered by events, both internal and external, but whatever we don't do ourselves is not our true self. This includes features that we would normally claim as parts of the self, such as our emotions or our past, since we didn't actively make or incorporate them. For Kant, we truly become ourselves when we separate ourselves from all of these factors that push on us and retreat to the noumenal self that, purified of all these factors, is impervious to external causes. Noumenally, we can't get pushed around; we do what we actually choose to do and this is when we are most our selves. Here we give ourselves the law and so are truly autonomous.

Taming the world requires us to separate ourselves from it. There must be a gap between ourselves as subjects and the world as object for us to understand and manipulate it. We know the world by representing it, taking conceptual or linguistic "pictures" of it which we bring back into our minds to ponder. Truth becomes the correspondence between these representations and their objects, and the reality of objects gets correlated with how well we can represent them.

> Knowledge as research calls beings to account with regard to the way in which, and the extent to which, they can be placed at the disposal of representation. Research has beings at its disposal when it can, through calculation, either predict their future or retrodict their past. . . . Nature and history . . . become objects of explanatory representation. . . . Only what becomes, in this way, an object *is* – counts as being. (OBT 65–6)

Thus, for Descartes the most real parts of physical reality are its quantifiable features because we can mathematically capture and digest these far better than the vague and changing perceptions of qualities like color or heat. Things like meanings or values get pulled out of the world and thrust into the mind as merely subjective projections. Kant takes this to its logical extreme to conclude that the only aspects of reality that we can take in are those that have been organized in such a way as to be comprehensible to our minds, and these are perfectly susceptible to scientific analysis.

Whereas the pre-Socratics were onto-centric and the medievals theo-centric, modernity is anthropocentric, due to the change in the understanding of being.

> The essence of humanity altogether transforms itself in that man becomes the subject. . . . He becomes that being upon which every being, in its way of being and its truth, is founded. Man becomes the relational center of beings as such. But this is only possible when there is a transformation in the understanding of beings as a whole.[17]

Being has become the object of our representations, rendering us the representing animal. Reason places us at the pinnacle of creation when we place ourselves there. Truth becomes something we initiate by making pictures of the world which must be true to its objects.

The forgetfulness of being

The overall arc of this story is one of the ever-growing oblivious-ness to being as humanity eclipses it. One thing to note is that although Heidegger attributes certain turns in the road to specific thinkers, he isn't exactly blaming them. As we will see, he does not believe that individuals determine the ideas they have but merely respond to what presents itself to them. Furthermore, metaphysicians are to be admired for turning from beings to their age's understanding of being; it's just that some of them are fated to articulate more or less destitute meanings. Finally, although covering over being increases over time due to philosophical changes, being itself is intrinsically inclined towards concealing itself, as we saw above. The fact that beings are manifest to us "withdraws" when we pay attention to the manifested beings. "It would lie then in the essence of being itself that being remains unthought because it removes itself" (OBT 197).

Still, being's tendency to hide has increased over the centuries. The pre-Socratics had the best sense of it, with a dynamic event of beings appearing that was dramatic, inspiring awe and wonder. The emergence of *physis* out of hiddenness reminds us that its manifestation is contingent, that it may have remained unrevealed, making us grateful for its appearance. When God creates the world, we still have the creation *ex nihilo*, although not of God or His Ideas, which gives us someone to be grateful to and something to be grateful for. In modernity we instigate these things ourselves which shuts down the space for wonder and gratitude. "The things for which we owe thanks are not things we have from ourselves. . . . But the thing given to us . . . is thinking. . . . How can we give thanks for this endowment, the gift of being able to think?" (WCT 142–3).

Now that we have traced the past, let us turn to the present. What is our age's understanding of being?

Further readings

Among Heidegger's writings, I recommend "The Age of the World Picture" in OBT; *Early Greek Thinking*; "Plato's Doctrine of Truth," "On the Essence and Concept of Φύσις in Aristotle's *Physics* B, I," "Hegel and the Greeks," and "Kant's Thesis about Being," all in PM.

For a general discussion of Heidegger's take on the history of philosophy, see Werner Marx's *Heidegger and the Tradition* or Otto Pöggeler's *The Paths of Heidegger's Life and Thought*. Karin de Boer's *Thinking in the Light of Time: Heidegger's Encounter with Hegel* addresses the same issue through the lens of Heidegger's interaction with Hegel, another philosopher who makes the history of philosophy central to his own thought.

A few works have come out dealing with Foucault's relationship to Heidegger, including my own *A Thing of This World* and the papers collected in Alan Milchman and Alan Rosenberg's *Foucault and Heidegger: Critical Encounters*. Michael E. Zimmerman's *Heidegger's Confrontation with Modernity: Technology, Politics, and Art* deals with Heidegger's involvement with the Nazis, as well as subjects from our next few chapters. John D. Caputo's excellent *Demythologizing Heidegger* connects Heidegger's changing narrative of the history of philosophy with his political decisions. Many of the relevant sources concerning Heidegger's relationship to Nazism have been gathered in Wolin's *The Heidegger Controversy*. Hugo Ott's *Martin Heidegger: A Political Life* and Rüdiger Safranski's *Martin Heidegger: Between Good and Evil* are generally considered to be his best biographies, at least until Iain Thomson's comes out.

9

Descartes, Thinking, and Free Will

Heidegger thinks about a wide variety of topics, but one that he spends a great deal of time on is thinking itself. Surely this, if anything, is the province of a thinker but on this topic, as on so many others, he finds previous philosophers' views wanting: "we can learn thinking only if we radically unlearn what thinking has been traditionally" (WCT 8). As in his early work, we find the truth by uncovering it, dismantling and scraping off centuries of distorted theories until we get to the way we actually experience it. This is the process he calls "destruction" in *Being and Time* and he continued to practice a version of it throughout his career. We will focus here on his destruction of Descartes, who plays an essential role in his history of philosophy: "with Descartes, there begins the completion of Western metaphysics" (OBT 75). Since, as we have seen, all thinkers reflect their era's ideas, we should find the entire mindset of modernity here, at least in embryo.

Descartes

Descartes inaugurates the modern age by overthrowing medieval ideas because they were not up to the task he thinks thinking should accomplish, namely, taming the wild profusion of the world into an orderly form that can be managed and controlled. The intrinsic *telos* of thought, as he sees it, is science. Comprehension orders phenomena intellectually and this gives birth to technology, which can structure the material world around us, thus easing the hardships and discomforts of mortal life. This drive to control the world is really an extension of his project of self-creation. The beliefs he had passively taken on in his childhood, "the opinions which may have slipped into my mind without having been intro-duced there by reason" (PWD I: 119), are problematic because they might be false having escaped any critical examination. But besides being dubious, the unthinking way he accepted them is in itself a problem because it means that they are not truly his beliefs.

In *Meditation IV*, Descartes gets out of the problem of error – that is, why an epistemologically benevolent deity would allow us to make mistakes – by making belief a fully voluntary activity. I am presented with propositions of varying plausibility – my cup appears to be gray and at hand, for example – but no perception or idea forces me to assent to it, no matter how obvious or persua-sive. To believe something requires, beyond grasping the content of the proposed claim, a *decision* to accept it as true. This is what shifts the blame for error from God onto us.

But this raises a problem since Descartes realizes that he did not go through the process of thinking about and agreeing to the vast store of ideas he finds his mind stocked with. They're just there, taken on unquestioningly by his lazy, gullible childhood self, accu-mulating in his mind like epistemological lint in a dryer.

> I reflected that we were all children before being men and had to be governed for some time by our appetites and our teachers . . .; hence I thought it virtually impossible that our judgments should be as unclouded and firm as they would have been if we had had the full use of our reason from the moment of our birth, and if we had always been guided by it alone. (PWD I: 117)

Descartes reverses that old saying about kittens: the problem with adults is that they were once children. During this unfortunate time we passively absorbed beliefs "under the control of" external agents rather than performing the labor for ourselves. Luckily, we can fix this.

Now that he has matured intellectually he resolves to put away childish beliefs. He must recapitulate his first acquisition of knowl-edge of the world and this time, do it right. Indeed, this time actu-ally *do* it rather than having it done for or to him by looking at his beliefs and *deciding* whether he actually believes them, ignoring those external agents who had controlled the process the first time through. "For since God has given each of us a light to distinguish truth from falsehood, I should not have thought myself obliged to rest content with the opinions of others for a single moment if I had not intended in due course to examine them using my own judgment" (PWD I: 124). He shall not cease from examination, and the end of all his examination will be to arrive at many of the beliefs he started with but now believing them for the first time. They may retain the same content but they will now actually be *his* beliefs since he will have made up his own mind to accept them. And in this way he will make his mind his own rather than passively receiving it, for a self that has been just given to you is not really yours. (Notice how similar this is to the account of authentic resoluteness in *Being and Time*.) His belief system will be built on certainty, while his self will be built on a foundation of will, leading to knowledge of the world on the one hand and autonomy on the other.

This act of self-reclamation that Descartes does for himself he also prescribes for Western civilization. Medieval knowledge was built on a foundation of sand; we must put it aside and start anew. Moderns should not accept ideas simply because they are written down in weighty tomes with impressive names attached to them, but find out what the world is like for themselves. "As soon as I was old enough to emerge from the control of my teachers, I entirely abandoned the study of letters. [I resolved] to seek no knowledge other than that which could be found in myself or else in the great book of the world" (PWD I: 115, see also 13–15). This disregard for the great, august authorities in favor of each individual's inherent ability to discern the truth is one reason he writes in French rather than in the more esoteric Latin. Descartes on an individual level and modernity on a cultural level will reboot the long, buggy history of knowledge and, relying on nothing handed down to them, pull themselves up by their epistemological bootstraps. As Heidegger puts it, "the essence of modernity can be seen in humanity's freeing itself from the bonds of the Middle Ages in that it frees itself to itself" (OBT 66).

Descartes even applies this, partially, to his own work. He decides not to publish some of his conclusions because "no one can conceive something so well, and make it our own, when he learns it from someone else as when he discovers it himself" (PWD I: 146). Despite their undeniable truth, revealing these discoveries to others harms them by preventing them from discovering the ideas for themselves, the only legitimate way of coming to know them) Descartes even says that if he had learned his own principles in his youth, which seemingly would have inoculated him against all the epistemological detritus he complains of, it would have squelched his intellectual gifts (PWD I: 148). Truths must come from oneself else they are not truly one's truths, in a sense. The rhetorical style of the *Meditations* solves this problem by allowing the reader to think along with him, reducing Descartes' role to that of a Socratic midwife who merely helps the reader see the ideas for herself.

The Scientific Revolution's ideal of intellectual maturity and independence blossoms into the dream of the Enlightenment, taking on a political and ethical form as well, all of which Heidegger finds concentrated in the idea that we are now a subject. "Man as the rational being of the Enlightenment is no less subject than man who grasps himself as nation, wills himself as people, nurtures himself as race and, finally, empowers himself as lord of the earth" (OBT 84). As we saw in Chapter 8, all the various aspects of a culture are merely manifestations of a single way of thinking, reflections of an individual understanding of being in multiple shards. To be modern is to think and choose for oneself in all of these various ways: it is to accept only what one decides to accept, whether this be a proposition, a moral law, a political ruler, or a judgment of beauty.

Heidegger detects an intrinsic problem in this outlook. Descartes got the ball rolling by demanding that the world do his bidding and that we become "lords and masters of nature" by taking control of ourselves. This power must not be simply given to us; we must take it.

> What is new, however, in this occurrence does not at all consist in the fact, merely, that the position of man in the midst of beings is other than it was for ancient or medieval man. What is decisive is that man specifically takes up this position as one constituted by himself) . . . Man makes depend on himself the way he is to stand to beings as the objective. What begins is that mode of human being which occupies the realm of human capacity as the domain of measuring and execution for the purpose of the mastery of beings as a whole. (OBT 69)

The particular position of subjectivity is new, but what's revolutionary is the insistence that we have placed ourselves there by our own efforts. According to the logic of autonomy, it must have been our achievement rather than our inheritance for it to be truly ours. Getting things for ourselves is the one thing that cannot be done for us by others. It must be of our doing.

But, Heidegger asks, where did this <u>impulse for control</u> come from? He writes that,

> Descartes can only be overcome through the overcoming of that which he himself founded, through the overcoming, namely, of modern (and that means, at the same time, Western) metaphysics. "Overcoming" means here, however, the primal asking of the question of the meaning of being, of, that is, the <u>sphere of projection and with it the truth of being</u>. This question unveils itself as, at the same time, <u>the question of the being of truth</u>. (OBT 76)

Now this sounds like his usual, knee-jerk invocation of the question of being and truth at every juncture. But we must keep in mind what Heidegger means by these terms. <u>Truth is the unconcealment of beings to us</u> in a particular way. <u>The way things are revealed – their beingness – determines how we interact with them.</u>

We rarely think about this dimension of experience, instead taking the meaning of various entities to be intrinsic to them, self-evident to all reasonable people. <u>We all start off taking the meaning of beings for granted, assuming that the way we experience them is just the way they are</u>, the view that Kant calls dogmatic naivety and Husserl the natural attitude. *Being and Time* showed us that hammers are not necessarily and intrinsically tools by pointing out how they transform into inert objects when we stop and stare at them. It is this change-over that reveals the fact that these modes of being come from us rather than being embedded in the essence of the entity, the way the necessity and universality of math and science demonstrated for Kant that space, time, and causality are our transcendental projections.

In his later work, Heidegger is still fighting against a kind of Kantian naivety where "the existing being is thereby taken as a thing-in-itself, i.e. without attending to the conditions of its possible givenness."[1] <u>The conditions of givenness are no longer in the subject, as they were for Kant and Husserl, but in a historical era's understanding of being.</u> People "already stand, without *their* knowing it, in a relation to being. Only from the truth of being that prevails on each occasion do they receive a light that first enables them to see and observe *as such* the beings represented by them" (PM 318). <u>Beings do not contain their own univocal meaning since their meaning differs depending on the particular kind of clearing they appear within.</u>

Heidegger is carrying out his usual method of what might be called, after Quine, "<u>ontological ascent</u>," moving from beings to beingness, and then to being itself. We make the first move when we examine the way beingness changes across time periods, parallel to the change-over from ready-to-hand tool to present-at-hand object in *Being and Time*. This keeps us from taking our own understanding of being as the only possible and obviously right one. "What did we seek from this 'historical reflection'? To obtain a *distance* from what we take as self-evident, from what lies all too close to us" (ET 6).

Heidegger illuminates the modern understanding of being by explaining how Descartes' project emerged out of the ashes of the medieval era. When revelation stopped counting as the highest form of knowledge, this created the need for a new foundation for knowledge. We needed a new source of certainty now that we could not rely on a divine guarantee of certain facts, and we appointed ourselves to perform that job. "This liberation *from* the certainty of salvation disclosed by revelation has to be, in itself, a liberation *to* a certainty in which man secures for himself the true as that which is known through his own knowing. . . . Descartes' metaphysical task became the following: to create the metaphysical ground for the freeing of man to freedom considered as self-determination that is certain of itself."[2] What Nietzsche dramatically calls the "death of God" created an epistemological vacuum which got filled by us. Self-reliance replaced trust in the divine, and autonomy rather than fidelity became the defining value of the age. Now, this explanation works as far as it goes, but it really just pushes the question back a step: why did revelation falter? Why was certainty felt to be necessary? Why did this certitude come to be planted in the self rather than somewhere else?

The answer lies in the way Heidegger defines truth: divine revelation appeared to Descartes as insufficient. We cannot say that this insufficiency was inherent in that form of knowledge that a millennium's worth of scholars had found perfectly adequate. It's not that the scholastics didn't realize that the Bible was of little aid in discovering cures for diseases; they didn't expect such things from knowledge. The revealed word hadn't changed, just the way Descartes and others heard it. The import of the Bible isn't an objective fact, out there in the world; rather, its significance is determined holistically, by the overall context or understanding of being it occurs within. This is a view Heidegger held throughout his career. His early work applies this analysis to the paradigm case of objective facts: science. "The rise of mathematical physics . . . lies rather in *the way in which Nature herself is mathematically projected.*

. . . Only 'in the light' of a Nature which has been projected in this fashion can anything like a 'fact' be found. . . . In principle there are no 'bare facts'" (BT 413-14/362). Facts are created; it's not that we just make stuff up, but that nature only yields scientific facts given certain attitudes and ways of observing on our part, in particular the disengaged stance that turns the subject of inquiry into present-at-hand objects. The dream of the innocent eye simply seeing what is really there without any kind of interpretation is the ultimate naivety: "in no case is a Dasein, untouched and unseduced by this way in which things have been interpreted, set before the open country of a 'world-in-itself' so that it just beholds what it encounters" (BT 213/169). This is why phenomenology must be hermeneutic: because experience itself is always interpretive.

He maintains this idea in his later work – "there are no mere facts, but . . . a fact is only what it is in the light of the fundamental conception" (BW 272) – only now tying interpretive schemes to epochal understandings of being rather than stances that Dasein takes up. These fundamental conceptions are expressions of a particularly shaped clearing, so to speak, that molds all that appears within it into a specific contour. In a new version of the Law of Transcendental Transitivity, differently shaped clearings will produce different experiences of the world, and hence different worlds. To illustrate this idea, Heidegger describes a point of transition when people of different understandings could be found side-by-side observing Galileo's famous experiment of dropping heavy bodies off the tower of Pisa:

> both Galileo and his opponents saw the same "fact." But they interpreted the same fact differently and made the same happening visible to themselves in different ways. Indeed, what appeared for them as the essential fact and truth was something different. . . . They thought something different, not only about the single case, but fundamentally, regarding the essence of a body and the nature of its motion. (BW 290)

This event straddled the medieval and modern epochs, so that some observers perceived it in the former context while Galileo saw it from within the new clearing, thus observing different events. In such cases, believing is seeing.

Thus even "objective" facts which are supposed to be independent of interpretive schemes are actually products of specific interpretive schemes, just as present-at-hand objects only exist when we observe entities. "The project first opens a domain where things – i.e., facts – show themselves . . . How they show themselves is prefigured in the project" (BW 291). Since this changes across history, what people see – and how they understand what they see – differs as well. While inertia is "self-evident" to us, "during the preceding fifteen hundred years it was not only unknown, but nature and beings in general were experienced in such a way that it would have been senseless" (BW 280). Inertia didn't fit into the ancient clearing and so didn't appear to them; when they looked at moving bodies they saw elements seeking their home regions.[3] The medievals weren't stupid or lazy in relying on revealed word instead of conducting experiments. Their whole way of thinking and experiencing told them that this was obviously the right thing to do. They possessed The Instruction Manual For Life, written by its inventor (who also happens to be omniscient), making it obviously the best possible source of truth.

Descartes isn't to be praised for seeing something that was right in front of previous thinkers' noses but that they stubbornly ignored. No, he saw something new because something new showed itself to him. He was able to see this because a new light shone upon the intellectual landscape of the time but, as usual, his focus on what was illuminated blinded him to the illumination itself. As a metaphysician, Descartes moved from beings to being-ness, defining a new understanding of subjectivity and what it means to be for his era. But he did not make the second move to the source of that understanding, to ask why he was able to think these new, never before thought ideas. Instead, he took credit for discovering them by his own intelligence and energy.

Thinking

To put Heidegger's idea in its most condensed and simplified form, he changes thinking from something fundamentally active to a passive process, something we receive or undergo or participate in rather than something we create, initiate, and control. Traditionally, thinking has been the bastion of genuine activity within the self as opposed to the body, the senses, emotions, etc. (the word "passions" shares an etymological root with "passivity"). These are things we simply find within ourselves, unchosen, like Descartes' stock of previously accepted beliefs; thinking on the other hand is something we do. It is our act which lets us most be our selves. As

Descartes writes, "nothing lies entirely within our power except our thoughts" (PWD I: 123).

This picture falls apart under a phenomenological description of the act of thinking. When I examine an argument, I quite literally *follow* its line of reasoning. I don't decide that there's something fishy with a particular premise or inference; it strikes me as wrong. Objections well up inside my mind the way melodies occur to composers (we'll talk more about artistic inspiration in Chapter 10). "Such thoughts do not first come to be by way of mortal thinking. Rather our mortal thinking is always summoned by that thought to correspond to it or renounce it. We human beings do not come upon thoughts; thoughts rather come to us mortals."[4] I don't make up my mind that 2 + 2 is 4, or that Socrates is mortal from the premises that Socrates is a man and that all men are mortal; my mind does the job for me the way my legs take over the act of walking. I reason on autopilot just as much as I usually drive a car without conscious interference. Think about having a conversation – do you consciously plan out what you're going to say before you say it? Or do you just sense that you have a response, open your mouth, and words come out? Even if you did deliberately plan your words out, this internal mental planning itself would depend on ideas and words presenting themselves to you as candidates, with certain options among them striking you as the best ones. This is why Heidegger argues that although "speaking and hearing are customarily set in opposition to one another," in fact "speech, taken on its own, is hearing. It is listening to the language we speak. . . . It is language that speaks."[5]

Heidegger applies this analysis of thought to the thinkers *par excellence*: philosophers. The great thinkers should be praised not for their creativity but for their sensitivity. They pick up and articulate the understanding of being that, concealed, forms and informs all that happens at that time. "What is great and constant in the thinking of a thinker simply consists in its expressly giving word to what always already resounds."[6] When Nietzsche, for example, thought about the world, the features that came to the forefront were flux and conflict. These features impressed themselves on him rather than him selecting them as most important; or rather, he selected them because they impressed him. "Nietzsche's thought has to plunge into metaphysics because Being radiates its own essence as will to power" (N IV: 181). What could he base this selection on except the fact that some characteristics seemed more significant than others? And he could not have decided *that* without slipping into an infinite regress of choosing the criteria for each choice. "We will have to rely on Being, and on how Being strikes our thinking, to ascertain from it what features essentially occur."[7] In general, we notice and think about "the sorts of things that are suggested by what is addressed . . . what the addressed allows to radiate of itself" (BW 409). Thus Nietzsche, the great philosopher of action, "neither made nor chose his way himself, no more than any other thinker ever did. He is sent on his way."[8]

Heidegger thus casts thought as a response to the way the world appears to us. "That Being itself and how Being itself concerns our thinking does not depend upon our thinking alone. That Being itself, and the manner in which Being itself, strikes a particular thinking, lets such thinking spring forth in springing from Being itself in such a way as to respond to Being as such."[9] This applies to all thinking but it is particularly interesting when applied to those who emphasize autonomy, one of the defining values of modernity, since this conception essentially compromises autonomy, more so than *Being and Time*'s account of thrownness. All actions are reactions, all thoughts and words responses. We are entirely reliant upon the fact that and the manner in which the world reveals itself to us. "The unconcealment itself, within which ordering unfolds, is never a human handiwork. . . . The unconcealment of the unconcealed has already propriated whenever it calls man forth into the modes of revealing allotted to him. When man, in his way, from within unconcealment reveals that which presences, he merely responds to the call of unconcealment."[10] This transference of agency away from the conscious subject is sometimes called "anti-humanism," partially because one of its most important statements comes in Heidegger's "Letter on Humanism."

The idea is captured in the title of the 1951–1952 series of lectures: *Was Heisst Denken?* This is usually translated as *What Is Called Thinking?*, a query into the nature of a phenomenon like many of his other titles: "What Is Metaphysics?", *What Is a Thing?*, *What Is Philosophy?*, and so on. However, in a rare word-play that survives translation into English, the word "call" means both to name and to call out to someone, to beckon, to attract and *call* someone's attention to something. So the title can also be translated as *What Calls Out to Thinking?* or *What Calls Upon Thinking?* The standard translation calls thinking into question, asking about the activity that has traditionally gone under this name, while the alternate reading of the same phrase contains the answer in embryo. Thinking is to perceive and respond to what calls upon us to think about it, what calls us to think in the first place.

Let us return to Descartes where we can find a tension between his conception of thought as essentially active and its necessarily passive nature.[11] As we have seen, he makes decision an essential part of good beliefs and yet the very best beliefs, the ones that must be in place for any others to be secure, are precisely those that we do not decide to believe because we cannot disbelieve them. What makes clear and distinct perceptions so distinctive is that they *command* assent from us, overriding attempts to step back and evaluate them, forcing us to acquiesce unquestioningly, just the kind of epistemological submissiveness that Descartes otherwise attacks. "I have already amply demonstrated that everything of which I am clearly aware is true. And even if I had not demonstrated this, the nature of my mind is such that I cannot but assent to these things, at least so long as I clearly perceive them."[12]

This is the nature of the optimal epistemological states. Although he feels that he has proven why we can legitimately rely on clear and distinct perceptions, Descartes admits that there is a sense in which this assurance does not matter. Regardless of our ability to legitimize them, we are simply hard-wired to respond to certain ideas by believing them. When it comes to proofs about triangles or God's existence, for example, "it is not that my thought makes it so, or imposes any necessity on any thing; on the contrary, it is the necessity of the thing itself . . . which determines my thinking. For I am not free to think of God without existence . . . as I am free to imagine a horse with or without wings" (PWD II: 46). Whereas our control of it is what makes thinking such an important part of us, in the realm of ideas the privilege gets reversed. It is precisely our power over the idea of a winged horse that shows that it spins freely, without catching on objective reality, whereas the fact that God's existence forces my thoughts down a specific path proves its truth. At one point, he even allows the compulsion that clear and distinct perceptions exert on his belief to trump the possibility that the idea is false absolutely, from God's point of view (PWD II: 103), a very interesting move given Heidegger's claim that Descartes is substituting our own knowledge for the medieval reliance on divine information.

Descartes also appeals to "the natural light" to justify certain inferences, many of which appear rather dubious to us: "now it is manifest by the natural light that there must be at least as much reality in the efficient and total cause as in the effect" (PWD II: 28), or God cannot be a deceiver "since it is manifest by the natural light that all fraud and deception depend on some defect" (PWD II: 35), or the claim that conservation and creation are essentially the same (PWD II: 33). This appeal may look like cheating – he sneaks whatever he needs for his argument past the skeptical guard by showing its stamp of approval by the light of nature – especially since these propositions hardly seem as self-evident to us as they did to him. But in fact, these passages paint a far more accurate picture of thinking than the more common descriptions of deliberate determination. For deliberation must be guided by the way ideas appear in a certain light. Especially convincing ones hijack our evaluation mechanisms, forcing us to cough up "4" to "2 + 2 = __." Although we today think of freedom as being completely unrestrained, Descartes defines freedom otherwise:

> The more I incline in one direction – either because I clearly understand that reasons of truth and goodness point that way, or because of a divinely produced disposition of my inmost thoughts – the freer is my choice. . . . The indifference I feel when there is no reason pushing me in one direction rather than another is the lowest grade of freedom. . . . For if I always saw clearly what was true and good, I should never have to deliberate about the right judgment or choice; in that case, although I should be wholly free, it would be impossible for me ever to be in a state of indifference. (PWD II: 40)

The proper use of freedom is to restrain my will from acting when it is not impelled to act. Ideally, I must only allow it to make the decision to believe when, paradoxically, I cannot make this decision because I am impelled to assent. Heidegger understands freedom in similar terms: "freedom is to be free and open for being claimed by something. This claim is then the ground of action, the motive" (Z 217).

Descartes says that among his faculties, only his will is absolute; only it approximates divine unlimitedness in being absolutely uncompromised. I may not be able to carry out what I will, but I can will whatever I want. Nothing can hinder it except clear and distinct perceptions which compel my assent whether I will it or not, somehow making them epistemologically optimal rather than compromising my autonomy. But Heidegger finds a problem in Descartes' way of setting up the issue.

As we have seen, Descartes is impatient with medieval ways of thinking because they yield no technological fruits, so he sets about constructing a new, more productive way of thinking. In this endeavor, Heidegger argues, Descartes is of necessity too late. For him to evaluate medieval philosophy in pragmatic terms of how well it enables control of the world is *already* to think technologically, in Heidegger's sense. It is to treat thought itself as a form of *Bestand* or resources to be shaped so that it will give us what we want. The medieval idea that it may be sacrosanct as a gift of God is itself part of the problem for Descartes; we must discard whatever ideas aren't pulling their weight. To think this way is already to see things through the lens of technological thinking which evaluates everything on the basis of how well it satisfies our desires and treats everything as resources to be arranged and deployed so as to better fulfill them. As we will see in more detail in Chapter 11, Heidegger's conception of technology applies to all sorts of things, not just electronic devices. In fact, he sees its most important applications to abstract phenomena like language, or thought.

Descartes can only consider reforming medieval thought to make it technologically oriented if he is already thinking technologically, that is, in terms of utility to us. But this means that he is (not) reconstructing his mind according to self-created ideals but following an ideal that had to be in place before he could even think about reforming his thinking, one he simply found to be appealing. In other words, he has to first think technologically for him to be able to think about making his thinking technologically apt; he must already be, at least to some extent, what he is trying to become. Because each epoch's understanding of being suffuses and guides all phenomena during that period, especially its way of thinking, this essential heteronomy applies to all epochs. No one can determine her own understanding of being since it is that understanding that determines the way they will try to shape it. "No human calculation and activity, in and of itself, can bring about a turn in the present world condition; one reason for this is the fact that the whole of man's activity has been stamped by this world condition and has come under its power. How then should he ever become master of it?" (EHP 224). This is why Heidegger says over and over again that we do not make our own clearing, as the Idealists believed. This is what he means by his infamous claim that only a god can save us (HR 326).

This also explains why "the essence of technology must harbor in itself the growth of the saving power. But in that case, might not an adequate look into what enframing is, as a destining of revealing, bring the upsurgence of the saving power into appearance?"[13]

We want to create our own way of thinking but "modern technology, as a revealing that orders, is thus no mere human doing. . . . This gathering concentrates man upon ordering the actual as standing-reserve" (BW 324). In other words, when we feel most active, making the earth over into a more tractable form, we are only reacting to the world's revealing itself to us as to-be-improved. "Technological activity . . . always merely responds to the challenge of enframing, but it never comprises enframing itself or brings it about."[14]

In building and creating, "we forget to ask: What is the ground that enabled modern technology to discover and set free new energies in nature?"[15] This forgetfulness of being is what Heidegger thinks of as nihilism, when the "totality of the world of technology is interpreted in advance in terms of man, as being of man's making. By this conception of the totality of the technological world, we reduce everything down to man. . . . We fail to hear the claim of Being which speaks in the essence of technology" (ID 34). An adequate look into the essence of technology shows us that we could not have made it since making a way of thinking is itself already a technological notion, and thus has to be in place for this project to appeal or make sense or even to occur to us. And this places an in principle limit on autonomy. When it comes to being and beingness, to the fact that beings appear to us and in the particular way they do, "the decision does not belong to humans. If this is to become clear, what is most important is the insight that man is not a being that makes himself."[16] Indeed, even the dream of autonomy is something heteronomously given to us: ("on one's own initiative' is already indicative of a way in which being itself lets human beings be in their essence" (HH 90). This applies to philosophy as well. Instead of just asking philosophical questions, Heidegger questions the act of questioning: "Why the Why?"[17] The answer: "we are constantly addressed by, summoned to attend to, grounds and reason."[18]

Reason, the traditional bastion of autonomy, is something we find compelling in that it compels us, attractive because it attracts us to it. And this means that when ideas strike us differently, we will think about them differently and find different kinds of actions and reasons reasonable, which is what happens when new epochs dawn. "Reason and its representational activity are only *one* kind of thinking and are by no means self-determined. They are determined, rather, by that which has called upon thinking to think in the manner of *ratio*" (PM 293). Whereas in *Being and Time* entities changed their mode of being depending on our stance towards them, now our whole way of being-in-the-world is like an echo, responding and conforming to the way beings manifest at that time.

One way to think about this is as a rejection of the view, common in early modern philosophy, of perception and judgment as separate phases. The idea is that first we see something and then we form a judgment about it, making perception conceptually innocent. Those cloaks and hats I see from my window in Descartes' example say nothing beyond themselves: in particular they make no claims about what lies unseen beneath them. It is a further, restrainable act of judgment that posits wearers beneath the hats. Kant depicts raw perceptions taken in by the intuition as getting structured by the understanding, with concepts super-added to it to form judgments. Perception says merely, "this rock" and "warmth;" the understanding forms it into an actual claim: "This rock is warm." Husserl, partially following Descartes, used the phenomenological reduction or epoché to get to the level of mere perception, which contains less than the unreduced natural perception purported to. Although in the natural attitude of daily life I think I see this cup, actually I'm only perceiving a side of the cup, what Husserl called an adumbration. It is my transcendental ego that fills in its backside according to what Heidegger calls "the old mythology of an intellect which glues and rigs together the world's matter with its own forms" (HCT 70).

Heidegger takes issue with this entire set-up. He rejects the idea that we get raw perceptions which we then form into macroscopic, familiar objects. Phenomenologically, we get the whole thing at one glance.

> We never really first perceive a throng of sensations, e.g., tones and noises, in the appearance of things – as this thing-concept alleges; rather we hear the storm whistling in the chimney, we hear the three-motored plane. . . . We hear the door shut in the house and never hear acoustical sensations or even mere sounds. In order to hear a bare sound we have to listen away from things, divert our ear from them, i.e., listen abstractly. (BW 151–2)

I don't first see individual features which I then piece together to infer a face; I immediately see my friend eating his favorite dish in the kind of holistic totality discovered by the Gestalt psychologists. Moreover, this perception is inherently meaningful: I see my friend whom I haven't seen in too long, or with whom I've been having a slight tiff which has strained relations. I register a gun pointed at me in my bowels, not my retinas.

This applies to intellectual pursuits as well. "$2 \times 2 = 7,287$" leaps out at me as wrong or, more precisely, as WRONG!, as $2 \times 2 = 7,287$ with sirens and spinning red lights going off. Perception already contains the seeds of conceptual development. When we negate or deny a proposition, that is because the proposition presents itself as negatable or to-be-denied, like the math mistake above.

> Negation does not conjure the "not" out of itself as a means for making distinctions and oppositions in whatever is given, inserting itself, as it were, in between what is given. How could negation produce the not from itself when it can make denials only when something deniable is already granted to it? (BW 105, see also BW 261)

Perception without concepts is not blind, as Kant had it; it's actually pretty brainy. This is what I have elsewhere called the perceptual model of thought where we see ideas directly (Braver 2012, 139–46). Although this view conflicts with Husserl's views of the transcendental ego uniting adumbrations, it is much closer to his notion of categorial intuition, an idea Heidegger often praises.

Free will

Just as we have been operating under a misguided notion of thinking, so Heidegger tells us that the same applies to our understanding of action. The "Letter on Humanism," which many consider the greatest single work of his later career, opens by telling us that, "we are still far from pondering the essence of action decisively enough" (BW 217). Much of Division 1 of *Being and Time* describes our daily behavior as on autopilot, which it criticizes as fallen in Division 2. The anxious encounter with death breaks this hypnotic inertia, allowing for explicit choice. His later work, on the other hand, deconstructs the very notion of explicit choice.

Deliberate decisions can only go back so far; they must bottom out on something like an automatic reflex or they will go on forever. Decisions must employ some kind of criterion, some way of selecting from among the options. But, Heidegger asks, where do these criteria come from? Why do we use one set instead of another? If our criteria are simply given to us – by our biology, society, God, or whatever – then, by the logic of autonomy, the decision is not itself decisive, not really *our* decision. While no one is forcing me to pick the chocolate ice cream rather than the Brussels sprouts, I do so because of the way my taste buds and upbringing formed me. It is, in a sense, *they* that are making the decision while I passively look on.

In order to make the act my own, it seems that I must actively choose the criteria as well. But how do I make *this* decision? How do I determine which considerations are paramount, taste or health? Let's say that, upon reflection, I now decide that health concerns outweigh the temporary pleasures of taste. I can certainly give reasons – health has longer benefits than the momentary delight of ice cream – but of course reasons can be given for the other side as well – I'd rather live well than live long. I have certain inclinations towards one over the other but these are features I simply find in myself, so relying on them cannot achieve the escape velocity for true autonomy.

Heidegger argues that we must rely on something like these inclinations that I have not chosen in order to act at all, siding with the intellectualists against the voluntarists in the great medieval debate about which faculty is decisive in decision-making.

> The inclination, that is, various directions of being inclined, are the presuppositions for the possibility of the decision of a faculty. If it could not and did not have to decide for one inclination or the other, that is, for what it has a propensity to, decision would not be decision, but a mere explosion of an act out of emptiness into emptiness, pure chance, but never self-determination, that is, freedom. (STF 148–9, see also STF 154–5)

If I remove all inclinations – all preferences, all emotional resonances, everything implanted in me by family, God, or nature – then I have at the same time bereft myself of the very features I need just to make a decision at all, like Buridan's ass who starves, paralyzed between two equally appetizing piles of hay. "Every decision, however, bases itself on something not mastered . . . else it would never be a decision" (BW 180). This is the Paradox of Complete Freedom: the absolute absence of all limitations on our actions proves to be an absolute limitation on our ability to act. Total power is impotence, not freedom. "I cannot exist at all without constantly responding to this or that address in a thematic or unthematic way; otherwise I could not take so much as a single step, nor cast a glance at something."[19]

This is one reason why Heidegger sees Nietzsche's solution to nihilism (the loss of values) as actually a worsening of the problem. Nietzsche argues that after the death of God, we can determine the value of everything rather than simply obeying archaic views. But when we must decide what value everything has, we end up surrendering the resources we need to actually find things to be of value, ending up in the empty tautology of wanting to get whatever we want or the will willing itself. If nothing in the world has intrinsic worth, then there can be no reason for me to prefer one state of things over another, paralyzing that creative impulse that Nietzsche relies on to reinvest the world with meaning.

Happily, we are not in the situation Nietzsche describes – a subject facing a featureless set of objects which make no claim on us. Actually, things are clamoring for our attention and our actions all the time.[20] I do not have to decide how to decide upon my lunch, disengaging from action to take up a purely reflective perspective the way staring turns the world into bare present-at-hand objects in *Being and Time*. Most of the time, the ice cream calls out to me, drawing my hungry grasp to it, demanding that it be eaten whereas the Brussels sprouts push me away. As in environmental psychologist J. J. Gibson's analysis, chairs "afford" sitting to entities with our skeletal structure, soliciting us to sit down when we are tired. This is not a subjective judgment added to the bare perception of intersecting planes of wood and fabric, but is the immediate way we perceive a chair. "In this openness, beings are familiar to us and known in different ways according to their different regions. Beings stand in a luminosity of knowledge and of sovereignty and afford ways and paths of penetration for the most diverse ways of being elaborated, formed, and considered" (BQ 178).

This applies to the situation where we feel ourselves most in control: making and using technology. "Beings themselves . . . make a claim on us with respect to their aptness to be planned and calculated" (ID 35). Our actions are reactions to the way things appear and appeal to us. Because the understanding of being has changed since the Middle Ages, the kinds of things that strike us as appropriate and desirable have changed as well. "The earth now reveals itself as a coal mining district, the soil as a mineral deposit. The field that the peasant formerly cultivated and set in order appears differently than it did when to set in order still meant to take care of and maintain" (BW 320). Carolyn Merchant gives a similar picture of this transition: the earth was a living thing for the medievals, a mother who grew metals in her womb, thus placing limits of decency on how much we should excavate. Thinking of rock as dead matter, on the other hand, releases us from any kind of obligation to it, allowing us to do with it what we will (Merchant 1990).

Sartre's early phenomenological work, *The Transcendence of the Ego*, describes action the same way. When I'm late for work and running after the bus that's pulling away, there's no "I" present, as in "I am running after the bus." This only appears later, on reflection. In the moment, there is only "bus-to-be-caught," which pulls me along in its wake. On a more ethical plane, it isn't that I see my friend Peter and make a judgment that he needs help.

> I pity Peter, and I go to his assistance. For my consciousness only one thing exists at that moment: Peter-having-to-be-helped. This quality of "having-to-be-helped" lies in Peter. It acts on me like a force. . . . There is an objective world of things and of actions, done or to be done, and the actions come to adhere as qualities to the things which call for them. (Sartre 1993, 56)

It is the things that call out to me, while my actions mesh into them like jigsaw puzzle pieces. Levinas is another philosopher who, practicing a variant of phenomenology, finds moral values in the world. The face of the other, in particular, issues the command that I not harm it. Once again, this is not my judgment but what the face itself says if you give a careful description of what actually appears (Levinas 1996).

Further readings

Heidegger's clearest treatments of these topics appear in "The Age of the World Picture" in OBT and "Modern Science, Metaphysics, and Mathematics" (an excerpt from *What Is a Thing?* in BW). Julian Young gives a very helpful explanation of Heidegger's views on action in *Heidegger's Later Philosophy*, as does Michel Haar in *Heidegger and the Essence of Man*. Bret W. Davis has also written on the topic in *Heidegger and the Will: On the Way to Gelassenheit*. Michael E. Zimmerman's *Eclipse of the Self: The Development of Heidegger's Concept of Authenticity* shows how Heidegger changed his mind about the nature of action, while Reiner Schürmann's *Heidegger on Being and Acting: From Principles to Anarchy* and my *A Thing of This World* take up the idea of acting, especially in relation to thinking. A number of books address the connection between Heidegger and Derrida, such as Herman Rapaport's *Heidegger and Derrida: Reflections on Time and Language*, or Paola Marrati's *Genesis and Trace: Derrida Reading Husserl and Heidegger*.

10

Gratitude, Language, and Art

In response to the complaint that philosophy is useless, Heidegger once responded, "even if *we* can't do anything with it, may not philosophy in the end do something *with us*?" (IM 13). Doing something with philosophy would be a form of technology in Heidegger's sense: treating it as *Bestand*, as a resource to be used in order to get what we want. True philosophizing means opening ourselves up to ideas, letting them develop and following them where they go, the way a phenomenologist studies experience or a painter patiently stares at a bowl of fruit until she actually *sees* it. This is a process that will change us.

Gratitude

Heidegger repeatedly emphasizes that philosophy should be less concerned with conclusions than with the process of thinking; "ways, not works," is the motto he chose for his Collected Works (*Gesamtausgabe*). Whereas the sole value of methods lies in the results they achieve, the activity of philosophizing has intrinsic value. This is why he reformulates the very idea of questioning as something that doesn't end when we get an answer, but goes on indefinitely. "Questioning here is no mere *prelude* in order to display something that is without question, as though that had been achieved. Questioning is here beginning and end."[1] Although he certainly makes a number of discoveries in his thought, these are not ultimately the point. For a phenomenologist anything that shows us something is informative, even if it doesn't conform to standard forms of content. The name of one of his collections of essays, *Holzwege* (translated as *Off the Beaten Track*), means the paths cut in forests by wood-cutters that end abruptly in dead-ends that can also be clearings.

His early work has a purpose or conclusion of sorts: it shows us the way to authenticity. This is, as we saw in Chapter 4, a form of perfectionist ethics. *Being and Time* sifts out our genuine essential structure from the misleading surface understanding embodied in traditional philosophy and in our culture so that we can intentionally live in harmony with the kind of beings we really are. We can choose a fitting life once we know the contours we must fit it to.

His later ethics cannot maintain this line of thought because his understanding of our nature has undergone a profound change. Man, the word that replaces "Dasein," is *fundamentally* historical rather than just assimilating historical content into an ahistorical structure. There is no deep set of *existentialia* or ways of being that define all people at all times. Now culture goes all the way down and culture changes with history, which means that human nature changes. The dream of finding our one true essence, the existential analytic, is dead.

But this change does not necessarily prevent perfectionist ethics. Although there is no single ahistorical essence, it is essential to us to be historically alterable. This is a little like authenticity in that it is a kind of meta-perfectionist ethics: no particular content is inherently natural or right for us, but this fact itself is inherently right. Each new epoch brings with it its own way of thinking that replaces the previous one and is, for its time, the right way to think. Each is true in Heidegger's sense of the word: each unconceals a world.

> This foundation happened in the West for the first time in Greece. . . . The realm of beings thus opened up was then transformed into a being in the sense of God's creation. This happened in the Middle Ages. This kind of being was again transformed at the beginning and during the course of the modern age. Beings became objects that could be controlled and penetrated by calculation. At each time a new and essential world irrupted. . . . At each time there happened unconcealment of beings. (BW 201)

What remains constant across history is change, historicity itself. This teaches us something about thought: "the thinking that thinks into the truth of Being is, as thinking, historical."[2]

Each epoch is a distinctive clearing with its own definition of beingness that determines how beings are for that time. In my numbering system, no. 1 (individual beings) and no. 2 (beingness) transform with the changing of the times. But what about no. 3, being itself, the simple fact of beings manifesting themselves to us at all, in any form whatsoever? In order for (no. 1) beings to appear to us with any form of (no. 2) beingness whatsoever, they manifestly must (no. 3) appear to us. No matter what changes, beings always have to appear to us for us to know and say anything about them. Thus the clearing is the ultimate always already: it must be in place for anything else to occur.

Our task is to be open to it. "Appropriating has the peculiar property of bringing man into his own as the being who perceives Being" (TB 23). Heidegger has retained from the early work the idea that we are the clearing, the place where beings emerge into the light.[3] It is within our awareness that beings are unconcealed. Initially, this takes place within a Kantian framework that attributes the clearing to us. It is because we care what happens to us that we project goals and roles by whose reflected light we see past inheritances and present opportunities. Our activity projects or opens up the space within which things can be seen and used, and our stance can cause a change-over in the mode of being of individual entities.

In the later work the emphasis shifts from our creation of the clearing to our reception of it. "How could man comport himself to beings – that is, experience beings as being – if the relationship to Being were not granted him?"[4] The central paradox of technology is the idea, expressed by Descartes, that we can formulate our own way of thinking under our own power and according to the dictates we choose, unimpinged upon by anything unchosen. As discussed in Chapter 9, for Descartes even to be able to think of this possibility he must already be thinking in technological ways, that is, seeking to transform materials into the right form to accomplish what we want. He could not have chosen this way of seeing things on pain of infinite regress.

We think, but only along the currents that originate with being. We could not have made ourselves thinking beings – we would have had to be able to perceive whatever resources and tools were needed and found the goal possible and attractive in order to do so, which would mean that we were already thinking – nor could we have made our particular way of thinking. All of this is "given" to us, a term Heidegger plays with. Before we can be

given anything specific we must be given the capacity to receive
the given, which is how he defines thought. "We receive many
gifts, of many kinds. But the highest and really most lasting gift
given to us is always our essential nature, with which we are gifted
in such a way that we are what we are only through it. . . . But the
thing given to us, in the sense of this dowry, is thinking."[5] Thus the
double meaning of the title of this book: when we think, we can
only think "of" or about being but in doing so, we are also thinking
the thoughts "of" as in belonging to or coming from being. We are
the organ by which the universe thinks its thoughts.
    There is a fundamental, inescapable interrelationship between
being and man, one that Heidegger insists on repeatedly throughout the later work.

Man *is* essentially this relationship of responding to Being, and he
is only this. . . . And Being? Let us think of Being according to its
original meaning, as presence. Being is present to man neither inci-
dentally nor only on rare occasions. Being is present and abides only
as it concerns man through the claim it makes on him. For it is man,
open towards Being, who alone lets Being arrive as presence. Such
becoming present needs the openness of a clearing, and by this need
remains appropriated to human being. This does not at all mean that
Being is posited first and only by man. . . . Man and Being are appropriated to each other. They belong to each other.[6]

Man and being are not two distinct entities or separable phases in
a process but rather flip sides of a single coin, different aspects of
an "event." Being is appearing and man is the appeared-to. Modi-
fying his earlier term, we can say that man and being are in-each-
case-mutual. Our seeing and thinking about the world in a sense
echoes the world's manifesting itself to us, in that we reveal being's
self-revelation. Whereas being presences beings, we can bring
being itself to presence by thinking it. That is why our "letting
beings be, is the fulfillment and consummation of the essence of
truth in the sense of the disclosure of beings."[7]
    Thus we *have* found an essence of man, the one feature that
continues throughout all historical changes: we are the clearing of
being, we are the circle of light in this dark universe. The epochs
of metaphysics cannot change this because for there to be metaphysics at all, there must be a clearing. Heidegger believes that he
has found the deepest condition of the possibility of experience
possible, beating Kant at his own game. Beings in their various
ways of being are the sets and characters that have their exits and
entrances, but the clearing is all the stage.

This is essential to the kinds of beings that we are; indeed, it is our essence as he says many times in the later works. There is no way for us not to be in the clearing, since in order to do or think or say anything we must have some awareness of the subject matter. From birth to death, from the moment you get up in the morning to the moment you fall asleep at night, and often some time in between, you are aware of something in some way; this is Heidegger's later appropriation of phenomenology's central idea of intentionality, the idea that all consciousness is consciousness of something. But it is also one of the basic laws of phenomenology that the features that are most pervasive in our experience are the hardest ones for us to become explicitly aware of – the inconspicuousness of the ubiquitous. This is why metaphysicians' ability to capture their epoch's sense of beingness, found in all phenomena of an age, is so impressive and valuable. This state of hiddenness in plain sight is a magnitude higher for the fact of awareness. Although we are always already within the clearing, i.e. in contact with beings, we take it for granted, ignore it in concentrating on the busyness of everyday life.

Heidegger wants to illuminate this light for us. "The clearing is the open region for everything that becomes present and absent. It is necessary for thinking to become explicitly aware of the matter here called clearing" (BW 442). While this does teach us a deeper understanding of our selves and our thinking, the ultimate reason is ethical – not in the sense of giving us rules to obey but in the sense of laying out the right kind of life. We should take up this fact of awareness in order to treasure and celebrate it. This is what he means when he calls us the shepherd or guard or preserver of being.

> The granting that sends one way or another into revealing is as such the saving power. For the saving power lets man see and enter into the highest dignity of his essence. This dignity lies in keeping watch over the unconcealment – and with it, from the first, the concealment – of all essential unfolding on this earth . . . Everything, then, depends upon this: that we ponder this rising and that, recollecting, we watch over it.[8]

We did not create it nor can we control it, but we do have the ability to dim it down or light it up. Paying attention to being is like blowing on a glowing ember, coaxing it into life, helping it expand into a full-fledged fire, an experience phenomenologists are familiar with. Our initial awareness of things is thin and diluted, taking hold of things by the most superficial handles. Here is an apple. I've known what apples are since a drawing adorned my kindergarten walls as an "A" word. Having that flash card knowledge – apples are round and red and you eat them – allows me to, in effect, ignore *this* apple in front of me. I already know what it's like so I have no need to examine it with any care.

But if I do look at it, *really* look at it, "staying with things" (353) as Heidegger says, it starts changing under my gaze. It unfolds new depths, layers, and aspects I passed by when I put it in my lunchbox. Now I see that its color is far from the simple red no. 5 that I, in essence, projected onto it, but is actually a complex array of colors, with inflections of green and yellow and shades I don't even have a name for, along with tiny dots and stretches of color like those in a sunset. How much it reveals depends largely on the care and patience with which I attend to it. It's the difference between gulping down a cold beer after mowing the lawn and a connoisseur swirling a mouthful of wine, detecting and sorting out half a dozen different tastes. Doing the latter is to celebrate having taste buds, truly appreciating the fact that we have this particular access to beings by using it to its fullest. A wine-taster is, in the terms of perfectionist ethics, tasting with excellence. She has developed this ability and uses it with great relish, achieving sensations and pleasures of a kind that I, wholly ignorant in such matters, never can.

Now, this is not an incitement to full-blown hedonism. The point isn't to get as much pleasure as possible but to excel in performing what Aristotle called our *ergon* or "distinctive function," that is, what makes us us and distinct from everything else. For Heidegger, it is clear what this is: "of all beings, only the human being, called upon by the voice of being, experiences the wonder of all wonders: *that* beings are."[9] We are the revealers of otherwise concealed beings and we ought to do this excellently. In this way, Heidegger still holds to the perfectionist motto, quoted in *Being and Time*, to become who we are.[10] We are always already the clearing but we rarely take ownership of it, truly making it our own. In terms from the early work, we can project this fact that we've been thrown into by becoming aware of it, celebrating it, and using it to the fullest extent. In an ontological reading of the US Army's motto, we should *be* all we can be.

This attitude instills a deep sense of gratitude, of thankfulness at this astonishing opportunity we've all been given. Usually when we're grateful, it is *to* the agent who brought about the boon, but thinking of being as *a* being commits the mistake Heidegger calls onto-theology. Just because there's no one to be grateful to, however, doesn't mean that we can't be grateful for the gift. In fact, Heidegger argues that the lack of an agent performing this favor actually heightens our sense of awe that it has happened. An agent responsible for the event clogs the arteries of gratitude: we can be appreciative of its actions, but its nature would explain their conferring of the favor. Platonic Ideas are intrinsically intelligible and, in the neo-Platonic reconstruction, naturally emanate lesser versions of themselves; God's goodness leads Him to create us. Oddly, the fact that these consequences follow from an agent makes it easier to take them for granted. A process just occurring, on the other hand, with no possible explanation, lets us be astounded that it has happened. Atheists sometimes make the similar argument that highly organized life emerging from an uncontrolled, unwatched-over process is far more awesome than a God making humans in His image. Note, however, that attributing it to external agents, as ancient Greece and the Middle Ages do, still allows far more gratitude than when we take credit for it, as modernity does.

Heidegger plays with the German expression for "there is:" "es gibt." Literally, this means "it gives" the way the English phrase "there is" literally refers to a spatial location. Heidegger seizes upon this as capturing what happens: being is a given in that it resists all explanation and must precede all else. Furthermore, it is a gift, a great boon to us. Being given the ability to think, we ought to use it as much and as fully as possible. In a word-play that survives translation, he connects thinking ("denken") with thanking ("danken") so that this activity is the "thanks that alone pays homage to the grace that being has bestowed upon the human essence in thinking" (PM 236). We all think in the sense of being aware of beings around us and having opinions about them, but few of us think about this thinking, or try to raise it to its highest forms. Few of us strive to think with excellence. Primarily, it has been philosophers who have guarded thought, preserving the spark across generations, occasionally blowing it into a fire. This is what it is to not take the ability to think for granted.

Language

Although Heidegger talks a great deal about language, his precise views on it can be rather difficult to pin down. There's no question that language is an important way in which beings appear to us;

the question is just *how* important it is to this process. In the early work, it's fairly clear that language is secondary to our practical engagement with the world. We understand a hammer by using it appropriately without any kind of internal or expressed verbalization necessary. While Heidegger says little about the body – a gap Merleau-Ponty tries to fill – you could say that it is our hand or arm that understands the hammer rather than our head or our tongue. Speaking of it comes afterwards and presupposes this more immediate, initial grasp of it. When we articulate it, "the totality-of-significations of intelligibility is *put into words*. To significations, words accrue" (BT 204/161).

In his later work language becomes far more important, and it is here that scholars disagree. Some believe that the same basic view of language as a secondary and derivative form of presencing holds.[12] The more common reading, however, is that his later work makes language primary to experience: it is what principally does the unconcealing: "language alone brings beings as beings into the open for the first time" (BW 198). Language, according to this interpretation, goes all the way down. There is no pre-linguistic level of experience that later gets articulated; from the first, we experience the world through our grammar and vocabulary. "The saying joins and pervades the open space of the clearing."[13]

This is a new phase in his attack on the naivety that thinks beings are just there, lying around for our inspection. Heidegger's Kantian question is always about the conditions of possibility that allow us to become aware of beings at all, as well as in this specific manner or, in his terms, their coming out of concealment into the clearing with a specific form of beingness. The later work makes language an essential part of this process rather than just attaching words like labels to an already opened world and set of entities arrayed before us. "The word, the name, sets the self-opening beings out of the immediate, overwhelming assault, back into their Being, and preserves them in this openness, delimitation, and constancy. Naming does not come afterward, providing a being that is already otherwise revealed with a designation and a token called a word."[14] Our world is organized at least partially because it comes linguistically structured, just as Kant said that we have orderly experience because our transcendental faculties order phenomena in space, time, causality, etc. and *Being and Time* had Dasein's activities projecting the world's equipmental lines of longitude and latitude. This is Heidegger's version of the old definition of humans as the *zoon logon*, or animal that speaks/thinks (both meanings of "*logos*"). "To be human means to be a sayer. . . . Even if we had a thousand eyes and a thousand ears, a thousand hands and many other senses and organs, if our essence did not stand within the power of language, then all beings would remain closed off to us" (IM 86). Since being only is if we reveal it and this revelation takes place via language, by the Law of Transcendental Transitivity this amounts to saying that being is itself linguistic, which is what I take his famous statement "language is the house of being" (BW 217) to mean.

Saying, he likes to say, is a showing, a word-play between the similar sounding "*sagen*" and "*zeigen*." This verbal showing or pointing can happen in relatively superficial ways. Telling you about my dog George, for example, creates a worm-hole clearing so to speak, allowing him to be present to you even though you're not in his presence nor have you ever seen him. Or I can direct your attention to something you had not seen or weren't paying attention to, the picture on the wall behind you, say, or a specific aspect of something we're looking at, or your shoes which had been there inconspicuously.

At a deeper level language sets up a taxonomy of the world, what Husserl calls ontological regions, that is, the different kinds of beings that are. *Being and Time* presented three ontological regions as different modes of being that beings can be, arguing there that our ability to interact appropriately with these entities rests on our (usually pre-ontological) understanding of their ways of being. Now he has transferred these understandings to language. Our language lays out – the more literal translation of "*auslegen*" or "interpret" – the lie of the metaphysical land, the various kinds of things there are. "Language speaks by pointing, reaching out to every region of presencing, letting what is present in each case appear in such regions or vanish from them. Accordingly, we listen to language in such a way that we let it tell us its saying" (BW 411). In this way, our grammar and vocabulary structure how we experience the world and all of our attempts to think and talk about it are guided by this ontological map. "Strictly, it is language that speaks. Man first speaks when, and only when, he responds to language by listening to its appeal" (PLT 216).

This also means that as language changes, so does being. Translations from one language into another never perfectly preserve the original meaning but transform it into a significance the new language can accommodate; every translation is an interpretation. Heidegger sometimes points to the translation of Greek into Latin as central to the epochal change from ancient to medieval.[15] In conversation with a Japanese philosopher, he says that "Eastasian man" lives in "an entirely different house" of being than Europeans, making "a dialogue from house to house . . . nearly impossible" (OWL 5). Here, Heidegger strongly disagrees with philosophers like Donald Davidson who argue that the ability to translate is necessary to the very concept of language, which would make the idea of an untranslatable meaning incoherent.[16]

As an example of this idea which we might call a linguistic antirealism, let's return to wine-tasting. A mouthful of wine says very little to me, yielding only a blunted, mish-mash of flavors. Were I to become educated in such matters, I would be able to discern a number of different tastes, pinpointing distinct shades of flavors that are mysterious to me at present: woody, high-note, etc. Heidegger's claim is that an essential part of learning to discern these experiences is acquiring a distinct vocabulary; the expert wine-taster would not be able to have these sensations without learning a new set of terms. It's not that she first gets a set of nameless experiences and then attaches labels to them, but rather that the very ability to discern them only comes with learning new names. The two processes of experience and speech are not sequential but mutually reinforcing and mutually illuminating. As Wittgenstein, also suspicious of pre-linguistic experience, puts it, "light dawns gradually over the whole" (Wittgenstein 1969, ¶141).

Language is an important part of beings coming into unconcealment, that is, into our awareness, but this can be done well or poorly depending on how fully and vividly it lights things up. Just as action in *Being and Time* had a tendency to fall into inauthentic automatism as lived by the they, so speaking succumbs to the gravitational pull of clichés and thoughtless talk. "It is as though man had to make an effort to live properly with language. It is as though such a dwelling were especially prone to succumb to the danger of commonness. The place of language properly inhabited, and of its habitual words, is usurped by common terms" (WCT 119). We use words so much that they lose their vibrancy, substituting for experience rather than enabling or heightening it. This allows us to talk of things without explicit awareness, dimming down the clearing and thus reducing being, similar to *Being and Time*'s idle talk. "In the word, in language, things first come to be and are. For this reason, too, the misuse of language in mere idle talk, in slogans and phrases, destroys our genuine relation to things" (IM 15).

The opposite of this worn-down thoughtless passing of words is poetry which, given the centrality of language, is the quintessential art form for Heidegger. Most of us allow the words we use to become inconspicuous, just like any other tool. When I ask my kids to pass the salt I give minimal attention to the salt and even less to the sound I form with my mouth. Poets on the other hand are alive to language; they remain awake in their speaking. This allows them to forge new words or use words in innovative ways, breathing life back into worn-away terms. These new connotations inevitably harden into denotations themselves; metaphors that, once fresh and alive, become stale, literal meaning. This is why Heidegger says that "everyday language is a forgotten and therefore used-up poem, from which there hardly resounds a call any longer" (PLT 208). The poet forges the paths that the rest of us tamp down and eventually lay asphalt over.

Art

So how should we speak? If everyday language is a dead poem, how do we breathe life back into it? How, more generally, should we light up the clearing if we are to clear excellently?

Heidegger's answer lies in an ingenious development of ideas from his early work. Recall that tools fade into inconspicuousness when they're functioning properly: the hammer "withdraws" from attention as long as everything is running smoothly. It's only when something goes wrong that the world "is lit up" (BT 105/75). This inconspicuousness which seemed fairly innocent in *Being and Time,* takes on sinister overtones in the later work as the forgetfulness of being. Unconcealment itself is what remains most concealed in its very act of unconcealing beings since we take this wondrous event for granted and pay it no mind.

He repeats this analysis of tools in his major statement on art, "The Origin of the Work of Art:" equipment and the material it's made of "[disappear] into usefulness."[17] While the wearer of a pair of shoes must understand its mode of being just to be able to wear them, "she knows all this without noticing or reflecting" (BW 160), i.e., pre-ontologically. This is natural since a tool that called attention to itself would be a faulty tool. But there is another kind of being which did not appear in *Being and Time* (at least not in this form) whose function is precisely to show and make conspicuous artworks. A good work of art, like a good phenomenological description, allows us to see our experience as we actually experience it without letting it sink into inconspicuousness, the way it does in the moment of having it, or distorting it, the way most theoretical reconstructions do afterwards. An artwork shows us (no. 1) a being in its (no. 2) beingness far more vividly and truly than normal activity (when it's inconspicuous) or disengaged accounts (which depict it with a different kind of being): "the equipmentality of equipment first expressly comes to the fore through the work and only in the work" (BW 161). Such unconcealment is why Heidegger concludes that "the essence of art would then be this: the truth of beings setting itself to work" (BW 162). Truth is beauty and beauty truth, not in the sense of accurate representation but in the sense of unconcealing what normally remains concealed, such as inconspicuous tools.

This revelation reaches its apex with no. 3 being itself, which is what Heidegger's later work is always moving towards. An artwork is a mini-clearing; it is the revelation of a being in its beingness. This is obvious when it comes to representational art, but it applies to non-representational art as well. These works show what he calls a world: a culture's general sense of how things work, what is noble and what base, how to live one's life. A Greek temple embodies the Greek worldview (a word Heidegger disliked, but that seems to me to capture what he's talking about) as much as a Jackson Pollock expresses the twentieth-century outlook. The former shows an orderly world, infused with values and meaning – a holistic significance Heidegger calls the presence of a god – whereas the latter tells of the fleeing of the gods, of the lack of life-sustaining narratives or a consensus on what makes a good life along with a celebration of freedom and dynamism and the wild fertility of chaos.

A representational tool such as a TV or photograph, as a piece of equipment, withdraws. It is not working correctly if I become aware of the screen or the piece of paper rather than looking through them as "magic windows" to what is depicted. Artworks, however, are not equipment. Their *proper* functioning consists in drawing attention to the medium instead of withdrawing. Think of the post-Impressionists who never let you forget that you're looking at a canvas covered with paint. Van Gogh, another of Heidegger's examples, makes each separate brush-stroke stand out *as* a brush-stroke.

Equipment takes into its service that of which it consists: the matter. In fabricating equipment – e.g., an ax – stone is used, and used up.

It disappears into usefulness. The material is all the better and more suitable the less it resists vanishing in the equipmental being of the equipment. By contrast the temple-work, in setting up a world, does not cause the material to disappear, but rather causes it to come forth for the very first time and to come into the open region of the work's world. The rock comes to bear and rest and so first becomes rock; metals come to glitter and shimmer, colors to glow, tones to sing, the word to say. (BW 171)

Artworks bring these materials – what Heidegger calls "earth" – into prominence instead of letting them fade into inconspicuousness. Representing something while simultaneously keeping the materials used from vanishing into the represented scene, artworks create a built-in tension. We alternate between looking *through* the painting to the scene depicted and looking *at* the paint used to depict it in a Gestalt switch Heidegger calls the strife between earth and world. The painting's resistance to inconspicuousness keeps the fact of its unconcealment (no. 3 being itself) explicit. Van Gogh's brush-strokes foreground the paintedness of the painting, the fact that someone used these materials to represent something, the fact that someone made this thing.

In contrast to all other modes of production, the work is distinguished by being created so that its createdness is part of the created work. . . . In the work, createdness is expressly created into the created being, so that it stands out from it. . . . The simple *factum est* is to be held forth into the open region by the work: namely this, that unconcealment of a being has happened here . . . or, that such a work *is* at all rather than is not . . . To be sure, "that" it is made is a property also of all equipment that is available and in use. But this "that" does not become prominent in the equipment; it disappears in usefulness. The more handy a piece of equipment is, the more inconspicuous it remains that, for example, this particular hammer is. . . . In general, of everything present to us, we can note that it *is*; but this also, if it is noted at all, is noted only soon to fall into oblivion. . . . In a work, by contrast, this fact, that it *is* as a work, is just what is unusual. (BW 189–90)

An artwork continually lives its birth, hovering over its non-existence. Its createdness reminds us of the fact that at one point it was not and that it might very well not have been, which makes us sharply aware of the fact that it is. In this way, artworks are like *a-lētheia* – they have a privative reference to non-being built into them.

Not only do they perspicuously show ways of being that are inconspicuous during use, not only does their own existence stand out, but the nature of artworks as clearings makes the clearing itself conspicuous. Artworks "do not simply make manifest what these isolated beings as such are . . . rather, they make unconcealment as such happen in regard to beings as a whole" (BW 181). A functioning representational tool like a TV becomes transparent, showing us only the content without showing us the showing itself; it's only when it malfunctions that we become aware of the fact that we're looking at miniature things on a screen. In artworks, on the other hand, earth is continuously striving with world; the inherently non-representational materials – globs of paint, blocks of stone – are constantly fighting with the scene being shown. As we vary our distance from and focus on a Van Gogh painting, it changes from thick brush-strokes on canvas to undulating trees in a vibrant landscape, and back again. The *factum est* of the clearing, the fact that beings are coming into unconcealment here, never recedes into the background because it is constantly being pulled back into its non-clearing aspect, which also comes into prominence in a way never seen before. "This setting forth of the earth is achieved by the work as it sets itself back into the earth. . . . The painter also uses pigment, but in such a way that color is not used up but rather only now comes to shine forth" (BW 173). The scene emerges from the materials with paint still dripping from it, so to speak.

We will see in Chapter 11 that technology leads to nihilism. We try to be entirely autonomous, determining our own values and organizing the world to be maximally compliant with our needs and desires, but this leads to an impoverished world of valueless values. There must be meaning and worth outside of ourselves for it to have true meaning and worth. Heidegger lists a number of ways to see this, and art is one of the best. While I have been focusing on representational art as an easier way to get a handle on the idea of works as mini-clearings, Heidegger applies his analysis to non-representational art as well. His example in the essay is a Greek temple that "in its standing there, first gives to things their look and to men their outlook on themselves" (BW 168). The temple manifests the Greek sense of what is important and what things mean, that is, their epoch's understanding of being. "This open relational context" (BW 167) provides "a guiding measure, a form in which what is essential gives guidance" (BW 169). Just as artworks take up non-representational materials and imbue them with a pictorial sense, so the temple takes up the "raw materials" of a human life – biological facts such as birth, aging, mating, eating, dying – and turns them into "paths and relations in which birth and death, disaster and blessing, victory and disgrace, endurance and decline acquire the shape of destiny for human being" (BW 167). The ceremonies carried out within the temple turn biological processes into cultural ones that unite a people with their community, with their ancestors, and with their god. This meaningfulness itself is what Heidegger means by "god," rather than a transcendent supernatural entity.

Artworks concentrate and embody a culture's understanding of being and its sense of good and bad, reminding us of the qualities that pervade our lives and thereby leading us out of nihilism. We receive "from Being itself the assignment of those directives that must become law and rule for man. . . . Only such dispatching is capable of supporting and obligating. Otherwise all law remains merely something fabricated by human reason."[18] Heidegger describes nihilism as a sense of homelessness, of not being at home in this world. In his early work, this existential *Unheimlichkeit* is endemic to the human condition: anxiety shows us that there is no such thing as a role "which belongs to existence" (BT 393/343), that is, that is written into our nature as our true occupation such as knowing the Forms or loving God. Grasping this, "one is liberated in such a way that for the first time one can authentically understand and choose among the factical possibilities lying ahead" and, in tune with modern autonomy, Dasein grasps "the possibility of taking over from itself its ownmost Being, and doing so of its own accord" (BT 308/263–4). Anxiety, literally not-being-at-home ("*Unheimlichkeit*"), cuts the claims that our society and tradition make upon us so that we can deliberately choose the roles we want to take up. Thus, "resoluteness constitutes the *loyalty* of existence to its own Self. As resoluteness which is ready for *anxiety*, this loyalty is at the same time a possible way of revering the sole authority which a free existing can have" (BT 443/391). We have been thrown into this world, abandoned, and it is up to us to furnish it.

In the later work, this existential homelessness becomes a contemporary rather than essential condition. We live in a destitute age from which the god has fled, but that itself can become the topic of our art. This very lack can replace what was formerly there, providing us with a sense of shared communal values. Indeed, much of existential philosophy and modernist art can be seen as doing just this (just think of Kafka or Beckett). Here, as with

technology, an adequate grasp of the problem turns into a kind of solution. We discover that these values cannot be determined by us since we must find them attractive and it is this given disposition that allows these notions to persuade and guide us. "Thus the dislocation of man back into his ground has to be carried out in the first place by those few, solitary, and uncanny ones, who in various ways as poets, thinkers, as builders and artists, as doers and actors, ground and shelter the truth of Being in beings through the transformation of beings" (BQ 181).

Furthermore, artistic creation is a paradigm of Heidegger's new conception of action. The Romantic notion of the artist as pure spontaneous creator is as faulty as the technological picture of the maker entirely in charge or the modern radically autonomous subject. Art is, essentially, inspiration: something enters the artist, gives them ideas, images, melodies, etc. "All creation, because it is such a drawing-up, is a drawing, as of water from a spring. Modern subjectivism, to be sure, immediately misinterprets creation, taking it as the sovereign subject's performance of genius" (BW 200). We all listen to language in speaking, but the poet listens the best, with the most patience, attention, and devotion. "The more poetic a poet is . . . the greater is the purity in which he submits what he says to an ever more painstaking listening" (PLT 216). The great artists do not control but submit, letting the marble guide their hammer to free what "wants" to be let out as Michelangelo did. Viewers must similarly submit, which lets the work "tell" them what it is, showing more and more detail and meaning. Since artworks are mini-clearings, this stance instantiates the proper way we should approach being itself. "Art must be measured as a way of letting truth come into being in these beings, which, as works, enchantingly transport man into the intimacy of Being while imposing on him the luminosity of the unconcealed and disposing him and determining him to be the custodian of the truth of Being" (BQ 164). Beauty is not just truth but goodness as well, in an interesting recasting of a doctrine called the unity of the transcendentals, found in the work of Duns Scotus, the subject of one of Heidegger's dissertations.

Further readings

"The Origin of the Work of Art" is the indispensable work for Heidegger's thoughts on art, although he also deals with the subject extensively, and relatively accessibly, in his lectures on Nietzsche. *What Calls for Thinking* represents his most sustained analysis of the nature of thought, although the topic runs throughout most of his works.

Many scholars discuss Heidegger's views on art. See Michel Haar's *The Song of the Earth: Heidegger and the Grounds of Being*, Julian Young's *Heidegger's Philosophy of Art*, as well as essays in Michael E. Zimmerman's *Heidegger's Confrontation with Modernity: Technology, Politics, and Art*; Karsten Harries and Christoph Jamme's *Martin Heidegger: Politics, Art, and Technology*; and Otto Pöggeler's *The Paths of Heidegger's Life and Thought*. For language, as well as history, see Mark Wrathall's *Heidegger and Unconcealment: Truth, Language, and History*.

11

Technology, Nietzsche, and Nihilism

For Heidegger, technology defines our age. Not because we are surrounded by electronic devices – that would remain at the ontic level of beings. Heidegger always wants to go beneath the surface level of particular things and actions to what makes them possible, seeking what leads us to act like this or to see the world as made up of these kinds of things. Explaining technology by appealing to science doesn't help either, but just pushes the question back a step: why do we have the kind of science that produces technology? Rather than tracing the development of particular forms of technology, we must ask why we find making such mechanisms such an obvious thing to do, why our default reaction to problems is to build devices to fix them. And the answer to this, of course, is our understanding of being.

Technology

Heidegger explains our technological orientation in terms of how beings appear to us, which he calls the "essence" of technology as opposed to particular devices. We today experience things in two primary ways: as problems and resources. The former means that we notice things when they resist us, when they interfere with our getting what we want like a tool becoming conspicuous when it breaks down. And we generally feel that this kind of obstruction shouldn't happen. We naturally see such obstacles as problems to-be-solved so that we can reenter the smooth, friction-less circuit of successful action.

This attitude extends modernity's emphasis on autonomy, as discussed in Chapter 9: it is up to us to make the world a more hospitable place, one more amenable to our desires. This fundamental attitude, which seems so obvious to us, clashes with the medieval understanding, for example, which sees the world as formed the way God deems it right, thus turning attempts to improve it into acts of hubris and rebellion. Suffering is there to temper the soul, to humble the flesh and bring down pride, making us God-fearing and modest enough to enter a heaven built for the meek. The emphasis then was on knowing our place rather than striving to rise above it by mastering the laws of nature. The moderns threw off these views as unfortunate restrictions that hampered our ability to improve our condition. Descartes announced the modern approach by proposing to use science to make ourselves "lords and masters of nature" (PWD I: 42–3).

Oriented towards the goal of fixing problems, we see the rest of reality as resources of varying usefulness in solving them. Heidegger calls our present understanding of being "Bestand," translated as "standing-reserve," "stockpile," or "resources." The idea is that things are just standing around, on reserve, waiting to be used by us. Trees are there to be turned into lumber, rivers are rushes of not-yet-bottled-water or not-yet-converted electricity. Of course, resources present problems of their own to the degree that they must be converted into more convenient forms to be used. The water in the river is drinkable, but I have to walk all the way there to retrieve it from the flowing stream. Much better to have an appropriately portioned amount in a handy bottle ready to be drunk standing there in my refrigerator, awaiting my thirst. Although the water and the act of drinking are basically the same whether drawn directly from the river or drunk from a plastic bottle, in the first version I have to conform to the world whereas in the second the world has been bent to my desires: I just reach out and grab what I want. The next step will be continuous IV drips so I won't even have to walk to the fridge. On Heidegger's view, technology obeys an intrinsic logic whereby materials are progressively transformed into increasingly useful and easily accessed forms.

Think of one of the signature pieces of twentieth-century technology: television. It brings the world to me, relieving me of the need to leave my house for engagement, information, and

entertainment. It takes over the burden of turning pages or imagin-
ing things, even of choosing what to look at by having the camera
do the focusing for me. Initially, however, the viewer still had to
conform to its schedule: one had to be in front of the TV at a certain
time in order to watch what were called "appointment shows." The
trend ever since – following a virtually inevitable development
on Heidegger's understanding of technology – has been to give
the viewer ever more power to mold TV's schedule around her
own. First came VCRs that could record shows, albeit through
cumbersome programming. Then seasons of shows were sold on
tape or DVD, allowing one to watch whenever one wanted, while
DVRs made programming a snap. Now the internet lets us watch
almost anything we want whenever we want to. Even the restric-
tion of being tied to a specific location is lifting as viewing gets
transferred to mobile devices that allow us to watch wherever we
want to as well. If Heidegger's analysis is right, he has given us
a formula to make fortunes: find some kink or friction in the use
or consumption of something popular and figure out a way to
straighten that kink (granted, this is the hard part). Anything that
makes acquisition and consumption easier and smoother will sell
like hot cakes.

Heidegger defines the essence of technology as "a way of revealing" (BW 318), which connects with his definition of truth as
unconcealment, rather than the set of electronic devices we use.
His point is that the making of contraptions – what we usually
think of as technology – only occurs if we are motivated to do so,
spurred by seeing inconveniences as in need of improvement.
While this is second nature to us, this way of seeing the world and
reacting to it is not necessary or universal, a fact we discover by
studying other ways of understanding being. "What is 'natural' is
not 'natural' at all, here meaning self-evident for any given ever-
existing man. The 'natural' is always historical" (WT 39). For the
medievals, the world called for forbearance, not ingenuity; it valued
the fear of God over the desires of the masses. Even today citizens
of other countries often scratch their heads at the way Americans
invent fixes for problems that never struck them as particularly
problematic.

The flip side of seeing problems in need of solutions is that the
rest of the world reveals itself to us as potential solutions for problems, materials at the disposal of our projects. Action, for Heidegger,
is always the reaction to the way something reveals itself, the way
his early work argued that all interactions with beings presuppose

an understanding of their mode of being. A sacred wood, for example, forbids being turned into toilet paper, but inefficiently stored wood product can and even should be pulped for whatever we need. Once again we see the importance of Descartes' metaphysics. His definition of all physical objects as dead, inert matter makes the world into the kind of thing that can't place restrictions on what we do with it. I am obligated to steward a land entrusted to me by God, but I can do whatever I want with spatio-temporally located bits of raw stuff. Following the intrinsic logic of technology, this leads to treating everything as nothing more than resources for us to get what we want. "The world now appears as an object open to the attacks of calculative thought, attacks that nothing is believed able any longer to resist. Nature becomes a gigantic gasoline station, an energy source for modern technology and industry" (DT 50).

The sense of which actions are sensible and which are beyond the pale emerges from our epoch's understanding of being. But Heidegger's analysis remains phenomenological, so he unpacks this understanding not on the cognitive level as a matter of subscribing to certain beliefs but at the far more basic level of seeing the world a certain way, just as our pre-ontological understanding of being resided in our interactions with beings in the early work. I don't exactly *believe* that as an American, I should not have to get up and walk to the TV to change the channel; that the TV must bend its cabled knee and do as I command so that I may become absorbed into a TV-self union where my slightest whim is instantly answered. Rather, any blockage in the process of changing channels simply appears as a nuisance, a wrinkle that should be ironed out the same way that chocolate ice cream radiates "to-be-eaten." With a remote control, a flick of the finger suffices; soon, that too will be effaced as too much work.[1]

Nietzsche

Heidegger spends a great deal of time reading and commenting on a wide variety of philosophers, but a few stand out as especially important: Plato, Aristotle, Kant, and Nietzsche. One reason for Nietzsche's prominence is that he closes off the entire history of metaphysics by ringing the final variation of the being-appearance dichotomy. As discussed in Chapter 8, Plato initiated metaphysics by prying apart the way things appear from the way they really are, and the history of philosophy for Heidegger consists in the various forms this distinction has taken – the different candidates philosophers have put into these slots. Nietzsche remains within metaphysics because he still subscribes to the division: he too is sifting out the real from the apparent, the true – despite all of his challenges to the very notion of truth – from the false. He completes this millennia-long project, however, and partially twists free of it by hitting on its final configuration: the complete reversal of Plato's version. For Nietzsche, it is the empirical and changing that is "really real," whereas the eternal is a wisp of conceptual smoke; when the truth is a lie, only lies can be true.[2]

Nietzsche's metaphysics makes him a transitional figure in Heidegger's telling, part Zarathustra foretelling the next phase and part *Übermensch* who enacts it. He engages in metaphysics by still sorting real from unreal, but ends it by the specific formulation he hits on. "Nietzsche's philosophy closes the ring that is formed by the very course of inquiry into being as such and as a whole" (N II: 200), but, "since all it does is turn metaphysics upside down, Nietzsche's countermovement against metaphysics remained embroiled in it and has no way out" (OBT 162). In short, "the true and the apparent worlds have exchanged their places and ranks and modes but in this exchange and inversion the precise *distinction* of a true and an apparent world is preserved" (N III: 124). In other words, by simply reversing the place of the real and the apparent, he still maintains the distinction and thus remains a metaphysician, albeit the final one. He does, however, open the door for the next great philosopher – who just happens to be Heidegger, as luck would have it – to think *post*-metaphysically by transcending the division entirely. This is what Heidegger calls "thinking," which can take place after "the end of philosophy," as the title of one of his late essays puts it.

Nietzsche is not only the last metaphysician; he is *the* philosopher of our era. We understand an epoch through its understanding of being, as we saw in Chapter 8, and our best access to this is always through that period's great metaphysicians. Now, as we saw in Chapter 9, these figures do not so much creatively come up with ideas on their own as capture the way the world appears to their culture as a whole. We today live in a technological world but this fact remains inconspicuous for most of us because it is ubiquitous. Nietzsche is the one who is so attuned to this fact that he is able to put it into words so that the rest of us can explicitly grasp the way we have already been living our lives, the way

phenomenology always works. Recall that the madman who
announces the death of God illuminates things with a lantern in
broad daylight (Nietzsche 1974, ¶125).

One of the most controversial features of Heidegger's reading
of Nietzsche – and there are a number – is his attempt to read him
systematically. Despite Nietzsche's own objections – "I mistrust all
systematizers. The will to a system is a lack of integrity" (Nietzsche
1954, 470) – Heidegger brings Nietzsche's main ideas into a coherent view grounded, as always, in an understanding of being. For
Nietzsche, being is will to power, a roiling chaos of forces spilling
into and pulling apart from each other, temporarily coagulating
into solid structures only to dissolve once more into new ones.

> And do you know what "the world" is to me? Shall I show it to you
> in my mirror? This world: a monster of energy . . . a play of forces
> and waves of forces . . . a sea of forces flowing and rushing together,
> eternally changing . . . as a becoming that knows no satiety, no
> disgust, no weariness: this, my *Dionysian* world of the eternally self-
> creating, the eternally self-destroying. . . . *This world is the will to
> power – and nothing besides!* And you yourselves are also this will to
> power – and nothing besides![3]

These forces continually struggle to impose themselves on each
other in contests that take many forms, with only the cruder ones
involving outright violence. Artistic creation and conceptual redefi-
nition are far more subtle, effective, and long-lasting ways of
sculpting chaos. Nietzsche ranks different psychological types of
people depending on how honestly they let their will flow out
unimpeded and how successfully they control the world. Strongest
is the *Übermensch* who grasps the world and herself as temporary
formations of will to power and joyfully takes up the task of
creation.

Heidegger points out that despite Nietzsche's provocative comments about the nature of truth, he assumes a fairly conventional
view of it when he praises some psychological types as correctly
understanding the nature of reality and themselves while others,
such as priests, dishonestly deny the way things are, misrepresent-
ing our natures by preaching virtues such as humility, meekness,
or charity that clash with how will to power actually operates and
obstruct its free flow. Heidegger's point is that Nietzsche can only
rank different types of ideas, actions, and people on the basis of
claims about how people ought to act, which is itself grounded in
views about their intrinsic constitution. "If there is no longer a

measuring and estimating with regard to something true, how is the world that arises from the 'action' of life still supposed to be branded and comprehended as 'semblance' at all?" (N III: 129). In other words, how can Nietzsche brand some as liars except by maintaining a truth they betray? This is how Heidegger teases metaphysical and epistemological views out of Nietzsche's ethical exhortations and condemnations, revealing a systematic philosophy that ironically explains his distrust of systems.

One of the more famous and important features of Nietzsche's thought is his proclamation that God is dead. This means that religion no longer occupies the central place in our lives that defines our place in the universe and the right way to live as it once did. Heidegger largely agrees with this analysis of the transition from medieval to modern times, as we saw in Chapter 8. This cosmic catastrophe leads to what Nietzsche calls "weak nihilism:" because Western civilization has tied our value and our values to some form of divinity for so long, anything that does not carry a deity's blessing – anything "human-all-too-human" – no longer seems weighty enough to anchor our lives. Rules must be handed down from on high if they are to command with authority; the will of the people is a paltry thing next to the laws written in stone by an omniscient and omnipotent God. But if God no longer commands our belief, then He cannot issue commands for our lives. He had anchored our lives, but now His death pulls down all the religiously sanctioned values with Him as He sinks away. Nietzsche predicted wars in the twentieth century the like of which had never been seen on Earth as cosmic despair dawned on humanity. This is nihilism, the loss of all values, and there is no going back.

We can move forward, however. We can, Nietzsche thinks, take back this power of creating new values from the divine sock puppet we gave it to so long ago, that we may wield it for ourselves, deliberately. This would be "strong nihilism" which allows the strong among us to become creators rather than followers. We can craft values more in tune with will to power and with the specific features of modern life, values that affirm life rather than denigrate it the way traditional philosophy and religion do. We can found a philosophy that makes the empirical changing world we live in the real one rather than a transcendent realm sucking out all truth and reality. Indeed, there are no restrictions on what we can do; this openness is what caused the problem but it also presents the chance for an entirely new way to live upon the earth. We, "we fearless ones," we "awesomely aweless" (Nietzsche 1974, 33) thinkers face a crisis that is also the opportunity of a lifetime, more – of a civilization, a race, a species.

> We philosophers and "free spirits" feel, when we hear the news that "the old god is dead," as if a new dawn shone on us. . . . At long last the horizon appears free to us again . . . at long last our ships may venture out again . . . the sea, *our* sea, lies open again; perhaps there has never yet been such an "open sea." (Nietzsche 1974, ¶343)

Creativity is once again possible, not in the service of a cruel and jealous God but for ourselves, creativity in that most difficult of media: (life.)

Nihilism

Now begins the most exciting and the most dangerous adventure the West has yet embarked upon: the attempt to grow up and live without a paternalistic deity telling us what to do, handing out gold stars of salvation and demerits of damnation. We sail out into waters not just uncharted but stripped of all orientation: the death of God "wipe[d] away the entire horizon . . . unchained this earth from its sun. . . . Is there still any up or down?" (Nietzsche 1974, ¶125). We lack not just maps but the magnetic poles that enable compasses to function at all. Where shall we get our good and evil if not from God or nature? What moral landmarks remain in this realm beyond good and evil? "If God . . . is dead . . . then there is nothing left which man can rely on and by which he can orient himself" (OBT 163).

Heidegger reads Nietzsche, as he does all philosophers, as following out the implications of a particular view of being. Nietzsche sees all of reality, including ourselves, as will to power and, in a version of perfectionist ethics, he derives values from this. The best person is the one who most fully actualizes their nature by embodying their own will to power, exercising it freely and successfully on their surroundings. This reaches its highest form not in enslaving or torturing those weaker – though Nietzsche does not condemn such actions *per se* – but in the making of new values. This is the greatest or most excellent kind of creation and the one that can benefit humanity the most. The values that have ruled the West so far conflict with the nature of life. They preach passivity, thus squelching the joy in activity; they teach humility and subservience, self-flagellation and guilt, with the overall result that "we are *neither as proud nor as happy* as we might be" (Nietzsche 1974, ¶301). Nietzsche constantly rails against pity because he himself suffers so much from it; his entire work is motivated by a heart-wrenching sorrow for humanity who, blocked from freely expressing aggression, directs it against themselves. "Oh this insane, pathetic beast – man! What ideas he has, what unnaturalness, what paroxysms of nonsense, what *bestiality of thought* erupts as soon as he is prevented just a little from being a *beast in deed!* . . . Too long, the earth has been a madhouse!" (Nietzsche 1967, I.23). Freed from the strictures of a sour God, we can now create anew. This has two benefits: the act of creation is itself one of the most intense pleasures in life given its affinity with the natural behavior of will to power, and we can now create values that affirm life and benefit us, provided that we understand what life is really like. "The sense for the real is the means of acquiring the power to shape things according to our wish. The joy in shaping and reshaping – a primeval joy!" (Nietzsche 1968, ¶495). Our orientation on this open sea comes from ourselves. We can remake the world so that it answers to our demands rather than the other way around; we can invent festivals to celebrate our lives rather than begging forgiveness from the bleeding, crucified God for being such wretched, unforgivable creatures.

This remaking of the world according to our desires is where Nietzsche's metaphysics meshes with technology. Technology is the concrete embodiment of will to power; it's where we physically restructure the world to meet our demands. Technology, broadly understood, is the natural tool of the *Übermensch* who refuses to settle for the world as it is, but reshapes it as he wishes it to be. "Nietzsche recognizes the historic moment in which man takes it on himself to assume dominion over the earth as a whole" (N II: 215). This happens as much in the forging of new values as in the bottling of water or the invention of new forms of energy or the founding of a nation.

Heidegger sees Nietzsche as bringing modern philosophy's emphasis on subjectivity and quest for autonomy to its culmination, as the death of God gives way to the birth of an independent humanity. We depend on no inheritance, whether it be from tradition, God, society, or nature. We will give ourselves the law through democratic government and humanistic ethics; we will secure our material comfort through science and technology, and our happiness by buying it (Heidegger doesn't talk about economics, but capitalism fits his picture nicely). This modern focus on each individual's right to acquire personal happiness is why popular revolutions swept across Europe in the eighteenth and nineteenth centuries and not in the eleventh and twelfth. A government of the people, by the people, and for the people only makes sense after a government of, by, and for God no longer appears self-evident.

Our desires become central in a way not allowed by previous epochs that lived in a world still redolent with intrinsic meaning and goals, a world laid out by God for a particular purpose. The death of God "disenchants" the world, leaving bare inert stuff or resources to be made more efficient for the only purposes that still exist: ours. Heidegger describes this as the oblivion or forgetfulness of being. The entire history of philosophy has been forgetting being more and more but the modern era represents the culmination of this tendency. "Beings *are*, yet they remain abandoned by Being and left to themselves, so as to be mere objects of our contrivance. All goals beyond men and peoples are gone) . . . What if the abandonment of beings by Being were the most hidden and most proper ground, and the essence, of what Nietzsche first recognized as 'nihilism?'" (BQ 159–60). This forgetfulness has the consequence that "one can no longer be struck by the miracle of beings: that they are" (BQ 169). We have an anthropocentric ontology in which beings are only real to the degree that they can be represented in such a way that we understand them and they aid us in our mastery of the world. Descartes determines mathematical properties to be the most real because they are most certain, most easily and reliably represented by our minds, and most useful to science; for Kant the mind structures things as they appear to us, while Hegel removes even that qualification. Finally Nietzsche gives us the power to control appearances consciously, to form new values deliberately. "Man fights for the position in which he can be that being who gives to every being the measure and draws up the guidelines" (OBT 71). Nothing tells us how things must be but ourselves and this power – according to Nietzsche – is what will enable us to overcome nihilism. The lack of values out there in the world allows us to make the values we want. *(should want)*

Heidegger believes that rather than saving us from nihilism, Nietzsche's solution actually intensifies it by denying us the resources we need to make a good life. We are to make the world over to satisfy our desires, so what do we desire? Ultimately, we want to fulfill our desires and to continue to do so. Heidegger thinks this project ends up collapsing on itself, the will willing only what it wills with no purposes higher than itself. It wills itself as sheer will because all specific values or goals that could guide our choices are extrinsic to it and hence cannot be accepted without compromising the integrity of the self-created self. All becomes instrumental means to acquiring ends which themselves dissolve into mere means for further ends. A fully autonomous being cannot accept *any* intrinsic or independently determined end or value, only those it explicitly wills. And it only wills that which contributes to getting what it wants. Everything becomes subservient to more and more control regardless of what or why you want to control it, which in the end makes all values valueless. All that is solid, as Marx wrote, melts into air.

Heidegger uses the word "value" to mean something that is only valuable because we value it, concluding that if things only have this kind of value, then nothing has genuine worth since all meaningfulness becomes arbitrary. We can have no reason to value any particular entities rather than others since nothing has intrinsic worth. "For it is precisely in the positing of new values from the will to power, by which and through which Nietzsche believes he will overcome nihilism, that nihilism proper first proclaims that there is nothing to Being itself, which has now become a value" (N IV: 203). We can see this in capitalism, for example. We want money to buy things but people get trapped in a feedback loop where they work harder and harder to make more and more money, to the point that their work deprives them of the opportunities to spend it or enjoy the things they can buy, an empty self-perpetuating circle slightly reminiscent of Nietzsche's eternal return of the same.

This deflation or cheapening of life is built into this Nietzsche's metaphysics for Heidegger. We devote ourselves to satisfying ourselves, but our desires have turned out to be less the great and noble goals of Beethoven and Goethe than the pedestrian and insipid ones of reality TV shows. Nietzsche foretold the *Übermensch* who would call down lightning to shake the very firmaments, but he got the "last man" who writes ad-copy and blinks. Happiness has become cheap and we are wallowing in it. "Creation, once the prerogative of the biblical God, has become the mark of human activity, whose creative work becomes in the end business transactions" (OBT 165). Throughout his career, Heidegger maintains an ambiguous attitude towards the mundane, as we saw in Part I. On the one hand, he celebrates it in contrast to its traditional denigration at the hands of philosophy; both phenomenology and existentialism are grounded in the concrete and specific, and his later works maintain this focus, adding some rather cheesy paeans to the peasant life-style. On the other hand, also in keeping with existentialism, there is a disdain for modern life with its newspapers and television, a distaste for media he inherited from Kierkegaard and a recoiling from the common in favor of the great he got from Nietzsche. Poets are the ones who truly speak whereas the rest of us just pass clichés back and forth, slowly wearing away words' gravitas. This tension is captured in the early idea of authenticity, which both is and isn't normal life.

Nietzsche's solution to nihilism is to put humanity in the place formerly occupied by God so that we now decree what shall be of worth. But this move reduces all worth to merely what we decree to be worthwhile. Recall Socrates' question to Euthyphro: is virtue good because the gods love it or do the gods love it because it is good? If its goodness is solely a result of their choosing it, then their choice cannot be called right or good; whatever they selected would have been good by fiat. Although "divine command theory" tries to explain goodness, it actually erases it, turning morality into divine whim, the gods' wills willing themselves. On the other hand, as "voluntarists" argue, simply recognizing an independent, preceding value is a rather modest job for omnipotent beings, one that we can surely take over for ourselves, making them superfluous. Furthermore, in a Judeo-Christian context, the question arises about the origin of these values – how could anything precede and bind God's decrees?

Nietzsche's thought is caught on the same dilemma: to the degree that the *Übermensch*'s decisions are purely willful with no imposition from anything external – to the degree that they fulfill the demands of autonomy – they ring empty and meaningless. On the other hand, to the degree that she responds to or recognizes inherent worth or meaningfulness, thus giving her choice validity, she compromises her own autonomy.

> Where beings have become objects of representation . . . a loss of being occurs. This loss – vaguely and uncertainly enough perceived – is correspondingly quickly made up for through the fact that we attribute to the object and the thus-interpreted being a value. . . . These become the general expression of the highest goals of creation devoted to the self-establishment of man as *subiectum*. . . . It is precisely "values" that are the powerless and threadbare mask of the objectification of beings, an objectification that has become flat and devoid of background. No one dies for mere values. (OBT 77, see also OBT 193)

Heidegger sees this problem at the heart of the very idea of autonomy and freedom; Nietzsche does not solve it, but it is to his credit that he exposes the problem. It becomes visible in his thought precisely because he brings the modern philosophy of subjectivity to its culmination. But Nietzsche also shows how modernity and technology end up eating themselves.

It is because he sums up the previous three centuries of the philosophy of subjectivity and brings the previous millennia of metaphysics to its completion that Nietzsche allows us to free ourselves from this long dead-end. "For as truly as he is the end, he is at the same time a transition" (BQ 169). In order to move on we need a new understanding of subjectivity, of being, and of action, since these are the elements that lead to the problems. Happily, we do not need to come up with a set of values ourselves; as Heidegger has always maintained, the world presents itself to us with meaning and worth. Ultimately, he thinks, we can't do anything but respond to being's solicitations that flood and permeate our every waking moment. Being has truly been generous in what it gives.

Further readings

The best texts for Heidegger's view of Nietzsche and, by extension, nihilism are "The Question Concerning Technology" in BW; the voluminous but surprisingly accessible lectures on Nietzsche; and "Nietzsche's Word: 'God Is Dead'" in OBT.

Charles Bambach addresses Heidegger's involvement with the Nazis and his views on the history of philosophy through his conversation with Nietzsche in *Heidegger's Roots: Nietzsche, National Socialism, and the Greeks*. The essays in David Allison's influential *The New Nietzsche* think about Nietzsche in ways that are influenced by both Heidegger and Derrida. A number of essays in James Risser's *Heidegger Towards the Turn: Essays on the Work of the 1930s*; Michael E. Zimmerman's *Heidegger's Confrontation with Modernity: Technology, Politics, and Art*; and Karsten Harries and Christoph Jamme's *Martin Heidegger: Politics, Art, and Technology* address the issues of nihilism and technology. Don Ihde's *Heidegger's Technologies: Postphenomenological Perspectives* takes up the topic of technology.

Allison: New Nietzsche (1985).
Reading the New Nietzsche
(2002)

Conclusion: Influences, Developments, and Criticisms

As we have seen, Heidegger's early work creates a stunning synthesis of what appear to be highly disparate, even incompatible ideas, at least they appeared that way before *Being and Time*. Perhaps the two most important pieces he brought together are phenomenology and existentialism, which looked very different beforehand. Phenomenology, in its founder Husserl's hands, was a highly technical philosophy, a method for systematizing certain features of experience that had been hidden and putting them into a scientifically rigorous order. Science was an ideal for Husserl, as it was for Descartes, one of the greatest influences on Husserl but whom Heidegger takes as a natural adversary on nearly every topic.[1] Husserl's work tended to be extremely methodical, sometimes rather plodding and tedious; Heidegger once ridiculed him for studying a mailbox for an entire semester.

Existentialism, on the other hand, was born of the wild rhetorical flights of Kierkegaard and Nietzsche, two superb stylists who eyed all systems with distrust. They believed that life was too messy for that kind of treatment. Besides, the questions that really count aren't about the correct analysis of the transcendental ego but the concrete self, the meaning of life and the inevitability of death. The existentialists want to make philosophy relevant to how we live our lives; no lengthy studies of mailboxes here! Descartes' dispassionate attempt to find absolute certainty was considered doubly wrong: we cannot find certainty in this world, which should turn us towards passion.

Heidegger's genius was to fuse these two approaches into an utterly natural philosophy that seems almost inevitable in hindsight. He dispensed with a lot of the more technical techniques of phenomenology, placing them instead in the more organic setting of our average everyday lives. We don't need to sit down and carefully perform a phenomenological reduction; we are all struck by anxiety at some point in our lives which accomplishes the same thing. In fact, phenomenology's method feeds into the traditional emphasis of disengaged theory over engaged action, making us sit back and observe rather than use. Its very attempts to describe experience faithfully introduce distortions.

Phenomenology for Heidegger means the attempt to overcome prejudices that force our thinking along certain ruts, reminding us of the true nature of our experience before we stopped it in order to examine it. And what we find when we look without the blinders of theory is pretty much the picture the existentialists had painted: inauthentic lives of conformism covering over anxieties about death and the meaninglessness of life. Although he rejects Husserl's emphasis on science, Heidegger did bring the elements together into a highly organized system more successfully than Husserl ever did; the architectonic of *Being and Time* approaches Kant's in beauty and magnitude.

Phenomenological existentialism went on to become one of the most important philosophical movements of the middle decades of the twentieth century. Under its banner, Jean-Paul Sartre (1905–80) became perhaps the best known intellectual in the world after World War II. His 1943 *Being and Nothingness* has been jokingly called a French translation of *Being and Time* because of how closely it follows Heidegger's ideas. However, unlike Heidegger's use of "Dasein" as a neutral place-holder to avoid traditional connotations, Sartre is happy to use "consciousness" (as well as the Hegelian "for-itself") and he places great emphasis on an extreme notion of freedom. In the eyes of many – myself included – most of the places where Sartre diverges from Heidegger represent losses and regressions. For example, Sartre reinstates a subject-object dichotomy, an idea that Heidegger went to great lengths to undermine. With this separation also comes the idea that consciousness projects subjective values onto an inherently meaningless world, another idea that Heidegger rejects. Interestingly, Sartre had an influence on Heidegger, albeit a negative one. Heidegger wrote "Letter on Humanism" partially to differentiate his thought from Sartre who claimed him as a fellow traveler. This helped spur Heidegger to his later understanding of agency discussed in Chapter 9.

The other major figure in phenomenological existentialism was Maurice Merleau-Ponty (1908–61), whose 1945 *Phenomenology of Perception* represents his big book (it seemed at the time that everyone had to have one to be a serious philosopher). Merleau-Ponty's main contribution is to show the importance of the body in our being-in-the-world. We live in the world that we do largely because of the nature of our bodies; a being with a different kind of body would live in a different world. And the "in" of our being-in-the-world, the ways we interact with the world, are fundamentally bodily for Merleau-Ponty. He speaks of "motor intentionality" to get intentionality out of the mind – it is my grasping hand that is directed towards the door-knob as I walk towards it, not my thoughts. Whereas Sartre's reputation dropped off sharply, Merleau-Ponty's has continued to rise. Phenomenology has also had a significant impact on cognitive science, often with explicitly Heideggerian themes as in the work of Hubert Dreyfus.[2]

The other great influence on Heidegger's early work is hermeneutics. Schleiermacher started this school as the study of understanding and interpretation because, with the Protestant Revolution and the printing press, people began to read the Bible for themselves rather than relying on priests to interpret it for them. Dilthey then broadened interpretation, seeing it as the essential method of the human sciences. Heidegger extends the reach further, arguing that every encounter with an entity takes place on the basis of a particular understanding of its being: we use a hammer intelligently because we have a pre-theoretical understanding of what it means to be a tool. This kind of interpretation lives in actions rather than ideas or overt acts of thinking about something, and it is constantly going on in the background of all of our encounters. Hence the boundaries of hermeneutics are coterminous with those of human life itself.

Hans-Georg Gadamer (1900–2002) was a pupil of Heidegger who went on to become the main figure of twentieth-century hermeneutics after him. His 1960 magnum opus, *Truth and Method*, is a wide-ranging, even rambling discussion of various forms of understanding which he generally models on having a conversation. Understanding for Gadamer is not formulaic; the title is actually meant ironically because truth doesn't yield to strict method but requires a flexible, *phronetic* approach. The key to

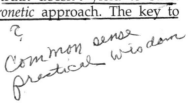

?,
Common sense
practical wisdom

understanding is to recognize your own fore-understandings, which he calls prejudices, as both necessary and limiting. They are necessary – as Heidegger argues – because they open up the field of inquiry in the first place but they can also function as blinders, sifting out all that clashes with what we already believe about the subject. While we can never rid ourselves of prejudices entirely – that was the Enlightenment's prejudice against prejudice – we need to always bring them into question, allowing them to be challenged and reformed to accommodate new ideas. This takes place paradigmatically in conversation when the participants open themselves to what the subject matter shows them and what their conversation partner can teach them, which is why Gadamer takes conversations to be the model of all understanding.

Emmanuel Levinas (1906–95) came to Freiburg to study with Husserl but, like many others, soon came under the spell of Heidegger. Like Heidegger, Levinas developed a highly unorthodox form of phenomenology but in a very different direction. Where *Being and Time* insists on the "mineness" of all experience, a version of traditional phenomenology's emphasis on the first-person perspective, Levinas believes that experience starts from the other. It is our encounter with other people that opens up our clearing, to use Heidegger's term; it is what keeps us out-in-the-world rather than encapsulated in ourselves like a substance. We are drawn out of ourselves by the challenges and demands of others; we are there for the other before we can be here for ourselves. Heidegger's emphasis on caring about our own fate is not just phenomenologically wrong, but unethical. For Levinas, the other comes first, in several senses.

As we have seen, Heidegger's work undergoes a significant change in the early 1930s. Experts disagree about the extent of the change, but it is unquestionable that the style of his writing altered. Although he continued to study previous philosophers meticulously, his relationship to them changed. He no longer depicted himself as a follower of any school, the way he had been a phenomenologist and, to a lesser degree, an existentialist and a hermeneuticist in *Being and Time*. Instead of aligning his work with pre-existing schools of thought, he started looking for an entirely new way of philosophizing which he called thinking. New schools continued to emerge from this later work. In particular, the loose grouping of figures under the title "post-modernism" works in its wake.

Michel Foucault (1926–84), one of the most influential intellectuals of the second half of the twentieth century, often cited Nietzsche as his main influence and there's no question that his ruminations on power, the body, and the inescapable interest of knowledge bear Nietzsche's stamp. But there is a strong Heideggerian element there too, as Foucault admitted on a number of occasions. Foucault's basic approach throughout his career was to analyze topics as divided into epochal slices. When he studied the subject, his main topic, he did not try to find the timeless essence of humanity but rather the various ways people have been formed as subjects at different points in history. Whereas Nietzsche certainly believed in the changeableness of reality in general and of subjectivity in particular, he did not arrange it in terms of epochs the way Heidegger did, and Foucault followed Heidegger in this.

Foucault did disagree on how to apply this technique, however. Where Heidegger found the most revealing texts of an epoch in its philosophical texts, Foucault sought out the forgotten obscure textual detritus of a society: prison timetables, shop inventories, handwriting instructions. These were the royal road to a culture's subconscious, whereas the philosophical works were epi-phenomena. He occasionally used philosophical works, but they were not as central for his work as they were for Heidegger's.

Nietzsche's description of the formation of modern subjectivity, the topic of *On the Genealogy of Morals*, imputes the alterations to conscious decisions made by individuals at a particular time for specific reasons: priests and slaves came up with a religion and ethics that favors the weak because they could not win in more open, honest forms of combat. Heidegger rejects such a notion as incoherent, focusing instead on the factors that made people find a different ethics attractive or plausible in the first place. Again, Foucault follows Heidegger's anti-humanism, constantly diminishing the role of the conscious, deliberate, autonomous decision maker in favor of the impersonal forces in a society that form all the individuals of the time.

Jacques Derrida (1930–2004) explicitly acknowledged his vast debt to Heidegger. He derived the term most associated with his work, "deconstruction," from Heidegger's own "*Destruktion*." He inherited from Heidegger the practice of extremely close readings of texts and the willingness to find surprising, unorthodox interpretations of them. Derrida also follows what he sees as Heidegger's suspicion of the metaphysics of presence. We can see one version of this in *Being and Time*'s analysis of presence-at-hand. Philosophy traditionally highlighted those features of reality that can be made fully present and unchanging: Forms, clear and distinct ideas, logic, etc. Yet fluctuating and even absent entities and features are far more prevalent and important to our ongoing experience. The tool that has withdrawn from express presence while I use it is much more commonplace and significant than the object I observe in reposed contemplation. Similarly, experiences of "nothingness" such as anxiety's meaninglessness or death's total absence are essential for teaching us about our lives. Derrida applies this idea to virtually every kind of apparently stable entity or system, especially language. He sees all meaning as riddled with absence, contradictions, and irreconcilable tensions, all of which texts deny in presenting themselves as simple, consistent entities. Just as Heidegger's *Destruktion* peels off the layers of falsifying theory to reveal the primordial experiences beneath, so Derrida's deconstruction removes the filters we use when we read to allow us to see the nest of contradictions.

In the early years of the twenty-first century, a new movement has been growing in continental philosophy called Speculative Realism. This loose school of thinkers sees the history of continental philosophy as largely a development of Kantian anti-realism. Anti-realism argues that we can only intelligibly talk about reality as we experience it without speculating about how things are independently of us, what Kant called things-in-themselves. The Speculative Realists believe that this movement has run its course and that it's time to go back to realism, albeit one that has learned the lessons of Kant and his intellectual offspring.

While most members of this movement classify Heidegger as a proponent of the anti-realism they want to move past, one of its founders, Graham Harman, finds realist resources within Heidegger's work. In particular, he broadens Heidegger's description of tool withdrawal to all encounters between entities, even when no Dasein or man or awareness of any kind is there to provide a medium of sentience within which they can encounter each other. Every time one object bumps into another, it only encounters those aspects it is open to. So, to take one of Harman's examples, flame only encounters the flammability of cotton, not its softness or its whiteness; these latter qualities withdraw from it. His project is to try to find the general laws governing all such events. This is just one example of the way Heidegger's work continues to offer new inspiration and insights well into the twenty-first century.

Further readings

There are a number of books dealing with Heidegger's entire career. Two classics are William J. Richardson's *Heidegger: Through Phenomenology to Thought* and Otto Pöggeler's *Martin Heidegger's Path of Thinking*. More recent books that I recommend are *Heidegger: An Introduction* by Richard Polt and *Heidegger* by John Richardson. Hubert Dreyfus and Mark Wrathall collected many of the best essays ever written on Heidegger in their four-volume anthology, *Heidegger Reexamined*, and produced another helpful collection in *A Companion to Heidegger*. Charles Guignon's *The Cambridge Companion to Heidegger* and Dreyfus and Hall's *Heidegger: A Critical Reader* are also helpful collections that cover a wide range of topics.

Notes

Introduction: An Initial Orientation

1 The one exception to this formula is being itself which can be made to appear but which can't be said to be, at least not in the sense that applies to beings. Thus beings are, but it would be a category mistake to say that "being is."

2 See Lackey 1999.

1 Introduction to *Being and Time*

1 The numbers in the margins of *Being and Time* are from the original German pagination so that people using different translations can synchronize citations. Quotes are usually given with both the page of the translation being used and the original pagination, separated by a slash, e.g. 19/1. Unless otherwise stated, all quotes in Part I of this book are from *Being and Time* and I will be using the standard Macquarrie and Robinson translation throughout.

2 There are some precedents of this conception of knowledge, such as Aristotle; see Braver 2012, 168–70. Other twentieth-century philosophers such as Ludwig Wittgenstein, Gilbert Ryle, and Michael Polanyi explore this distinction as well.

3 I will refer to sections of the book by division number, then chapter number (in Roman numerals), and then paragraph number (that is, the continuously numbered sections denoted

by "¶") when relevant, all separated by periods. So the chapter referred to above is Division 1, ch. IV.

4 We can piece together some of what Part II would have been from contemporary lecture series that deal with these figures.

5 This name plays on Kant's categorical imperative, the second form of which is to treat rational beings (as ends-in-themselves) as fundamentally different from non-rational beings (as means only), which may have been one of the influences on Heidegger's uncompromising dichotomy between Dasein and everything else.

6 Perhaps the classic statement of this reading of *Being and Time* is *Heidegger's Temporal Idealism* by Bill Blattner. It's an idealism because reality derives certain features from us, and it's a temporal idealism because temporality is the central, unifying feature derived. Many scholars have commented on the connection between Heidegger and Kant; book-length studies include Schalow 1992, Sherover 1971.

7 This is explained more clearly in *History of the Concept of Time* ¶9 if you're interested.

2 *Being and Time* 1.I–IV: Being-in and the World

1 Two of the best books on this topic, indeed on Heidegger in general, are Guignon 1983 and Richardson 1986.

2 This idea has important implications for artificial intelligence which have been explored in Hubert Dreyfus' work. See especially Dreyfus 1992.

3 On this topic, see Braver 2007, ch. 5.

4 Nietzsche, mocking Mill's Utilitarianism, once wrote that "man does *not* strive for pleasure; only the Englishman does" (Nietzsche 1954, 468).

5 Jeff Malpas has forcefully argued that space plays a more important role than Heidegger acknowledges. See Malpas 2008, 2012.

6 See Blakeslee and Blakeslee 2008, 140. Although Heidegger does not do this, other phenomenologists such as Merleau-Ponty and contemporary figures like Shaun Gallagher and Dan Zahavi carry on a rich dialogue with neuroscience. See, e.g., Merleau-Ponty 1962, Gallagher 2006, Gallagher and Zahavi 2012.

7　Hegel too embraced a deep holism which, in the realm of politics, makes society primary rather than building it up by aggregating individuals (Hegel 1969, 167; 2002, ¶75, ¶156, ¶273, ¶276, ¶331).
8　This is an important topic for Michel Foucault and Pierre Bourdieu. See Foucault 1978, 1995, Bourdieu 1977.
9　The importance of norms to having a world forms a central subject of John Haugeland's very interesting reading of Heidegger. See Haugeland 2013.
10　Emmanuel Levinas, an important French philosopher who studied with both Husserl and Heidegger, develops this line of thought in his quasi-phenomenological ethics of the other. See Levinas 1996.

3　*Being and Time* 1.V–VI: The There and Care

1　Russell discusses how "the subject–predicate logic" of our language leads to a "substance-attribute metaphysic," even though it is an accidental feature of our syntax: "language misleads us both by its vocabulary and by its syntax. We must be on our guard in both respects if our logic is not to lead to a false metaphysic" (in Ayer 1959, 38). For Nietzsche, "formerly, one believed in 'the soul' as one believed in grammar and the grammatical subject: one said, 'I' is the condition, 'think' is the predicate and conditioned – thinking is an activity to which thought *must* supply a subject as cause" (1966, ¶54).
2　Wittgenstein 2001, 5.6331. Sartre's early phenomenological work, *The Transcendence of the Ego*, also captures this well.
3　Hegel makes a similar argument in the Introduction to *Phenomenology of Spirit*.
4　Williams 1978, 65.
5　For more on this topic see Braver 2007, 181–98.

4　*Being and Time* 2.I–III.¶64: Authenticity

1　This is one reason why, as I said above, 1.V can be seen as the heart of the book, or at least a privileged section. Haugeland makes a similar point (2013, 147).

2 Note too that he mentions here a third possible state – undifferentiated – whereas he sometimes acknowledges only authentic and inauthentic states.

3 Levinas actually argues that this is our primary access to death. See Critchley's second essay in Levine 2008 for a helpful discussion.

4 For more on this, see Braver 2012, especially ch. 5 and the Conclusion.

5 This is a constant theme in Derrida's thought, using examples like one's native tongue or name as features that we experience as deeply ours even though they were chosen for us. See esp. Derrida 1978, 278–94.

6 Thoreau 1992, 86.

7 Compare to a similar comment Heidegger made towards the end of his career: "In this domain, one cannot prove anything. One must abandon the belief that only what can be proved is true. . . . We are not dealing with a theory here, but with the insight into what we ourselves always already are" (Z 217).

8 Like Heidegger's making truth and being Dasein-dependent in 1.VI.¶¶43–4, Kant says of the phenomenal realm that, "external objects (bodies), however, are mere appearances, and are therefore nothing but a species of my representations, the objects of which are something only through these representations. Apart from them they are nothing" (Kant 1965, A370–1; see also ibid. A42/B59, A383).

9 Heidegger extensively discussed Aristotle in a number of courses throughout the 1920s and early 1930s. For more detailed examinations of the pair, see Brogan 2006, McNeill 1999, Sadler 2001.

10 This realization is the key to what Richard Rorty calls irony. See Rorty 1989.

5 *Being and Time* 2.III.¶65–VI: Temporality as the Meaning of Existence

1 Heidegger even calls "tautological thinking . . . the primordial sense of phenomenology" (FS 80).

2 Nietzsche 1954, 486. On this, see Braver 2012, ch. 4.

3 Sartre 1956, 41–2.

4 For more on this, see Braver 2007, ch. 1.

5 See Crowell 2001 for more on this pair.

6 In fact in his later work, he comes to reject this attempt to derive space from time (TB 23). I am grateful to an anonymous reader for this reference. See Malpas' excellent essay in Kiverstein and Wheeler 2012 for details.

7 Putnam 1981, 49.

8 In the Preface to his breakthrough work, *Ideas*, Husserl says of phenomenology, "there lies embedded in its meaning as philosophy a radicalism in the matter of foundations, an absolute freedom from all presuppositions, a securing for itself an absolute basis: the totality of presuppositions that can be 'taken for granted'" (Husserl 1962, 20).

9 Nietzsche 1954, 251. For more on this connection, see Braver 2007, 510.

10 See Barash 2003 on this topic.

11 Augustine 1961, XI.15, 264–6.

12 Technically, Descartes did not subscribe to a container theory of space, as Newton did, but he did remove the kind of qualitative distinctions that Aristotle's space had.

13 Foucault examines just such transformations.

6 *Being and Time*: Conclusion

1 If you want to see the answer a number of prominent Heidegger scholars give, see Braver forthcoming.

7 Introduction to the Later Heidegger

1 Even here there is disagreement. Richard Rorty, for example, writes that, "I greatly admire the later work, even though I could do without all the stuff about 'the question after the meaning of Being'" (Rorty 2006, 94) and more generally that, "the word 'Being' is more trouble than it is worth. I would be happy if Heidegger had never employed it" (Rorty 1991, 71). This contrasts with commentators like John Haugeland for whom the question of being is absolutely central to *Being and Time* and everything in it needs to be read from that perspective.

8 History, Nazism, the History of Being and of its Forgetting

1 OBT 57, see also OBT 79, N II: 80, N II: 131, N IV: 7, 100, 205, WT 95–6, BW 330, PR 55, 87, 94, CP 169/¶122, ET 150, FS 61, WCT 66.
2 I called this idea Impersonal Conceptual Scheme and discussed it at length in Braver 2007, 284–91.
3 Foucault did use philosophical texts, they just were less important than more mundane documents and much less important than in Heidegger's system. In his final works, Foucault relies more on philosophical works than previously.
4 For a helpful and brief discussion of these matters, see "Heidegger and the Nazis" by Thomas Sheehan, *The New York Review of Books*, 35 (10) (June 16, 1988): 38–47. Many relevant sources have been gathered in Wolin's *The Heidegger Controversy*. Victor Farias' *Heidegger and Nazism* is generally regarded as poor scholarship and should not be relied upon.
5 Ott 1993, 187; HR 323; Sheehan 1988, 39.
6 IM 213, M 102/¶47; Löwith 1994, 60.
7 See Lang 1996.
8 HR 313–18, 270; Davis 2010, 110; Wolin 1991, 164.
9 HR 322; Davis 2010, 107–8.
10 PLT 116, 166, 170, HR 325.
11 PM 321, see also BW 363, WCT 66. Heidegger also says that the worst thing that could happen to humanity is that technology could "render the human condition, man's being, tolerable for everybody and happy in all respects" (PLT 116).
12 "On the general question of the relation between Heidegger's thought and his Nazism, I am not persuaded that there is much to be said except that one of the century's most original thinkers happened to be a pretty nasty character. . . . The relation between a writer's books and other parts of his life [is] contingent" (Rorty 1989, 113n. 13, see also Harries and Jamme 1994, 36–7).
13 Pierre Bourdieu has given a nuanced version of this claim in *The Political Ontology of Martin Heidegger*.
14 Löwith 1994, 60.
15 "Each individual is the son of his people and, at the same time, insofar as his state is in development, the son of his

age. No one remains behind it, no one can leap ahead of it. This spiritual being is his – he is one of its representatives – it is that from which he arises and wherein he stands" (Hegel 1953, 66).

16 TB 52, see also TB 6, 33, BW 433, IM 30, FS 9, CP 171/¶125, M 17, 206, PR 91, 108, WIP 63, QT 39.
17 OBT 66–7, see also QT 151, PR 76–7. For more on Heidegger's history of truth, see Braver 2007, 291–306.

9 Descartes, Thinking, and Free Will

1 EF 159, see also BW 132, 196, BQ 170, WCT 66, PM 231, 313, CP 80–1/¶55, IM 138, M 75, 125.
2 OBT 81, see also OBT 66, BW 295–6.
3 This resembles Foucault's later idea of ideas being "within the true" for certain periods. See Foucault 1972, 224.
4 PR 53, see also PLT 6, PT 53, BW 372. See also Braver 2013. Timothy J. Nulty has been working on similar ideas in his unpublished paper, "Hubert Dreyfus and the Last Myth of the Mental," which he kindly let me see.
5 BW 410–11, see also BW 418, 423, PR 96, N IV: 200, PT 25, PLT 181, 209.
6 PR 24, see also N IV: 7, QT 54.
7 N IV: 214, see also BW 384, BQ 105.
8 WCT 46, see also WCT 65, 164.
9 PM 279, see also BW 217, 384, IM 166–7.
10 BW 324, see also PLT 171, BQ 179, ET 229, 325–7.
11 This is just the kind of internal tension that Derrida's deconstructive readings seek.
12 PWD II: 45, see also PWD II: 48, PWD II: 147.
13 BW 334, see also QT 41, M 56.
14 BW 326, see also BW 323, OBT 188.
15 DT 50, see also QT 42–3, N II: 223, N III: 181.
16 FS 56, see also WCT 115, 126, 142, OWL 76, BW 136, CP 167/¶120.
17 IM 5, see also M 237/¶74, MFL 214–15, KPM 199.
18 PR 3, see also PM 293, PLT 112, CP 88/¶61, 92/¶67.
19 Z 217, see also BW 330, 360–1.
20 See BW 251, 262, N IV: 44, N IV: 202–3, BQ 159, TB 77, PM 313, 319.

10   Gratitude, Language, and Art

1   CP 242/¶222, see also IM 44, N II: 192, WCT 169, BQ 9.
2   BW 238, see also CP 123/¶87, 168/¶120, EGT 27, ID 51.
3   BT 171/133, 182/143, 187/147, 214/170, 263/220, 355/307, 401/350.
4   N IV: 152, see also N III: 68.
5   WCT 142, see also WCT 151, FS 73, PM 279, 294, DT 64, PR 69, 75, CP 167/¶120.
6   ID 31–2, see also BW 228–9, 235, DT 84, Z 176–80, CP 169/¶123.
7   BW 127, see also BW 217, 245, EGT 36, PM 236.
8   BW 337, see also BW 231, 234, 239, 245, 252, 259, 329–30, BQ 132, 163, CP 169/¶122, PM 257.
9   PM 234, see also BW 170, IM 86.
10   BT 186/145, BW 256, 416, N I: 194, N IV: 94, FS 73, CP 163/¶118, 169/¶122, 211/¶175, M 176, HH 76, ET 153, ID 33.
11   See Merleau-Ponty 1962.
12   Wrathall 2010 presents an extremely well-argued case for this interpretation.
13   BW 414, see also BW 230, IM 15, 57, 167, 198, PLT 189, OWL 66, 73, 155.
14   IM 183, see also PLT 198.
15   BW 149, 226, HR 331.
16   For more on this, see Braver 2007, 228–53; Braver 2011.
17   BW 171, see also BW 159, 173.
18   BW 262, see also BW 132, 251, 331, FS 56.

11   Technology, Nietzsche, and Nihilism

1   At the time of this writing, XBOX has a Kinnect attachment that allows voice commands to control one's entertainment center. Its operation is presently spotty, which means that they are working on a new version that will work more smoothly.
2   I try to sort through these convoluted moves in Braver 2007, 128–30.
3   Nietzsche 1968, ¶1067, see also 1966, ¶259. Another controversial aspect of Heidegger's reading is that he concentrates on the *Nachlass*, the unpublished portions of Nietzsche's writings, more than the published books. He does give a justification for this focus, but many find it objectionable.

Conclusion: Influences, Developments, and Criticisms

1 Some have suggested that Heidegger's criticisms of Descartes are disguised attacks on Husserl.
2 See Kiverstein and Wheeler 2012 for a survey of this work.

References

Heidegger, Martin. 1956. *What Is Philosophy?* trans. William Kluback and Jean T. Wilde. New College and University Press.

——1959. *An Introduction to Metaphysics.* trans. Ralph Manheim. New Haven: Yale University Press.

——1962. *Being and Time.* trans. John Macquarrie and Edward Robinson. San Francisco: HarperSanFrancisco.

——1966. *Discourse on Thinking.* trans. John M. Anderson and E. Hans Freund. San Francisco: Harper Torchbooks.

——1967. *What Is a Thing?* trans. W. B. Barton Jr. and Vera Deutsch. Chicago: Henry Regnery.

——1968. *What Is Called Thinking?* trans. J. Glenn Gray. New York: Harper and Row.

——1969. *Identity and Difference.* trans. Joan Stambaugh. New York: Harper Torchbooks.

——1971. *On the Way to Language.* trans. Peter D. Hertz. San Francisco: HarperSanFrancisco.

——1971. *Poetry, Language, Thought.* trans. Albert Hofstadter. New York: Harper and Row.

——1972. *On Time and Being.* trans. Joan Stambaugh. New York: Harper Torchbooks.

——1975. *Early Greek Thinking: The Dawn of Western Philosophy.* trans. David Farrell Krell and Frank A. Capuzzi. San Francisco: HarperSanFrancisco.

——1976. *The Piety of Thinking.* trans. James G. Hart and John C. Maraldo. Bloomington: Indiana University Press.

——1977. *The Question Concerning Technology and Other Essays.* trans. William Lovitt. New York: Harper Torchbooks.

——*Nietzsche.* 4 vols. 1979, 1984, 1987, and 1982. ed. David Farrell Krell. San Francisco: HarperSanFrancisco.

——1985. *History of the Concept of Time.* trans. Theodore Kisiel. Bloomington: Indiana University Press.

——1985. *Schelling's Treatise on the Essence of Human Freedom.* trans. Joan Stambaugh. Ohio University Press.

——1990. *Kant and the Problem of Metaphysics.* 5th enl. edn. trans. Richard Taft. Bloomington: Indiana University Press.

——1991. *The Principle of Reason.* trans. Reginald Lilly. Bloomington: Indiana University Press.

——1992. *The Metaphysical Foundations of Logic.* trans. Michael Heim. Bloomington: Indiana University Press.

——1993. *Basic Writings.* rev. edn. ed. David Farrell Krell. San Francisco: HarperSanFrancisco.

——1994. *Basic Questions of Philosophy: Selected "Problems" of "Logic."* trans. Richard Rojcewicz and André Schuwer. Bloomington: Indiana University Press.

——1996. *Hölderlin's Hymn "The Ister."* trans. William McNeill and Julia Davis. Bloomington: Indiana University Press.

——1998. *Pathmarks.* ed. William McNeill. Cambridge University Press.

——1999. *Contributions to Philosophy (From Enowning).* trans. Parvis Emad and Kenneth Maly. Bloomington: Indiana University Press.

——2000. *Elucidations of Hölderlin's Poetry.* trans. Keith Hoeller. Amherst: Humanity Books.

——2001. *Zollikon Seminars: Protocols – Conversations – Letters.* trans. Franz Mayr and Richard Askay. Evanston, Ill.: Northwestern University Press.

——2002. *Mindfulness.* trans. Parvis Emad and Thomas Kalary. New York: Continuum.

——2002. *Off the Beaten Track.* trans. and ed. Julian Young and Kenneth Haynes. New York: Cambridge University Press.

——2002. *The Essence of Human Freedom: An Introduction to Philosophy.* trans. Ted Sadler. New York: Continuum.

——2002. *The Essence of Truth: On Plato's Cave Allegory and "Theaetetus."* trans. Ted Sadler. New York: Continuum.

——2003. *Four Seminars.* trans. Andrew Mitchell and François Raffoul. Bloomington: Indiana University Press.

——2009. *The Heidegger Reader.* ed. Günter Figal. Bloomington: Indiana University Press.

Other works

Allison, David B., ed. 1977. *The New Nietzsche.* New York: Dell.

Augustine. 1961. *Confessions.* trans. R. S. Pine-Coffin. New York: Penguin Books.

Ayer, A. J., 1959. ed. *Logical Positivism.* New York: Free Press.

Bambach, Charles R. 1995. *Heidegger, Dilthey, and the Crisis of Historicism.* Cornell University Press.

——2005. *Heidegger's Roots: Nietzsche, National Socialism, and the Greeks.* Cornell University Press.

Barash, Jeffrey Andrew. 2003. *Martin Heidegger and the Problem of Historical Meaning.* Fordham University Press.

Blakeslee, Sandra, and Matthew Blakeslee. 2008. *The Body Has a Mind of Its Own: How Body Maps in Your Brain Help You Do (Almost) Everything Better.* New York: Random House.

Blattner, William D. 1999. *Heidegger's Temporal Idealism.* New York: Cambridge University Press.

Bourdieu, Pierre. 1977. *Outline of a Theory of Practice.* Cambridge University Press.

——1991. *The Political Ontology of Martin Heidegger.* Stanford University Press.

Braver, Lee. 2007. *A Thing of This World: A History of Continental Anti-Realism.* Evanston, IL: Northwestern University Press.

——2011. "Davidson's Reading of Gadamer: Triangulation, Conversation, and the Analytic-Continental Divide." In *Dialogues with Davidson.* ed. Jeff Malpas. Cambridge, MA: MIT Press.

——2012. *Groundless Grounds: A Study of Wittgenstein and Heidegger.* Cambridge, MA: MIT Press.

——2013. "Never Mind: Thinking of Subjectivity in the Dreyfus-McDowell Debate." In *Mind, Reason and Being-in-the-World: The McDowell-Dreyfus Debate.* ed. Joseph K. Schear. New York: Routledge.

——Forthcoming. *Division III of Being and Time: Heidegger's Unanswered Question of Being.* Cambridge, MA: MIT Press.

Brogan, Walter A. 2006. *Heidegger and Aristotle: The Twofoldness of Being.* State University of New York Press.

Caputo, John D. 1993. *Demythologizing Heidegger.* Indianapolis: Indiana University Press.

Carman, Taylor. 2007. *Heidegger's Analytic: Interpretation, Discourse and Authenticity in Being and Time.* Cambridge University Press.

Crowell, Steven, and Jeff Malpas, eds. 2007. *Transcendental Heidegger.*
Stanford University Press.

Crowell, Steven Galt. 2001. *Husserl, Heidegger, and the Space of Meaning: Paths Towards Transcendental Phenomenology.* Northwestern University Press.

Damasio, Antonio. 2008. *Descartes' Error: Emotion, Reason, and the Human Brain.* Penguin Books.

Davis, Bret W. 2007. *Heidegger and the Will: On the Way to Gelassenheit.* Northwestern University Press.

—— ed. 2010. *Martin Heidegger: Key Concepts.* Durham: Acumen Publishing.

De Boer, Karin. 2000. *Thinking in the Light of Time: Heidegger's Encounter with Hegel.* State University of New York Press.

Derrida, Jacques. 1978. *Writing and Difference.* trans. Alan Bass. London: Routledge.

Descartes, René. 1984. *The Philosophical Writings of Descartes.* 3 vols. trans. John Cottingham, Robert Stoothoff, and Dugald Murdoch. Cambridge University Press.

Dreyfus, Hubert L. 1992. *What Computers Still Can't Do: A Critique of Artificial Reason.* Cambridge, MA: MIT Press.

——1990. *Being-in-the-World: A Commentary on Heidegger's Being and Time, Division I.* Cambridge, MA: MIT Press.

Dreyfus, Hubert, and Mark Wrathall, eds. 2002. *Heidegger Reexamined.* 4 vols. Routledge.

——2005. *A Companion to Heidegger.* Oxford: Blackwell.

Dreyfus, Hubert L., and Harrison Hall, eds. 1992. *Heidegger: A Critical Reader.* Oxford: Blackwell.

Farias, Victor. 1991. *Heidegger and Nazism.* Philadelphia: Temple University Press.

Foucault, Michel. 1978. *The History of Sexuality: An Introduction.* Vol. 1 of *The History of Sexuality.* trans. Robert Hurley. New York: Vintage Books.

——1995. *Discipline and Punish: The Birth of the Prison.* trans. Alan Sheridan. New York: Vintage Books.

——1972. *The Archaeology of Knowledge.* trans. A. M. Sheridan Smith. New York: Harper Colophon Books.

Gadamer, Hans-Georg. 2013. *Truth and Method.* Bloomsbury Academic.

Gallagher, Shaun. 2006. *How the Body Shapes the Mind.* Oxford University Press.

Gallagher, Shaun, and Dan Zahavi. 2012. *The Phenomenological Mind,* 2nd edn. Routledge.

Guignon, Charles B. 1983. *Heidegger and the Problem of Knowledge.* Indianapolis: Hackett.

—— ed. 1993. *The Cambridge Companion to Heidegger.* New York: Cambridge University Press.

——2009. "The Body, Bodily Feelings, and Existential Feelings: A Heideggerian Perspective." *Philosophy, Psychiatry, & Psychology,* 16 (2) (June): 195–9.

——2004. *On Being Authentic.* Routledge.

Haar, Michel. 1993. *Heidegger and the Essence of Man.* trans. William McNeill. State University of New York Press.

——1993. *The Song of the Earth: Heidegger and the Grounds of Being.* trans. Reginald Lilly. Indiana University Press.

Harman, Graham. 2002. *Tool-Being: Heidegger and the Metaphysics of Objects.* Open Court.

Harries, Karsten, and Christoph Jamme, eds. 1994. *Martin Heidegger: Politics, Art, and Technology.* Holmes & Meier.

Haugeland, John. 2013. *Dasein Disclosed: John Haugeland's Heidegger.* ed. Joseph Rouse. Harvard University Press.

Hegel, G. W. F. 1953. *Reason in History: A General Introduction to the Philosophy of History.* Englewood Cliffs, NJ: Prentice Hall.

——1969. *Hegel's Science of Logic.* trans. A. V. Miller. London: G. Allen & Unwin.

——2002. *Hegel's The Philosophy of Right.* trans. Alan White. Newburyport, Mass.: Focus Philosophical Library.

Husserl, Edmund. 1962. *Ideas: General Introduction to Pure Phenomenology.* trans. W. R. Boyce Gibson. New York: Collier, Macmillan.

——1977. *Cartesian Meditations: An Introduction to Phenomenology.* trans. Dorian Cairns. Martinus Nijhoff Pub.

Ihde, Don. 2010. *Heidegger's Technologies: Postphenomenological Perspectives.* Fordham University Press.

Kant, Immanuel. 1965. *Critique of Pure Reason.* trans. Norman Kemp Smith. New York: St Martin's.

Kiverstein, Julian, and Michael Wheeler, eds. 2012. *Heidegger and Cognitive Science.* Palgrave Macmillan.

Lackey, Douglas P. 1999. "What Are the Modern Classics? The Baruch Poll of Great Philosophy in the Twentieth Century." *The Philosophical Forum,* 30 (4) (December 1999): 329–46.

Lang, Berel. 1996. *Heidegger's Silence.* Cornell University Press.

Levinas, Emmanuel. 1996. *Basic Philosophical Writings.* ed. Adriaan T. Peperzak, Simon Critchley, and Robert Bernasconi. Bloomington: Indiana University Press.

Levine, Stephen, ed. 2008. *On Heidegger's Being and Time.* New York: Routledge.

Löwith, Karl. 1994. *My Life in Germany Before and After 1933: A Report.* trans. Elizabeth King. Chicago: University of Illinois Press.

MacIntyre, Alasdair. 1984. *After Virtue.* University of Notre Dame Press, 2nd edn.

Malpas, Jeff. 2008. *Heidegger's Topology: Being, Place, World.* Cambridge, MA: MIT Press.

——2012. *Heidegger and the Thinking of Place: Explorations in the Topology of Being.* Cambridge, MA: MIT Press.

Marrati, Paola. 2005. *Genesis and Trace: Derrida Reading Husserl and Heidegger.* Stanford University Press.

Marx, Werner. 1971. *Heidegger and the Tradition.* trans. Theodore Kisiel and Murray Greene. Northwestern University Press.

McNeill, William. 1999. *The Glance of the Eye: Heidegger, Aristotle, and the Ends of Theory.* State University of New York Press.

Meillassoux, Quentin. 2010. *After Finitude: An Essay on the Necessity of Contingency.* Bloomsbury Academic.

Merchant, Carolyn. 1990. *The Death of Nature: Women, Ecology, and the Scientific Revolution.* HarperOne.

Merleau-Ponty, Maurice. 1962. *Phenomenology of Perception.* trans. Colin Smith. London: Routledge & Kegan Paul.

Milchman, Alan, and Alan Rosenberg, eds. 2003. *Foucault and Heidegger: Critical Encounters.* Minneapolis: University of Minnesota Press.

Moran, Dermot. 2000. *Introduction to Phenomenology.* Routledge.

Nietzsche, Friedrich. 1954. *The Portable Nietzsche.* ed. and trans. Walter Kaufmann. New York: Penguin Books.

——1966. *Beyond Good and Evil: Prelude to a Philosophy of the Future.* trans. Walter Kaufmann. New York: Vintage Books.

——1967. *On the Genealogy of Morals/Ecce Homo.* trans. Walter Kaufmann and R. J. Hollingdale. New York: Vintage Books.

——1968. *The Will to Power.* ed. Walter Kaufmann. trans. Walter Kaufmann and R. J. Hollingdale. New York: Vintage Books.

——1974. *The Gay Science.* trans. Walter Kaufmann. New York: Vintage Books.

Ott, Hugo. 1993. *Heidegger: A Political Life.* trans. Allan Blunden. Basic Books.

Petzet, Heinrich Wiegand. 1993. *Encounters & Dialogues with Martin Heidegger 1929–1976.* University of Chicago Press.

Pippin, Robert B. 1997. *Idealism as Modernism: Hegelian Variations.* Cambridge University Press.

——1999. *Modernism as a Philosophical Problem: On the Dissatisfactions of European High Culture*, 2nd edn. Wiley-Blackwell.

Polt, Richard. 1999. *Heidegger: An Introduction.* Cornell University Press.

Pöggeler, Otto. 1991. *Martin Heidegger's Path of Thinking.* trans. Daniel Magurshak and Sigmund Barber. Humanity Books.

——1998. *The Paths of Heidegger's Life and Thought.* trans. John Bailiff. Amherst: Humanity Books.

Polanyi, Michael. 1966. *The Tacit Dimension.* Routledge.

Putnam, Hilary. 1981. *Reason, Truth and History.* New York: Cambridge University Press.

Raffoul, François, and Eric Nelson, eds. 2009. *Rethinking Facticity.* State University of New York Press.

Rapaport, Herman. 1991. *Heidegger and Derrida: Reflections on Time and Language.* University of Nebraska Press.

Richardson, John. 1986. *Existential Epistemology: A Heideggerian Critique of the Cartesian Project.* Oxford: Clarendon.

——2012. *Heidegger.* Routledge.

Richardson, William J. 2003. *Heidegger: Through Phenomenology to Thought*, 4th edn. Fordham University Press.

Risser, James. 1999. *Heidegger Towards the Turn: Essays on the Work of the 1930s.* State University of New York Press.

Rorty, Richard. 1989. *Contingency, Irony, and Solidarity.* Cambridge University Press.

——1991. *Objectivity, Relativism, and Truth: Philosophical Papers Volume 1.* Cambridge University Press.

——2006. *Take Care of Freedom and Truth Will Take Care of Itself: Interviews with Richard Rorty.* ed. Eduardo Mendicta. Stanford: Stanford University Press.

Sadler, Ted. 2001. *Heidegger and Aristotle: The Question of Being.* Continuum.

Safranski, Rüdiger. 1998. *Martin Heidegger: Between Good and Evil.* trans. Ewald Osers. Harvard University Press.

Ryle, Gilbert. 1949. *The Concept of Mind.* University of Chicago Press.

Sartre, Jean-Paul. 1956. *Being and Nothingness: A Phenomenological Essay on Ontology.* trans. Hazel E. Barnes. Washington Square Press.

——1993. *The Transcendence of the Ego: An Existentialist Theory of Consciousness.* trans. Forrest Williams and Robert Kirkpatrick. New York: Hill and Wang.

Schalow, Frank. 1992. *The Renewal of the Heidegger–Kant Dialogue.* State University of New York Press.

230 References

Schürmann, Reiner. 1987. *Heidegger on Being and Acting: From Principles to Anarchy*. Indiana University Press.

Sheehan, Thomas. 1988. "Heidegger and the Nazis." *The New York Review of Books*, 35 (10) (June 16, 1988): 38–47.

——2001. "A Paradigm Shift in Heidegger Research." *Continental Philosophy Review* 34: 183–202.

Sherover, Charles M. 1971. *Heidegger, Kant, and Time*. Bloomington: Indiana University Press.

Stapleton, Timothy J. 1984. *Husserl and Heidegger: The Question of a Phenomenological Beginning*. State University of New York Press.

Taylor, Charles. 1989. *Sources of the Self: The Making of the Modern Identity*. Cambridge University Press.

Thomson, Iain D. 2011. *Heidegger, Art, and Postmodernity*. Cambridge University Press.

Thoreau, Henry David. 1992. *Walden and Other Writings*. Brooks Atkinson edn. Modern Library.

Williams, Bernard. 1978. *Descartes: The Project of Pure Inquiry*. Pelican.

Wittgenstein, Ludwig. 1969. *On Certainty*. ed. G. E. M. Anscombe and G. H. von Wright. trans. Denis Paul and G. E. M. Anscombe. New York: Harper Torchbooks.

——2001. *Tractatus Logico-Philosophicus*. trans. D. F. Pears and B. F. McGuinness. New York: Routledge.

Wolin, Richard, ed. 1993. *The Heidegger Controversy: A Critical Reader*. Cambridge, MA: MIT Press.

Wrathall, Mark A. 2010. *Heidegger and Unconcealment: Truth, Language, and History*. Cambridge University Press.

——2013. *The Cambridge Companion to Heidegger's Being and Time*. Cambridge University Press.

Young, Julian. 2001. *Heidegger's Philosophy of Art*. Cambridge University Press.

——2002. *Heidegger's Later Philosophy*. Cambridge University Press.

Zimmerman, Michael E. 1986. *Eclipse of the Self: The Development of Heidegger's Concept of Authenticity*, rev. edn. Ohio University Press.

——1990. *Heidegger's Confrontation with Modernity: Technology, Politics, and Art*. Indiana University Press.

Index

Index